ISBN 978-1-333-82519-5
PIBN 10702504

English
Français
Deutsche
Italiano
Español
Português

www.forgottenbooks.com

Mythology Photography **Fiction**
Fishing Christianity **Art** Cooking
Essays Buddhism Freemasonry
Medicine **Biology** Music **Ancient
Egypt** Evolution Carpentry Physics
Dance Geology **Mathematics** Fitness
Shakespeare **Folklore** Yoga Marketing
Confidence Immortality Biographies
Poetry **Psychology** Witchcraft
Electronics Chemistry History **Law**
Accounting **Philosophy** Anthropology
Alchemy Drama Quantum Mechanics
Atheism Sexual Health **Ancient History**
Entrepreneurship Languages Sport
Paleontology Needlework Islam
Metaphysics Investment Archaeology
Parenting Statistics Criminology
Motivational

The Publications of
The Yorkshire Parish Register Society.

VOL. LIV.

Issued to Subscribers for the year 1916.

The Boundaries of

... Greece ... 480-146

VOLUME

II

The Register

OF THE

Chapelry of

EAST ROUNTON

in the Parish of Rudby-in-Cleveland,

CO. YORK.

1595-1837.

TRANSCRIBED AND EDITED BY THE

REV. WILLIAM THOMAS ROBSON, M.A.,

Rector of West Rounton.

PRIVATELY PRINTED FOR

THE YORKSHIRE PARISH REGISTER SOCIETY.

1916,

J. WHITEHEAD AND SON, LEEDS AND LONDON.

PREFACE.

East Rounton is a township and chapelry, situated in the North Riding of Yorkshire, and district of Cleveland.

It is a modern as well as a model village, and extends along the north bank of the Wiske to the borders of West Rounton.

It is in the Cleveland division of the Riding, Stokesley union and county court district, the Archdeaconry of Cleveland and Diocese of York.

The lord of the manor of both East and West Rounton is Sir Hugh Bell, Baronet, who is also Lord-Lieutenant of the North Riding ; his residence is Rounton Grange, about half a mile from the village. The estate of East Rounton was purchased by the late Sir Lowthian Bell, of the late John Wailes, Esq., in the year 1865.

The church dates from the thirteenth century, and was restored on the model of the ancient structure by the late Sir Lowthian Bell, under the direction of Robert J. Johnson, architect, of Newcastle-on-Tyne, in the year 1884, and consists of a chancel, nave, south porch, and a western turret containing one bell.

East Rounton was formerly a chapelry in the parish of Rudby-in-Cleveland, about four miles distant, the last incumbent being the Rev. John Johnson, who resigned it in the year 1912, and by an Order in Council, dated 11th October in that year, East and West Rounton were united as one parish, the patron being the Archbishop of York.

The Registers date from the year 1595, and embrace the parish of Rudby up to the year 1813, when each parish had its own separate register. The entries in the early Registers are in Latin. Baptisms, marriages, and burials are entered indiscriminately. There was no burial-ground enclosed until the year 1880 ; previous to that the funerals took place either at Hutton Rudby or at West Rounton.

The Society is indebted to Sir Hugh Bell for kindly giving a donation of £10 towards the cost of printing this Register.

The Index has been kindly prepared by Mr. John Charlesworth, of Horbury.

W. T. R.

REGISTERS OF EAST ROUNTON,

IN THE PARISH OF RUDBY.

Anno Domini 1595.

Baptizatus fuit Thomas Ridley filius Lionelli. xxx⁰ Die Maij.

Baptizat Richardus Coverdall filius Thomæ. xxviij⁰ Octobr.

Baptizatus Gulihelmus Campion filius Roberti. vij⁰ Decembris.

Sepultus fuit predictus Gulihelmus Campion. xxix⁰ Decembris.

Baptizata Anna Rountrie filia Johanis. xix⁰ Martij.

Sepulta fuit predicta Anna Rontrie. xxiiij⁰ Martij.

Anno Domini 1596.

Baptizatus Jacobus Tomson filius Jacobi. xxviij⁰ Martij.

Coniugati Thomas Simson et Anna Warde. Do Diæ Maij.

Jacobus Hemsley et Anna Kendraw. Nono Diæ Maij.

Gulihelmus Hugell et Francisca Midleton. xvj⁰ Diæ Maij.

Sepulta fuit Anna Buttrie uxor Richardi. xv⁰ Junii.

Sepultus fuit Jacobus Tomson. xxiv⁰ Augusti.

Baptizata Elizabetha Lever filia Rodolphi. xxx⁰ Augusti.

Baptizatus fuit Rowlandus Tomson filius Leonardi. xij⁰ Sep.

Sepulta Margareta Simson filia Johanis senioris. xxvij⁰ Oct.

Baptizata Anna Campion filia Roberti. xxvj⁰ Novembris.

Baptizata Anna Trughet filia Jacobi. xxviij⁰ Novembris.

Sepulta fuit Anna Hemsley uxor Jacobi. xiij⁰ Decembris.

Sepulta Anna Buttrie filia Roberti. xxiv⁰ Decembris.

Anna Truhet filia Jacobi. primo Januarii.

Sepultus Jacobus Tomson filius Jacobi et Janæ. xxviij Jan.

Baptiza Isabella Midleton filia Nicholai. secundo die Februarii.

Sepulta fuit Alicia Allene uxor Gulihelmi. vj⁰ februarij.

Sepult. Robertus Aplebee. xxviij februarij.

Johanes Rontrie filius Johanis. iiij⁰ Martij.

Baptizata Isabella Trughet filia Georgii. vj⁰ Martii.

Thomas Hugell filius Gulihelmi. ix⁰ Martii. Susceptores, Jacobus Trughet, Robertus Buttrie et Isabella Warde, vidua.

Sepultus Thomas Ridley filius Lionelli. xvij⁰ Martij.

Robertus Stevenson sepultus fuit. xxij⁰ Martij.

Anno Domini 1597.

xxiiij⁰ Martij. Baptizatus Robertus Simson filius Thomæ.

xxv⁰ Martij. Sepulta Isabella Midleton filia Nicholai.

primo Aprilis. Margareta Sherwood uxor Richardi.

Et v⁰ Aprilis. ipse Richardus sepultus fuit.

v⁰ Julii. Sepultus fuit Robertus Buttrie.

xvij⁰ Julij. Coniugati Georgius Yewen et Isabella Kaye.

A

xxxj⁰ Julii. Baptizatus Robertus Buttrie filius defuncti.

xiij⁰ Novembris. Sepulta fuit Alicia Midleton.

iiij Decembris. Coniugati Gulihelmus Hemsley et Manda Best De Hornbie.

xxviij⁰ Decembris. Sepultus fuit Jacobus Trughet. Colomī præstatissimus suæ ætatis.

Quarto Januarij. Baptizata Katerena Truhet filia defuncti.

xv⁰ Januarii. Baptizata ad motionæ Rogeri Elwod, Anna Douglas filia Annæ, ex fornicatione, ut fertur Johanis Truhet sed credibilior fama est ipsa Rogeri Elwod adulterio geminisse.

xij⁰ februarij. Baptizata Seith Johnson filia Jacobi.

xv⁰ Martij. Sepulta Katerena Trughet filia Jacobi defuncti.

Anno Domini 1598.

xxij⁰ Maij. Baptizatus Johanes Midleton filius Nicholaii.

xxx⁰ Maij. Coniugati Carolus Kendraw et Elina Truhet vidua Jacobi.

xviij⁰ Junij. Henricus Atkinson et Seitha Buttrie.

xix Novembris. Thomas Kilburn et Elizabetha Hudson.

xix Novembris. Baptizatus Johanes Ridleye filius Leonelli. Susceptores Johanes Roddam et Rodolphus Foster et Jana Hugell.

xxvj⁰ Novembris. Baptizat' Jacobus Coverdell filius Thomæ.

xvj⁰ Decembris. Elisia Kendraw uxor Caroli infantula. ad sepulturam ducta ut inde dîvesa nō sine violetia suspitione.

xvij⁰ Decembris. Coniugati Richardus Buttrie et Margareta Apleton De Brunton vidua.

xix⁰ Martii. Baptizatus Johanes Rontrie filius Johanis.

xij⁰ Decembris. Coniugati Jacobus Hemsleie et Elizabetha Maston Kirklevington Vidua.

Anno Domini 1599.

xxxj⁰ Martij. Sepultus fuit Idem Johanes infantulus.

xvij⁰ Junij. Baptizatus Egidius Hugell filius Gulihelmi.

xiiij⁰ Augusti. Jana Hemsleye filia Jacobi, et [blank]

Secundo Novembris. Jana Simson filia Thomæ.

vj Octobris. Sepulta fuit Jana Hemsleye filia Jacobi.

xxiij⁰ Octobris. Baptizatus Gulihelmus Paul . . . . filius.

iij Februarii. Baptizati Egidius Midleton filius Nicolai et Maria Truhet filia Georgii.

1600.

Coniugati xxij⁰ Aprilis. Gulihelmus Hunter et Elinora Hemsleye et

xix⁰ Maij. Gregorius Motherson et Isabella Warde Vidua.

Maij xxxj⁰. Robertus Warde et Elizabetha Gaile.

Novembris xviij⁰. Richardus Kendraw et Margareta Burton de Bushie, vidua.

Baptizati.

xxv⁰ Aprilis. Giliana Tomson filia Gulihelmi de West Akland, et

Primo Februarij. Anna Hemsleye filia Jacobi.

Anno Domini 1601.

xxv⁰ Aprilis. Baptizati Georgius Hemsley filius Gulihelmi, et

xxix Augusti. Egidius Simson filius Johanis Junioris.

x Maij. Coniugati Henricus Boomer de Martin et Giliana Hale de East roncton.

ix⁰ Augusti. Sepultus Egidius Hugel filius Gulihelmi.

29º Augusti. Baptizatus Egidius Simson filius Johanis. Susceptores Egidius Hugell, Robertus Ripley et Anna Simson.

iijº October. Sepultus fuit idem Egidius.

primo Novembris. Richardus Kendraw sepultus fuit.

xvijº Novembris. Coniugati Carolus Kendraw de East roncton et Jana Truhet parochiæ de Harlsey.

Anno Domini 1602.

iij Die Junij. Coniugati Edwardus Lambe De parochia Burnholme [sic] et Anna Simson filia Johanis de Eastroncton.

vj Die Julij. Christoferus Milner et Jana Gowland servi et famuli Thomæ Hugill parochiæ de Burnholme banis matrimonii ter p. Roberti Harton.

xxvº Julii. Baptizata fuit Anna Pauli filia Roberti. Susceptores Gulihelmus Thornabîe, Anna Bonwell et Anna Stockton.

xxijº Augusti. baptizatus fuit Egidius Hugill filius Gulihelmi. Suscep. Johanes Stockton, Robertus Warde et Francisca Hastings.

vijº Decembris. Sepulta fuit Margeria Wilsona Vidua.

xxº Decembris. baptizatus fuit Gulihelmus Kendraw filius Caroli. suscep. Gulihelmus Huthwait, Jo : Butrie, et [blank].

xijº febr. Alisia Tomson, Vidua.

xiijº febr. baptizata fuit Isabella Hemsley filia Jacobi. susceptores Robertus Warde, Anna Buttrie et Jana Kendrawe.

Anno Domini 1606.

vjº die Aprilis. Baptizata fuit Elizab : Bootra filia Johanis Trughet, Rogero Elwoodi marito fornicatione emesse Janæ. Susceptores Gulihelmus Hugill, Elizab : Rontrie et Isabella Tomson.

xxvijº Die mensis Aprilis. Sepulta fuit Elizabetha Warde uxor Roberti.

Quarto Die mensis Maij. Baptizati Johanes Warde filius Robti. susceptores Johanes Rothomund, Thomas Stockton et Anna Tunstall.

Et eodem tempore, Anna Hugyll filius Gulihelmi, susceptores Johanes Rothomund, Anna Jesse et Anna Stockton.

3º Die mensis Octobris. Sepulta fuit Elizabetha Campion filia Robti.

vº Die mensis Octobris. Baptizatus Robertus Kendraw filius Caroli. Susceptores Robertus Warde, Gulielmus Buttrie et Anna Stockton.

xxvjº Octobris. Baptizatus Thomas Simson filius Robti. suscep. Egidius Hugyll, Johanes Warde et Katerena Trughet.

xxviij Die Januarii. Baptizatus Christopherus Buttrie filius Gulihelmi. suscept. Jacobus Hemsleye, Georgius Trughet et Jana Cotes soror Gulihelmi.

vijº Die mensis februariï. Sepultus fuit Robertus Kendraw infantulus.

xxvº februarii. Baptizatus Jacobus Hemsley filius Jacobi. susceptores Laurentius Pearson, Edmondus Hemsley et Margareta Aplebie.

Anno Domini 1607.

xxº Die mensis Aprilis. Baptizatus fuit Richardus Simson filius Johanis. suscept. Richardus Kendraw, Richardus Warde et Margareta Apleby.

2º Die Augusti. Matrimonio Coniugati Thomas Wilson et Katerena Allen.

xvjº Octobris. Baptizata fuit Anna Roger filia Robti. Susceptores Gulihelmus Walker, Anna Turner et Elizabetha Aplebie.

xvº Die mensis Novembris. Baptizata fuit Elysabetha Wilson filia Thomæ. Susceptores Robertus Warde, Elizabetha Hemsley et Margareta Aplebie.

xxº Die mensis Novembris. Sepultus fuit Richardus Hemsleye plenus dier.

vjº Die Decembris. Coniugati Nycolaus Graye et Mauda Hemsley Vidua Gulihelmi.

xxº Decembris. Baptizatus Gulihelmus Kendraw filius Caroli. Susceptores Gulihelmus Thornabie, Gulihelmus Hugylle et Anna Jaire uxor Davidis.

Anno Domini 1608.

viij Die Maij. Baptizatus fuit Richardus Hemsley filius Jacobi. Susceptores Richardus Warde, Richardus Kendraw et Anna Atkinson.

xxivº Julij. Baptizatus fuit Gulihelmus Hugyll filius Gulihelmi. Susceptores Gulihelmus Huthwaite, Gulihelmus Thornabie et Katerena Trughet.

xixº Aug. Baptizatus Margareta Greye filius Nicolai. Susceptores Jacobus Hemsley, Margareta Aplebie et Emma Simson.

xixº Augusti. Sepultus fuit Gulihelmus Hugylle infans filius Gulihelmi.

Sept. v. Baptizatus fuit Gulihelmus Huthwayt filius Francisci. Susceptores Gulihelmus Hugyll, Robertus Warde et Katerena Trughet.

xxiijº Octobris. Matrimonio Coniugati Gulielmus Heron et Francisca Tomsone.

xxvjº Octobris. Baptizatus fuit Robertus Parkin filius Christoferi. Susceptores Robertus Hemsley, Robertus Hindman et Anna Garnet.

vijº Januarij. Baptizatus fuit Richardus Simson filius Robti. Susceptores Richardus Warde, Gulihelmus Walker et Margereta Aplebie.

xiijº Januarij. Sepultus fuit Idem Richardus Simson infantulus sex dierum.

29º Januarij. Baptizatus fuit Robtus Buttriæ filius Gulihelmi. Susceptores Robertus Warde, Johanes Wynde et Margareta Aplebie.

Anno Domini 1609.

xxº Augusti. Baptizata fuit Jana Trughet filia Georgij. Susceptores Jo: Warde, Jana Kendraw et Margereta Aplebie.

vijº Februarij. Baptizata fuit Elizabetha Simson filius Roberti. Susceptores Gulihelmus Buttrie, Isabella Hyndman et Elizabetha Rontrie.

Anno Domini 1610.

primo Aprilis. Baptizatus fuit Richardus Kendraw filius Caroli. Susceptores Richardus Porter, Edmondus Hemsley et Christabella Tyrrie.

Quarto Aprilis. Sepulta fuit Elyzabetha Simson infantula filia Roberti.

vijº Aprilis. Sepultus fuit Richardus Kendraw infantulus 7 dierum.

3º Junij. Baptizatus fuit Johannes Hemsleye filius Jacobi. Susceptores Johannes Hindman, Jo: Hebden et Isabella Hyndman uxor Jacobi.

xvijº Junij. Baptizata fuit Maria Tomson filia Gulihelmi de Swaynbie. Susceptores Carolus Midleton, Armiger, Maria Phillippot et Anna Tomson soror Gulihelmi predictus.

xxº Junij. Baptizata fuit Jana Athie filia Johanis de Sedburie, Elizabethæ Stevenson in fornicatione suscepta. Susceptores Gulihelmus Hugyll, Jana Hugyll et Katerena Trughet.

Jane Herone baptized the second day of August 1610.

xxiiij Septembris. Sepultus fuit Richardus Warde.

Primo Januarij. Baptizata fuit Francisca Hughyll filia Michaelis. Susceptores Robertus Warde, Francisca Hugylle et Elizabetha Warde.

xxvij⁰ Januarij. Baptizatus fuit Thomas Buttrie filius Gulihelmi. Susceptores Thomas Hastings, Willimus Walker et Alicia Buttrie.

Tertio Die mensis Februarij. Sepultus fuit Richardus Buttrie.

xxvij⁰ Die mensis Februarij. Baptizata fuit Elizabetha Humphreye filia Francisci. Susceptores Johanes Warde, Elizabetha Humphrey et Jana Hadocke.

Anno Domini 1611.

v Die Maij. Baptizata fuit Jana Kendraw. Susceptores Georgius Trughet, Francisca Trughet et Anna Bonwell.

2⁰ Die mensis Junij. Baptizata fuit Sara Wilson filia Thomæ. Susceptores, Richardus Porter, Sara Bradsonne et Anna Bonwell.

xx⁰ Die mensis Augusti. Baptizatus fuit Carolus Walker filius Gulihelmi. Susceptores Carolus Hastings, Robertus Nycolson et Anna Stockton.

xxvij⁰ Die mensis Augusti. Baptizatus Gulihelmus Simson filius Robti. Susceptores Gulihelmus Hughyll, Gregorius Mothersall et Elizabetha Hemsley.

xiij⁰ Octobris. Matrimonio coniugati Johanes Coulson de Hutton Rudbie et Elizabetha Tomson de Eastroncton.

xxij⁰ Decembris. Baptizata Tomasin Buttrie filia Robti. Susceptores Thomas Tomson, Katerena Trughet et Elizabetha Warde.

Anno Domini 1612.

viij⁰ Aprilis. Sepulta fuit Jenetta Simson vidua uxor Johanis defuncti.

20 Aprilis. Sepulta fuit Anna Warwick vidua parochiæ de Leedes.

vij⁰ Junij. Baptizata fuit Margeria Campion filia Robti. Susceptores Thomas Wilson, Margareta Humfrey et Jana Paule.

xxviij⁰ Die mensis Junii. Baptizata fuit Anna Hastings filia Caroli. Susceptores Egidius Hugyll, Anna Fowlgrove et Faitha Cutler.

27⁰ Julij. Sepultus fuit Gulihelmus Ælleni.

29⁰ Sepulta fuit. Jana Kendraw filia Caroli.

primo Augusti. Sepultus fuit Johanes Hemsley filius Jacobi.

vj⁰ Die Augusti. Sepulta fuit Tomasine Buttrie infans filia Rohti.

xiij⁰ Sept. Baptizatus fuit Georgius Trughet filius Georgii. Susceptores Edmundus Hemsley, Richardus Kendraw et Sara Bradforde.

xxix⁰ Octobris. Baptizatus fuit Simon Foxe filius Johanis. Susceptores Carolus Jarie, Thomas Hastings et Anna Bonwell.

fortio Januarij. Baptizatus fuit Georgius Parkino filius Christoferi. Susceptores Georgius Trughet, Rodolphus Turner et Maria Hastings.

xix⁰ Januarij. Sepulta fuit Elizabetha Stevenson.

xxvj⁰ Januarij. Baptizatus fuit Richardus Kendraw filius Caroli. Suscept. Thomas Hastings, Jacobus Hemsley et Margareta Kendraw uxor Robti.

xvj⁰ Martij. Sepulta fuit Elizabetha [nuyet].

Anno Domini 1613.

xxvij⁰ Martij. Sepulta Sara Wilson filia Thomæ.

vj⁰ Aprilis. Baptizatus fuit Egidius Walker filius Gulihelmi. Suscept. Egidius Hugyll, Edmondus Hemsley et Elizabetha Warde.

xj⁰ Aprilis. Baptizatus fuit Edmundus Hugill filius Gulihelmi. Suscept. Edmundus Rothomond, Armiger, Georgius Kendall et fides Cutler.

xxx⁰ Die mensis Maij. Sepultus fuit Franciscus Humfreye.

Quinto Die mensis Junii. Baptizatus fuit Ægidius Butrie filius Robti. Suscept. Ægidius Hugylle, Johanes Warde et Maria Hastings.

Decimo sexto die Junii. Sepulta fuit Anna Buttry filia Gulielmi Buttry.

Anno predict.

xviijº Julij. Sepultus fuit Rodolphus Turner.

xxiijº Julij. Sepultus fuit Ædmundus Hugyll Infans filius Gulihelmi.

xxxº Die mensis Julij. Baptizatus fuit Jacobus Hemsley filius Jacobi. Suscept. Carolus Hastings, Johanes Warde et Katerena Trughet.

xxvjº Septembris. Baptizatus Jacobus Humfreye filius Francisci defuncti. Susceptores Jacobus Hemsley, Georgius Trughet et Elizabetha Warde.

xvijº Octobris. Baptizatus fuit Lucas Hugyll filius Michaelis. Suscept. Ægidius Hugyll, Georgius Trughet et Margareta Hugyll.

29º Octobris. Sepultus fuit Rogerus Elwood.

31º Octobris. Baptizatus fuit Symon Buttrie filius Robti. Suscept. Edmondus Hemsley, Johanes Hebden et Anna Jarie.

vjº Octobris. Sepulta fuit Anna Hale vidua in multa nive.

In Die Sti. Thomæ Apostoli. Coniugati fuerunt Robertus Warde et Gyliana Athi parochiæ de litle Haughton in eadem palia.

viijº Januarij. Sepultus fuit Gulihelmus Walker.

30º Januarij. Baptizatus Johanes Graye filius Nicholai. Suscept. Jo : Warde, Rich. Kendraw et Gyliana Warde.

Anno Domini 1614.

xxvijº Martij. Baptizatus fuit Johanes Wilson filius Thomæ. Suscept. Johanes Turner, Thomas Garnet, francisca Hastings.

xxº Die Maii. Sepultus fuit Egidius Hugylle filius Gulihelmi.

xxvjº Maij. Baptizata fuit Maria Wetherell filia Thomæ. Suscept. Thomas Hugyll, Maria Byrd et Juliana Warde.

xiiijº Junij. Sepulta fuit Margeria Campion filia Roberti.

iijº Julij. Matrimonio coniugati Thomas Tomson et Anna Cotes.

4 Die Octobris. Baptizata fuit Maria Tomson filia Thomæ. Suscept. Thomas Hugyll, Maria Kendraw et Isabella Trughet.

2º Die Octobris. Sepultus fuit Henricus Coulsone.

30º Die mensis Octobris. Sepulta fuit Alicia Buttrie.

viijº Januarij. Baptizata fuit Giliana Hugyll filia Gulihelmi. Susceptores Thomas Hastings, Gyliana Warde et Maria Kendraw.

Anno Domini 1615.

Aprilis 23. Robertus filius Roberti Simpson baptizatus fuit.

Maij 3. Thomas filius Roberti Paul sepultus.

Julij 16. Georgius filius Jacobi Trewhayt baptizatus.

Julij 26. Henricus filius Roberti Buttry baptizatus.

28th Augusti. Baptizatus Robertus Warde filius Roberti. Susceptores Georgius Trughet, Gulihelmus Hugill et Jana Hugill.

Nov. 5. Robertus Coulson et Helena Shepheard matrimonio juncti.

Nov. 12. Elizabeth Hugill filia Guilielmi Hugill Sepulta.

Decem. 26. Juliana Coulson filia Roberti Coulson baptizata.

Janij 21. Elizabeth Trewhayt filia Georgij Trewhayt baptizata.

Janij 21. Egidius filius Michailis Spooner baptizatus.

Janij 28. Robtus. Kendray filius Caroli Kendray baptizatus die 28.

Feb : 3. Juliana filia Roberti Coulson sepulta die 3 Febru :

Feb : 11. Thomas filius Jacobi Hemsley baptizatus Febr. 11.

Anno Domini 1616.

March 26. Jana Elwood vidua sepulta fuit. March 26.

Novemb. 17. Johanes Fox et Jana Yowland matrimonio juncti.

Novemb. 21. Baptizati Richardus Colson et Margeria Colson nati Roberti Colson.

Jana Allenie sepulta fuit.

Anno Domini 1617.

viij⁰ Die Maij. Baptizata fuit Jana Hugill filia [*blank*]

Jaine Hugill the daughter of Thomas Hugill was buried the xvjth day of August.

Mary Simson the daughter of Willyam Simson was baptized the xvijth day of August.

Thomas Hugill senior was buried the xvijth day of October.

Thomas Mothersall of Kirkleaventon & Margery Humphrey were married the ixth day of November.

Jaine Thomson the daughter of Thomas Thomson was baptized the sixth day of November.

Anne Warde the daughter of Robert Warde was baptized the xxiijth day of November.

Mary Spooner the daughter of Michaell Spooner was baptized the xjth day of March.

Thomas Truhit the sonne of James Truhit was baptized the xth day of May.

Anno Domini 1618.

Margery Allen widdowe was buried the xxvjth day of May.

Juliana Hugill filia Thomæ Hugill baptizata fuit x^{mo} die Augusti. Susceptores Thomas Merrowe, Juliana Warde et Isabella Truhit.

Richardus Simson filius Roberti Simson baptizatus xvjth die Augusti. Susceptores Richardus Kendray, Richardus Porter et Isabella Truhet.

Ædward Coverdell the sonne of Thomas Coverdell was buried the xxijth day of September.

Ælizabeth Foxe the daughter of John Foxe was baptized the viijth day of October.

Julian Hewgill the daughter of Thomas Hewgill was buried the viijth day of October.

Christoferus Wilson filius Thomæ baptizatus xviij die Octobris. Susceptores Christopherus Walker, Robertus Paule et Philotis Thomson.

Margaret Mothersall the daughter of Thomas Mothersall was baptized the xxiiijth day of February.

Robert Cowlson was buried the xxiiijth day of February.

gillian Trewhit daughter of George Trewhit was buried the iiijth day of March. Thomas Coverdell, John Simson, Churchwardens. John Hesloppe, Curate there.

Anno Domini 1619.

Julian Spooner the daughter of Michael Spooner was baptized the xiijth day of August.

Marie Thomson the Daughter of Thomas Thomson was buried the xxviijth day of August.

Richard Swainson of Thornaby & Margaret Walker were married the xxxjth day of October.

Anno Domini 1620

Baptizatus xxj^{mo} die Maij. Georgius Thomson filius Thomæ Thomson. Susceptores Georgius Truhit, Richardus Porter et Guliana Warde.

xxx^{mo} Die Julij. baptizata Ælizabetha Swainson filia Richardi Swainson. Susceptores Robertus Buttrie, Ælizabetha Applebie et Isabella Truhit.

Thomas Laburne & Joane Shephearde were married the xxjth day of January.

Margaret Warde was buried the xixth day of March.

Anno Domini 1621.

Robert Paul the son of Robert Paul was buried the ixth day of May.

Christabell Tirry the wife of John Tyrry was buried the vjth day of June.

Giles Thomson & Anne Persevell were married the viijth day of July.

Richarde Warde the sonne of Robert Warde was baptized the thirde day of September.

Raphe Wilson was buried the xiiijth day of September.

James Truhit the sonne of James Truhit was baptized the xijth day of October.

Anne Laburne the daughter of Thomas Laburne was baptized the xxviijth day of October.

Richarde Buttry the son of William Buttry was baptized the xvijth day of March.

Francis Hugill the wife of William Hugill was buried the xxiijth of March.

Mary Simson the daughter of Robert Simson was baptized the xxiiijth day of March.

John Hesloppe, Curate.   Giles Hugill, Churchwarden.

Anno Domini 1622.

Inprimis William Humfreye of Hutton juxta Rudby & Isabell Truhit of this Chappelrie were married the xijth day of May.

Marie Thomson the daughter of Thomas Thomson was baptized the seventh day of July.

An Infant of George Truhitt was buried the seconde day of November.

Richarde Swainson the sonne of Richarde Swainson was baptized the 3 day of November.

Anno Domini 1623.

Inprimis Nicholas Middleton was buried the xxvth day of April.

Robert Ransonne the sonne of Robert Ransonne was baptized the xxvij day of April.

Francis Simson the wife of John Simson was buried the first day of May.

Willyam Armstrong the son of Willyam Armstrong was baptized the xvijth day of May.

John Rowntree was buried the first day of June.

Willyam Hugill & Florence Campion were marryed the xijth day of October.

Willyam Laburne the sonne of Thomas Laburne, was baptized the xxiijrd day of November.

Anno Domini 1624.

Inprimis Christofer Coates was buried the xxviijth day of March.

Widdowe Cowlson senior was buried the xijth day of Aprill.

Mary Simson the daughter of Robert Simson was buried xvth day of April.

John Hesloppe, Clerke, Curate.
Wiliyam Hugill, Willyam Truhit, Churchwardens.

Jaine Hugill the wife of Giles Hugill was buried the first day of May.

Willyam Warde ye sonne of Robert Warde was baptized ye first day of August.

Willyam Thomson the sonne of Thomas Thomson was baptized the xvij[th] day of November.

Anno Domini 1625.

Inprimis Isabell Swainson the daughter of Richarde Swainson was baptized the xxiiij[th] of March.

George Armestronge the sonne of Willyam Armestronge was baptized the seconde day of October.

Richarde Laburne the sonne of Thomas Laburne was baptized the sixth day of October.

Joane Kendray the daughter of Richarde Kendray was baptized the ninth day of October.

John Simson the sonne of Robert Simson was baptized the nineteenth day of October.

Willyam Paule and Ælizabeth Baine of Cuckwolde were married the xxiij day of October.

George Hesloppe the sonne of John Hesloppe, Clerke, Curate of Eastrounton, was baptized the first day of November.

Jaine Harryson widdowe was burryed the 28th of November.

Raph Lainge & Jaine Campyon were married the 25th of November.

Margaret Coates the daughter of James Coates begotten in Adultery was baptized the 31st day of December.

Richard Ranson & Elizabeth Ranson the sonne & daughter of Robert Ranson were baptized the 8th day of January.

Richarde Lainge the sonne of Raph Lainge was baptized the 26th day of February.

Anno Domini 1626

Inprimis Widdowe Hugill was buried the first day of July.

Thomas Paule the sonne of Willyam Paule was baptized the tenth day of September.

Jaine Kendray the daughter of Richarde Kendray was buried the eleventh day of September.

John Hesloppe, Curate.
Raphe Watters, George Truhit, Churchwardens.

Margery Colthurst the daughter of Edward Colthurst was baptized the xxj[st] day of December.

Jaine Hugill was buried the 1st day of January.

An Infant of Giles Thomson was buried the 19th of January.

Barbara Roddam the daughter of Ædmonde Roddam Æsquire was baptized the fourth day of February.

Barbara Swainson the daughter of Richarde Swainson was baptized the xviij[th] day of February.

Anno Domini 1627.

Inprimis Ailse Thomson the daughter of Thomas Thomson was baptized the xv[th] day of July.

Jaine Kendray the daughter of Richarde Kendray was baptized the xxij[nd] day of July.

Widdowe Appleby was buried the 13th day of February.

Anno Domini 1628.

Inprimis Francis Hesloppe the sonne of John Hesloppe, Clerke, Curate of Eastrounton, was baptized the first day of April.

Thomas Roddam Æsquire was buried the 26th day of April.

Raphe Warde the sonne of Robert Warde was baptized the 24th day of August.

Katherine Roddam the daughter of Ædmonde Roddam Æsquire was baptized the 7th day of September.

Henry Robbinson of Ingleby under Arncliffe & Jaine Simson were married the 9th day of November.

Steven Merington the sonne of Matthew Merington & Joane Swainson the daughter of Richarde Swainson were baptized the first day of January.

Jaine Thomson the daughter of Giles Thomson was baptized the 20th day of January.

Elizabeth Ranson the wife of Robert Ranson & an Infant of the said Robert Ranson were buried the 27th of January.

Robert Paule the sonne of William Paule was baptized the 1st day of February.

Widdowe Coates was buried the 20th day of February.

Thomas Merrowe was buried the ninth day of March.

John Hesloppe, Clerk, Curate.
Raphe Watters, Robert Paule, Churchwardens.
Anno Domini 1629.

Inprimis Jaine Kendray the daughter of Richarde Kendray was buried the 17th day of Aprill.

John Simson and Ailse Wilson were marryed the 16th day of June.

Febra. 9no. Sepultus fuit John Heslop, Cleric', in Cemeterio de West Rounton.

Ego Georgius Nedham in artibus Magister, admissus fuit ad Capellam de East Rounton, vacantem per mortem John Heslop; decimo die Februarij 1629.

Anno Domini 1630. Guardianus Tho : Tompson.

Aprilis 11o. Sepultus fuit Franciscus Heslop infantem cemiterio de West Rounton.

May 23. Baptizata fuit Juliana Robinson filia Henrici et Janæ Robinson. Susceptores fuerunt Gulihelmus Paul, Juliana Ward et Anna Paul.

July 4to. Coniugati fuerunt Gulielmus Heron et Margarett Gray hujus Capellæ.

August. Baptizata fuit Anna Kendray filia Richardi Kendray et Dorothea uxoris ejus. Suscepterunt Christofer Tompson de West Rounton et Margareta Swainson et Maria Merington.

Sept. 26. Baptizatus fuit Willimus Armstrong filius Bartholomæi et Anna uxoris ejus. Susceptores Willimus Hugill, Willimus Paul et Tamisana Tod.

Feb. 6to. Sepulta fuit Dorothea Rodam filia Mrs Rodam.

Anno Domini 1631.

Aprilis 28. Sepultus fuit Richardus Ranson infans boni viri Roḃti Ranson.

July 17. Coniugati fuerunt Thomas Campershine de Parochia de Sigston et Barbara Wilkinson hujus Capellæ banis matrimonii ter publicis editis juxta hujus Ecclesiæ.

July 23. Coniugati fuerunt Thomas Stainthorp Capellæ de Whorlton et Ellena Shawe parochiæ de West Rounton virtute licentiæ illie concessa et Decano et Capitalo Ecclesiæ Cathedrae beati Petri Ebor p.p. sede Archiepali et seriati dati 23 hujus mensis Julii per Signata W. Easdall.

Sept. 25. Baptizata fuit Elizabetha Paul filia Gullielmi et Elizabetha. Suscepterunt Robertus Day de Welbury et Elizabetha ejusdem parochiæ et Anna Paul hujus Capellæ.

Nov. 6to. Baptizata fuit Anna Gedling filia Richardi de Highgate Hill hujus Capellæ. Susceptores Richardus Porter, Anna Swalwell et Elizabetha Weldon.   George Nedham, Curate.

Nov. 27. Coniugati fuerunt Johannes Ward hujus Capellæ et Alicia Smith de Crathorne banis matrimoniis ter publicis editis.

Decemb. 17. Baptizata fuit Anna Armstrong filia Bartholomæi. Suscepterunt Johannes Truhit, Anna Paul et Anna Ward filia Roberti, omnes hujus Capellæ.

Decemb. 29. Sepultus fuit Ægidius Hugill in Cæmeterio de Hutton juxta Rudby.

Feb. 13. Sepulta fuit infans Thomæ et Barbara Campershine abortiue in Cæmeterio de West Rounton.

Anno Domini 1632.

April 15. Baptizata fuit Mathilda Merington filia Mathæi Merington et uxoris ejus. Suscepterunt Johannes Truwhayt et Anna Swalwell hujus Capellæ et Thomas Fowler de Stockton.

Aug : 31. Baptizata fuit Gratia Ranson filia boni viri Ranson et uxoris ejus. Suscepterunt Johannes Ward Senior et Anna Paul et Jana Weldon parochiæ de West Rounton.

Sept. 18. Sepulta fuit Jana Tompson hujus Capellæ in Cæmeterio de West Rounton.

Octob. 1°. Baptizata fuit Jana filia Isabellæ Heslop viduæ.

Octob. 7mo. Baptizatus fuit Robertus filius ejusdem Isabellæ viduæ ex eodem illigitimo partu Roberto Weldon de West Rounton fuit fertur genitore.

Octob : 24. Sepultus fuit Johes Ward hujus Capellæ.

Novemb. 18^{uo}. Decimo octavo Baptizata fuit Elizabetha Truhitt filia Johannis Truhitt.

Novemb. 19no. Sepulta fuit Alicia Apleby in Cæmiterio de West Rounton.

Decemb. 9no. Sepulta fuit Anna Walker vidua in Cæmiterio de West Rounton.

Decemb. 10mo. Sepultus fuit Robertus Paul Senior.

Decemb. 23. Baptizatus fuit Thomas Ward filius Johannis Ward Junioris.

Jan : 6to. Sepulta fuit Elizabetha Waters vidua.

Jan : 23to. Sepultus fuit Guilielmus Truhitt.

Anno Domini 1633.

Aprilis 17mo. Sepulta fuit Juliana Robinson filia Henrici et Jana Robinson.

Junij 16to. Baptizatus fuit Richardus Kendraw filius Richardi et uxoris ejus. Suscepterunt Richardus Lodge et Guilielmus Thornaby et Anna Truwhit uxor Johannis hujus Capellæ.

Julij 21no. Baptizata fuit Elizabetha Campershine filia Thomæ Campershine.

Sept :   8no.   Baptizatus fuit Richardus Hemslye filius Richardi.
Nov : 17mo.   Baptizata fuit Tamiesina Robinson filia Henrici.
                     Georg. Nedham, Curat.   Rich. Gedling, Guardian.
Novemb. 29.   Baptizata fuit Jana Armstrong filia Bartholomæi.
Jan. 26.   Baptizata fuit Anna Paul filia Gulielmi.

Anno Domini 1634.

April 1mo.   Baptizata fuit Elizabetha Ward filia Robti. Seniores.
Junij 5no.   Sepultus fuit prematurus partus Rich : Hemsley.
Nov. 3.   Sepultus fuit Robertus Simpson Senior.
Nov. 16to.   Baptizatus fuit Guilielmus Gedling filius Richardi.
Jan. 18no.   Sepultus fuit Guilielmus Heron in Cæmeterio de West Rounton.
Martij 1mo.   Baptizata fuit Elizabetha Ward filia Johannis.
Tho : Truwhit the son of John Truwhit baptized August the first.

Anno Domini 1635.   Guardianus Johes Simpson.

April 22do.   Sepultus fuit filius Thomas Laborni in Cæmeterio de West
                     Rounton sine Baptizando mortuus.
Junij 7mo.   Baptizata fuit Jana Hemslye filia Richardi.
Julij 4to.   Sepulta fuit eadem Jana Hemslye.
Aug : 26to.   Baptizata fuit Margaret Campershine filia Thomæ.
Aug : 22.   Baptizata fuit Florentia Smith filia Menilla Smith in fornica-
                     tione p. Gullielmi Paul ut dicito.

Anno Domini 1636.   Guardianus Johannes Ward.

July   27.   Baptizata fuit p' matura Jaine Guilielmi Masterman et uxoris
                     ejus.
Aug. 13.   Sepulta fuit Anna Paul filia Guilielmi.
Aug. 14.   Baptizata fuit Elizabetha Robinson filia Henrici.
Sept. 29.   Baptizata fuit Joanna Heron filia Jaine Heron in fornicatione
                     per Thomas Butry de Stokesley fuit dicito.
Aug : 28.   Baptizatus fuit Richardus Ranson filius Robti.
Feb : 2.   Baptizata fuit Anna Paul filia Guilielmi.

Anno Domini 1637.

Aprilis 2do.   Baptizata fuit Maria Truhit filia Johanis.
May 14.   Bapt. [blank].
Octob. 1mo.   Coniugati fuerunt Egidius Walker et Alicia Morly de Par-
                     ochiæ de Guisbrough.
Jan.   1mo.   Baptizatus fuit Franciscus Getling filius Richardi.
Jan. 29no.   Sepulta fuit Magdalena Gray uxor Nicholai.
July 10mo.   Baptizata fuit Anna Walker filia Egidii.
                     Guardianus Gulielmus Hugill.

Anno Domini 1638.   Guardianus Guilielmus Masterman.

April 3lo.   Coniugati fuerunt Johannes Hirdman et Anna Ward.
May   6.   Baptizata fuit Maria Forsitt filia Roberti.
August 28uo. Sepultus fuit Richardus Kendra.

Anno Domi. 1639.   Guardianus Robertus Ward.

Junij 16to.   Baptizata fuit Margareta Paul filia Guilielmi.
Aug : 23lo.   Sepulta fuit Elizabetha Apleby in Cemeterio de West Rounton.
Sept : 1mo.   Sepultus fuit Guilielmus Hugill.
Octob. 7mo.   Sepultus fuit Thomas Tompson in Cæmeterio de West Rounton.
Octob. 27mo. Baptizata fuit Margareta Hindman filia Johanis.

Nove : 10mo. Matrimonio conjuncti fuere Florentia Hugill hujus Capellæ et
    Johanes Tayler Parochiæ de West Rounton banis matri-
    monialibus ter interrogatis.
Nov. 18^{uo}. Baptizatus fuit Thomas Blades filius Leonardi.
Decemb. 8^{uo}. Baptizata fuit Anna Truhitt filia Johanis.
Feb^r 2do. Baptizata fuit Jana Walker filia Egidii.
Feb^r 11mo. Baptizatus fuit Guilielmus Ward filius Johannis.
        Anno Domini 1640. Guardianus Johannes Hindman.
Aprilis decimo secundo Coniugati fuere Robertus Cotes Capellæ Dighton-
    ensis et Dorothea Kendra hujus Capellæ. Banis matrimo'libus utrima
    ter interrogatis.
Augusti secundo Baptizatus fuit Guilielmus Ranson filius Roberti.
Augusti sexto Sepultus fuit Franciscus Masterman filius Guilielmi.
Augusti vicessimo Sepultus fuit predictus Guilielmus Ranson filius Robti
Junij. Vicessimo Octavo. Coniugati fuere Guilielmus Coverdale hujus
    Capellæ et Dorothea Rogerson de Ingleby subter Arnclif banis matri-
    monialibus utrima ter interrogatis.
January. Ultimo. Baptizata fuit Maria Merrington filia Mathæi.
           Anno Domini 1641.
Aprilis undecimo. Baptizatus fuit Franciscus Coverdale filius Guilielmi.
Junij vicessimo quinto. Sepulta fuit Maria Weldon filia Richardi in
    Cæmeterio West Rountonensi.
Septemb. undecimo. Sepultus fuit Thomas Laborn.
Decemb. vicessimo sexto. Baptizatus fuit Robertus Blades filius Leonardi.
           Guardianus Carolus Kendra.
           Anno Domini 1642.
Maij primo. Baptizatus fuit Georgius Truhit filius Johannis.
Julij decimo. Baptizata fuit Elizabetha Apleby filia Egidii.
Augusti decimo quarto. Baptizata fuit Jana Ward filia Johannis.
Octob. vicessimo tertio. Baptizata fuit Jana Hindman filia Johannis.
Jan. vicessimo decimo. Sepulta fuit Jana Paul.
Febru. quarto. Baptizatus fuit Henricus Weldon filius Richardi.
           Guardianus Carolus Kendra.
           Anno Domini 1643.
Maij treginta decimo. Coniugati fuere Alicia Gedling hujus capellæ et
    Thomas Tunstall Parochiæ de Hutton Rudby.
Junij decimo octavo. Sepultus fuit Richardus Weldon hujus Capellæ in
    Cæmeterio de West Rounton juxta natus fuit.
Julij undecimo. Coniugati fuere Elizabetha Kendra hujus capellæ et
    Henricus Heborn Parochiæ de Ingleby Arncliffe licentiæ obtenta a dno.
    per Easdale sigello et solvit decem solidos mihi.
Aug : vicessimo septimo. Baptizata fuit Phylis Robinson filia Henrici.
Nov. decimo novo. Baptizata fuit Johannes Gedling filius Johannis.
Decemb. Baptizatus fuit Robertus Co[? tes] filius Johannis' Sen.
Mart. septimo. Baptizata fuit Alicia Tod filia Christoferi.
        Anno Domini 1644. Guardianus Carolus Kendra.
Junij undecimo. Baptizata fuit Joanna Wright filia Antony.
Junij vicessimo. Baptizatus fuit Christoferus Jackson filius Johannis ut
    sus[cipit] et Janæ Tompson in fornicatione genitus fuerant Welburyensis.
August decimo. Sepultus fuit Michaell Hugill.

August. vicessimo quinto. Baptizata fuit Averilla Coverdale filia Guilielmi.
August. ultimo. Sepulta eadem Averilla in Cæmeterio W. Rountonensi.
Octob. vicessimo septimo. Baptizata fuit Maria Ward filia Johannis.
Nove. nono. Sepultus fuit Mathewus Merington filius Mathewi.
Dec. decimo quinto. Baptizatus fuit Guilielmus Apleby filius Ægidii.
Jan. primo. Baptizatus fuit Thomas Gedling filius Johannis.
Jan. tertio. Sepulta fuit Maria Gedling uxor Johannis.
Jan. duodecimo. Baptizata fuit Barbaria Truhit filia Johannis.
Jan. vicessimo sexto. Baptizatus fuit Johannes Parlour filius Ranulphi.
Feb. vicessimo sexto. Sepultus fuit Thomas Welbury in Cæmeterio W.
Rounton.   Guardianus Johannes Hirdman.

Anno Domini 1645.

April. decimo tertio. Baptizatus fuit Christoferus Blades filius Leonardi.
Junij vicessimo secundo. Coniugati fuere Anna Ranson hujus Capellæ et
Guilielmus Grason Parochiæ de Eston Banis matrimonilib9 ter utring̃:
interrogatis.
Decimo octavo. Baptizatus fuit Guilielmus Sutlington filius Thomæ de
Dumfrise in Scotia.
ultimo. Baptizatus fuit Gabriell Chalk filius Francisci.
Jan. vicessimo sexto. Sepultus fuit Robertus Ward.
Feb. octavo. Baptizatus fuit Thomas Coverdale filius Guilielmi.
Martij vicessimo quarto. Baptizatus fuit Johannes Tod filius Christoferi.
Guardianus Johannes Gedling.

Anno Domini 1646.

Maij Decimo nono. Matrimonii Coniugati fuere Johannes Lawson
parochiæ de Leak et Anna Hugill hujus Capellæ banis matrimonialibus
ter interrogatis.
August. vicessimo tertio. Baptizata fuit Anna Gedling filia Johannis.
Junij vicessimo secundo. Baptizatus fuit Robertus Hirdman filius
Johannis.
Octob. vicessimo septimo. Baptizatus fuit Jacobus Makelyn filius cor-
poratis Makelyn Scoti p. uxorem Scotiana.
Dec. ultimo. Sepultus fuit Johannes Simpson Senioȓ tima morti ereptus.
Jan. secundo. Sepultus Richardus Gedling fuit intestatus.
Jan : quinto. Matrimonii Coniugati fuere Henricus Faithy e. Regimento
Generalis Lashby miles et Isabella Swan filia Richardi hujus Capellæ
Banis Matrimonialiabus ter interrogatis.
Jan : undecimo. Baptizata fuit Anna Boons filia Guilielmi.
Feb : Decimo sexto. Baptizatus fuit Georgius Chalk filius Francisci Chalk.
Mart. Primo. Coniugati fuere Thomas Ridett et Margareta Cotes Banis
Matrimonialibus ter interrogatis.
Mart : septimo. Baptizata fuit Alicia Ward filia Johannis.
Mart : undecimo. Sepultus fuit Richardus Porter.

Anno 1647.

April quarto. Baptizata fuit Jana Wright filia Antonii.
Aprilj vicessimo. Sepulta fuit vidua Spooner in Cæmeterio West Rounton.
Julij quarto. Baptizata fuit Jana Truhit filia Johanis.
Nov. vicesimo primo. Baptizatus fuit Johannes Walker filius Egidii.
Nov. vicesimo septimo. Baptizata fuit Anna Faithy filia Henrici genilitis
e. Regimento Generalis Lashby desent qui ut creditus viri.

Jan : primo. Baptizata fuit Margareta Ridett filia Thomæ.
Feb : vicesimo sexto. Sepulta fuit Alicia Simpson vidua Johannis.
Baptizata fuit Guilielmus Blades filius Leonardi.
Guardianus Johannes Gedling.
Anno 1648.
Aug : Decimo tertio. Baptizata fuit Elizabetha Parlor filia Ranulphi.
Sep : tertio. Baptizata fuit Jana Dobson filia Johannis.
Octob. octavo. Baptizatus fuit Jacobus Gedling filius Johannis.
Martij vicesimo. Sepulta fuit vidua Blades in Cæmiterio West Rounton.
Anno 1649.
Aprilis 1649. Sepultus fuit Thomas Blades Ibidem ejusdem.
Maij nono. Sepulta fuit Joanna Blades filia Leonardi.
Junij tertio. Baptizatus fuit Robertus Ward filius Johannis.
Junij vicesimo tertio. Sepult. fuit Dobson.
Aug : Tertio. Sepulta fuit Margareta Ridett filia Thomæ in Cæmeterio W.
Rounton.   John Stockton, curate of East Rounton.
1654.
Elizabeth filia John Gedlin Baptized.
John the sonn of John Truwhitt baptized the first day of June 1651.
1655. Thomas Swale et Margarett Corner m^d 13 die November.
Mathew the sonne of Steven Merrinton of Harlsey baptized the 2nd day
    of December 1655 by me John Stockton.
Elizabeth Paul Sepultus 10 die Augusti 1662.
Robt. the sonn of John Truwhitt baptized the second of October 1653.
Thomas Truwhitt & Elizabeth Todd married the 5th May 1657.
Alis the wife of John Ward Buried the 15th of February 1663.
Thomas Marsterman and Averill Fawcitt married the 4th of August 1657.
1655. Maria filia John Parkin bapt^d 23 die Septembris.
1656. Jone the daughter of John Truwhitt bap. 24 die Maij.
1656. James the sonn of Willm. Ward baptized the 17 day of August.
1656. Mary the daughter of Willm. Tomson 2 day of November.
Johñay the Daughter of John Truwhitt Baptized the 29th of May 1656.
John the sonn of Thomas Truwhitt Baptized the 26th of October 1660.
1662. Willm. Myles of London and Catheren Pinckney of Inglebie married
    2nd of March.
1662. James filius Willimus Marsterman bap. 27 die Aprilis.
Thomas filius Willimus Tomson eodem die.
Thomas filius Willimus Shiphard de Harlsey grange 16 October.
James filius John Rilton bap. 10 die Novembris Englyby Arncliffe.
Christofer the son of Mathew Wilkinson of Mount bap. 22 day February.
1660. William the sonne of William Masterman Baptized 2 day of Febru-
    ary.
James Bowes Barne the ending of february 1649.
    John Trewhit of East Rounton elected by the Parishioners to be
parish Register of the said place the 24th May 1657, was approved and
sworn to the due execution of the office and trust aforesaid, before me
the 25th of May 1657. .   F^r Lascelles.
Anno Domini 1657. Margarett Masterman buried the 2^d of July 1658.
Marie the daughter of John Gedlinge bapts. the 5 die June 1657.
Alis the daughter of Gulielmus Walker bapt. the 18th day of April 1658.

Jane the daughter of Willim Tomson bapt. the 2^d day of May 1658.

Michell the sonn of Willim Masterman Sen. baptized the second of August 1663.

1662. Elizabeth the daughter of Christofer Lambart bap. 26 day of February.

1663. Thomas the sonn of William Labourn baptized the 18th of September.

Mr Henry Ogle minister of East Rounton chosen by the consent of the Inhabitants the first of August 1663.

John Hindman chosen by Mr Ogle to be Clarke of East Rounton and Register, the 8 day of Aprill in the year of our Lord God 1664.

Anno Domini 1664.

John Thompson the sonne of William Thompson Baptized the last day of September.

The burial of William Ward the sonne of John Ward the 25 of October.

Margrett the Daughter of William Masterman Jun. Baptized the 20th of November.

The buriall of Barbary the wife of William Ward the 29th of December.

Henry Palmer and Jane Ward of East Rounton was married with a lycense the 7th of February.

Willm Lyklay & Elizabeth Robinson was marryd the 19th of May 1666.

Thomas Ward and Mary [blank] was marryed the 8th of June with a lycense in the yeare 1666.

Anno Domini 1665.

Robt. Ward was buried the 10th of May 1665.

Robt. Symson of Haygarth Hill and Hanna Robinson of West Rounton was married the 23rd of May.

Richard the sonn of Willm Labourn baptized the 26th of November 1665.

Richard Simson & Mary Flintoft married the 30th of May 1665.

John the sonn of John Swan baptized the 21st of January 1665.

Henry Robinson buried the 20th of May 1666.

Lenard the sonn of Robt. Blades baptized the 6th of February 1665.

Margreet the daughter of Francis Coverdaile baptized the 19th of March 1666.

Jane the daughter of Tho : Blades baptized the 25th of March.

Jane the daughter of Tho : Blades buried the 28th of March.

Willm the sonn of Richard Symson baptized the 22nd of Aprill.

Willm the sonn of Robt. Symson baptized first of July.

Alce the daughter of John Ward buried the 30th of July.

Mary the daughter of John Ward buried the 13th of November.

James Hunter & Margreet Paull married the second of October.

Willm the sonn of Willm Licklay baptized the 9th of February.

Ann the daughter of Willm Maisterman Seno : baptized the 3rd of March.

Francis the sonne of William Maisterman Junio. baptized the 30th of November.

1667.

Elizabeth the daughter of Richard Sympson baptized the 22nd of September.

William Maisterman' Senio. buried July the 22nd.

Elizabeth daughter of James Hunter baptized the 4th of August.

John Gedling buryed the 23 day of August.

An the daughter of Robert Hemsley buried the 29th of September.
Thomas Whorlton and Dorothy Liddale married November the 1st.

1668.

An the daughter of Thomas Whorlton baptized the first day of January.
An the daughter of William Maisterman baptized the 19th of January.
William the son of Francis Coverdale baptized the seventh day of February.
An the daughter of Thomas Whorleton buried the eight day of February.
William Paull buryed the 21 day of March.

Anno Domini 1669.

James the son of William Ward buried the 10 of May.
Jane the daughter of William Lickly baptized the 23 of May.
Charles the son of Thomas Hall buried the 17 day of June.
An the daughter of Thomas Ward baptized 23 day of June.
George the son of Robert Simpson baptized the 4th of July.
William the son of William Laburn baptized the 19 of September.
William the son of James Hunter baptized the 26 of September.
Elizabeth the daughter of John Swan baptized the x of October.

1670.

Christopher the son of Robert Blades baptized the 17th of Aprill.
Margret the daughter of Thomas Whorleton baptized the 21 of Aprill.
Margret the daughter of John Hirdman buryed the 17 of June.
An the wife of Robert Hemsley buryed the 8 of September.
Joane Laburne buryed the 22 day of September.
Julian Ward buried the 10th of November.
Francis Chalke buried the 29 of January.
William the son of William Laburn buryed the 7 of February.

Anno Domini 1671.

Thomas the son of Willi Maisterman baptized March 26.
Elizabeth Lickly buried the 26 of April wife of William Lickly.
Alis the daughter of Giles Walker buryed the 3d day of June.
[blank] the son of Robert Sympson baptized the 21 of May.
Thomas Bowes buryed the 19th of September.
An the wife of Georg Hemsley buried the third day of January.
James and Mary the children of James Hunter baptized the 18th day of February.
Georg Liddale the elder buried the same day.

1672.

James the son of James Hunter buryed July the 10 day.
John Ridley buryed the 17th day of July.
An the wife of John Truhit buryed the 27th of July.
Thomas the son of Thomas Ward baptized the six of October.
Robert the son of Willi Lickly baptized the 13 day of October.
Mary the daughter of Tho : Whorleton baptized the [blank].
Mary the said daughter of Tho : Whorleton buryed the 9 of February.

1673.

Elizabeth the Daughter of Robert Blades baptized the 12 of Aprill.
Sara the Daughter of William Maisterman baptized the 25 of May.
The buryall of Willi Ward the 24 of July.
Elizabeth the Daughter of John Gedling baptized the 11 of October.
Dorothy the Daughter of Thomas Whorleton baptized the 10 of March.

1674.

John Robinson buryed the 30th Day of March.

Hannah the Daughter of James Hunter baptized the 7th Day of May.

George Hemsley buryed the 4 Day of June.

Mary the Daughter of Robert Sympson baptized the 14th of June.

An the wife of William Rennison buryed the 20 Day of June.

Thomas the son of William Lickly baptized the 11 Day of October.

Tho : the sd. son of William Lickly buried the 15 Day of October.

Asqueth Cotome and Jane Harker marryed the 29 of November.

Thomas the son of Thomas Coverdale baptized the last of January.

William Laburne buried the 7 Day of February.

1675.

Robert the son of Robert Hemsley baptized the 15 of Aprill.

John the son of William Maisterman baptized the 20 Day of May.

Alice the Daughter of Tho : Ward baptized the 23 Day of May.

Willi Coverdale buried the 24 Day of May.

Robert the son of Robert Hemsley buried the 11 day of July.

An Marsterman buried the 14 Day of September.

Mary the Daughter of John Gedling baptized the 17 Day of October.

Margret the Daughter of William Lickly baptized the 8 of February.

1676.

Margret the Daughter of James Hunter baptized the 11 of June.

Margery Chalke buried the 6 Day of July.

Abygale the Daughter of Thomas Whorleton baptized July 13.

An the Daughter of Robert Hemsley baptized the 20 Day August.

John the son of George Truhit baptized the 22 day of August.

John Truwhit buried the 29 Day of August 1676.

John and Margret the children of Robt. Blades baptized November the first.

1677.

Leonard Blades buryed the first Day of May.

Margret the Daughter of James Hunter buryed Septem. 17.

Jane the Daughter of William Marsterman baptized November 13.

Sara the Daughter of John Gedling baptized December 9 Day.

An Paul buried the 9 Day of March.

1678

Margret the Daughter of Tho : Coverdale baptized July 7 Day.

Mary the Daughter of Thomas Ward baptized August the 4 Day.

Elizabeth the Daughter of Tho : Whorleton was baptized the 23 Day of September.

James the son of James Mellanby baptized November the 24.

Georg the son of Georg Truwhit buried December 4.

Georg the son of Robt. Hemsley baptized February the 23 Day.

1679.

An the wife of Willi Lickly buried the first Day of May.

Elizabeth the Daughter of John Gedlin buried the 14 of May.

Margret the Daughter of James Hunter baptized the 17 of August.

Sara the Daughter of John Gedlin buried the 16 of Septem.

Francis Cort buried the 29 of September.

An the Daughter of Tho : Whorlton baptized the 14 of February.

was buried the next day being the 15 of February.

Thomas the son of William Walker buried the 20 of February.
John the son of John Gedlin baptized March the 26.

1680.

Thomas Ward buryed the third of September.
Jane Thomson buried the 24 of September.
Syeth Parler buried the 6 Day of October.
Widd' Blades buried the 14 Day of October.
Richard Ward buried the 20 Day of October.
Giles Walker buried the 4 Day of November.
Alice Walker buried the 10 Day of November.
Ellis Truwhit buryed the 14 Day of December.
Margret the Daughter of Mary Ward bapt. the 29 of December.
Elezabeth Bowes buryed the 30 Day of December.
Margret the Daughter of Mary Ward buried the last of December.
Mary Ward the wife of Thomas Ward buried 15 of February.
John Hirdman was buried the 7 of March.

1681.

Ellis the Daughter of George Truwhit buried the 23 of February.
Elizabeth Gedlin baptized the 28 of February.
Daniel Whorlton baptized the 1 of November.
Francis Masterman was buried the 28 of July 1685.
Daniel Whorleton son of Thomas Whorleton buried the 3^d day of Feb : 1682.
Elizabeth Daughter of Thomas Whorleton buried the 9th of May 1682.
Isabell Swan of East Rounton buried the 8th day of July 1683.
Jane Swan daughter of John Swan buried the 31 day of March 1683.
Dorathy Walker buried the 14th day of April 1683.
George Truhit and Margret Dauson married the 24th of October 1683.
Elizabeth Daughter of Thomas Whorleton baptized the 27th Day of May
    1684.
Jane Daughter of George Trewhit ye 2^d Day of September 1684.
[blank] Trewhit son of George Trewhit baptized ye 12th day of April 1685.
Willyam son of George Brown buried ye 13th Day of July 1685.
Francis Masterman son of Willyam buried ye 28th Day of July 1685.
Willyam Midleton and Margret Masterman maried 18th day of November
    1685.
Dorathy Liddill buried ye 2nd day of April 1686.
Mary daughter of Thomas Whorleton baptized 1st day of July 1686.
Mary Brown buried ye 14th day of December 1686.
Margret daughter of Will. Masterman Junior baptized ye 15th day of
    February 1689.
Elizabeth Blades wife of Robert Blades buried October ye 14, 1689.
Isabell Tompson buried ye 15th Day of February 1689.
Jane Lebron buried ye 15th Day of February 1689.
Margret daughter of James Frankland baptized ye 20 of March 1689.
Elizabeth daughter of George Trewhit baptized ye 8th day of April 1690
Jane daughter of Willyam Masterman junior baptized ye 2th day of January
    1691.
Mary daughter of George Trewhit baptized ye 7th day of March 1691.
Willyam son of Francis Coverdill buried ye 26th day of February 1691.
Willyam son of Willyam Masterman Senior buried ye 24th day of April 1692.

Margret Masterman daughter of Willyam Masterman buried ye 9th of
  February 1692.
James son of Willyam Hunter baptized ye 13th day of June 1693.
Jane wife of Thomas Coverdill buried ye 13th day of July 1693.
Thomas son of John Trewhit buried ye 24th day of October 1693.
Willyam son of James Frankland baptized ye 1st day of January 1693.
Thomas son of Thomas Masterman junior baptized ye 28th day of January
  1693.
Anne daughter of Richard Shippley baptized y^e 25th day of March 1694.
[blank] daughter of Thomas Masterman baptized May the 13 day.
Catherine daughter of George Truwhit baptized February y^e 23 day.
Thomas & William sons of Thomas Masterman baptized February y^e
  4th day 169$\frac{6}{7}$.
William y^e son of Thos Masterman buried March y^e 15th day 1697.
Henry son of Tho : Masterman baptized March the 20th 169$\frac{7}{8}$ born March
  y^e 3^d day.
Robert Hemsley buried February y^e second day 169$\frac{7}{8}$.
Mary y^e daughter of Henry Herrison baptized September y^e 17th day
  1698.
William the son of George Truwhit baptized October the 2^d day 1698.
Thomas Masterman & Jane Thomas marred 11 July.
Margret y^e daughter of Thomas Masterman baptized the 11th day of June
  1699.
Mary the daughter of Thomas Masterman baptized the 18th day of August.
Jane the daughter of Henry Herryson baptized ye 5th day of January 1701.
William the son of Tho : Masterman baptized ye 30th day of March 1701.
Tho : the son of Tho : Masterman of Hagget Hill baptized ye 20th day of
  December 1701.
Tho : son of Tho : Masterman of Hagget Hill buried y^e 26 of December 1701.
Orpah y^e wife of Peter Atkinson buried y^e 30th day of June 1702.
Ann y^e daughter of Geo : Truwhit buried y^e 3rd day of September 1702.
Thomas y^e son of Tho : Masterman baptized y^e 11th day of September 1702.
William son of Wm Wright born y^e 8th day of January 170$\frac{2}{3}$.   Quaker.
Tho : y^e son of Tho : Masterman was buried y^e 24th of Aprill 1703.
Peter y^e son of Peter Atkinson baptized y^e 3 day of [blank].
James the son of Thomas Masterman baptized the 16th day of March 1704.
Tho : son of Tho : Clerk baptized y^e 10 day of September 1704.
Will Masterman buried the 30 day of September 1704.
Katherine daughter of Tho : Masterman baptized ye 8 day of January 1706.
Elizabeth daughter of George Truhit baptized ye 10 day of February 1706.
John son of John [blank] baptized ye 2 day of February 1706.
Una daughter of Tho : Clerk baptized ye six day of February 1706.
George ye son of Tho : Masterman baptized y^e 29th of October 1708.
George Trewhitt of Hagget Hill and Ann Smith of West Harlsey maried
  November y^e 16, 1704.
Elizabeth y^e daughter of George Trewitt baptized y^e 10 day of January
  1706.
George Trewitt y^e son of George Trewitt baptized October y^e 23rd 1707.
W$\tilde{m}$ y^e son of John Stainthorp buried May y^e ninth 1709.
[blank] y^e son of Joseph Chapman babtized 8th of September 1709.

Tho : y^e son of George Trewhit of Hagget Hill baptized y^e eight day of November 1709.

George y^e son of Tho : Masterman buried March 13th 1710.

Thomas son of Tho : Masterman baptized y^e 26 day of September 1710 and buried y^e 12th day of January 17$\frac{10}{11}$.

Margret Campershine buried y^e 8th of January 17$\frac{10}{11}$.

Nathaniel Trewhit son of Geo : Truwhit baptized February y^e 19th 17$\frac{11}{12}$.

John the son of John Sanderson baptized March y^e 18th 17$\frac{11}{12}$.

Jane y^e daughter of Tho : Masterman baptized y^e 28th of October & buried December 17th 1712.

Jane the daughter of Luke Rawlin baptized y^e 6th day of January 17$\frac{12}{13}$ and buried the 13th day of January 1712.

James y^e son of Ralph Elgy baptized y^e 16 day of March 1712.

Una the daughter of Thos Coverdale baptized May 26th 1713.

Rebeckah the dauter of George Trewhit baptized March y^e 2^d 171$\frac{3}{4}$.

John the son of Robt. Jackson baptized the 8th day of February 171$\frac{3}{4}$.

Benieyman y^e son of Raph Elgey, husbandman, buried Novembris 2^d 1714.

John son of William Proud, hus., baptized February y^e eight.

[blank] spinster, daughter of William Tomson December the 30th 1714.

John the son of Wm Proud, husbandman, buried May the fourth day 1715.

William son of John Lowder baptized 21st day of December 1715.

Thomas the son of Marmaduke Gill baptized the 9th day of Feby 1715.

Deborah the daughter of George Trewhit baptized the 3rd day of June 1716.

James ye son of William Stocktill baptized ye 29th day of June 1716.

Deborah the daughter of George Trewhit buried ye 6th day of November 1716.

Thos Coverdale Senr buried the 30th day of December at West Rounton 1716.

Saray the daughter of Wm Proud baptized 5th day of February 1716.

Elizabeth Trewhit buried the 4th day of Aprill 1717.

George ye son of John Lowder bapt. ye 9th day of March 1717.

Dorothy ye daughter of George Flower baptized ye 29th day of March 1718.

Peter Atkinson was buried the 16th of June 1711.

Joseph Chapman son of Joseph Chapman was baptized the 4th day of August 1711.

Rebeckah the douter of George Trewhit buried May the 5 day 1717.

Rebeckah the douter of Georg Trewhit, yeoman, baptized October y^e 22, 1717.

John y^e son of John Fantrape buried November the 5 day 1717.

Isaack y^e son of Joseph was buried y^e 11 of June 1718.

Jo : y^e son of J$_0$: Bardrum buried y^e 16th of June 1718.

William son of Wm Proud bapt. July 8th 1718.

Elizabeth y^e daughter of George Trewhitt was buried Novemb. 4th 1718.

Mary y^e daughter of Francis Wilkinson baptized March y^e 24th 1719.

Sarah y^e daughter of John Lawder baptized April 25th day 1720.

Benjamin ye son of George Trewhitt baptized April the 26th 1720.

Dorothy ye daughter of Geo : Flower baptized November 4th 1720.

Mary ye daughter of Francis Wilkinson was buried ye 8th day of June 1721.

Anne ye daughter of William Stocktill buried ye 30 day of December 1721.

John the son of Joseph Chapman baptized 2nd day of May 1717.

Else Coverdil the wife of Francis buried the 27th day of September 1724.

Wm Sayer and Eliz : Willis married April 1730.

Jerome Ewbank and Eliz : Stockton married April 1730.

Ann the daughter of Tom Wright buried October the twenty-first 1726.

Mathew the son of John Lowder baptized November 29th 1726.

John Sayer and Elizabeth Trewhit married the 25th of April 1727.

Elizabeth the daughter of James Proud baptized the first day of June 1727.

Jane the daughter of George Wood baptized July ye 6th 1727.

Elizabeth the daughter of Henerey Sadler baptized the 23rd of July 1727.

Ann the daughter of George Trewhit baptized September the 16th 1727.

Thomas the son of John Rountree baptized the eight day of October 1727.

James ye son of James Proud baptized August 21 in 1729.

James Sayer and Eliz : Wood married Novemb. 1731.

John Walker and Eliz : Sayer married January 1731.

George Allan and Eliz : Baker married Novemb. 1731.

John Green and Eliz : Truhit married January 1731.

Mary Hemsley buried ye 8th day of May 1727.

Eliz : Frankland.

Dorothy ye daughter of Geo : Flower buried March ye 16th 1719.

Jane Allison wid : buried Octob^r 3^d 1720.

Jane Mellanby buried Octob^r 29th 1720.

John ye son of Simon Sanderson baptized November 3^d 1719.

Christopher ye son of John Lowder baptized ye 12th of December 1721.

December 11th 1722. Hannah ye daughter of William Proud baptized.

November ye 5th 1722. Eliz : Langrill was buried.

Decr ye 17th 1722. Fran : Coverdill was buried.

Christopher the son of George Trewhitt baptized Aprill the twenty-fifth
    1723.

John the son of John Nelson baptized August the eighteenth day 1723.

Mary the daughter of George Flower baptized November the twenty-first
    1723.

Tamer the daughter of Will. Proud baptized January the twenty-ninth
    1723.

Margret the daughter of Joseph Chapman baptized December 31st day 1724.

George Flower buried September ye 24, 1725.

Thomas the son of James Proud baptized October ye 31, 1725.

Elizabeth the daughter of James Elderson baptized the 28 day of Decemb^r
    1725.

Henery the son of Henery Sadler baptized 30 of December 1725.

Catheran the daughter of John Nelson baptized January the 24th 1725.

Mary Chapman buried [blank] 1732.

Alse ye daughter of James Proud baptized February first.

Rebeckah ye daughter of George Trewhitt buried February 17.

Nathaniell ye son of George Trewhitt buried February 19.

George Trewhitt buried April 21, 1732.

Margret Wright buried [blank] 1732.

Dorothy Whorlton buried [blank].

Ann the daughter of Robert Fisher baptized April 10, 1733.

William the son of James Proud baptized the second of August 1734.

John the son of Robert Fisher baptized the 2^d day of March 1734/5.

Ann the daughter of John Lowder baptized the 25th day of November 1734.

Ann the daughter of Joseph Metcalfe baptized October the 17, 1733.

Elizabeth the daughter of Joseph Metcalfe baptized December the 29, 1735.

Jane the daughter of George Wood baptized ye 17 of May 1727.

Sarah the daughter of George Wood baptized July the 22 day 1730.

Mari the daughter of Leonard Edon was baptized the 29 day of April 1734.

John son of Henry Sadler baptized June 20, 1736.

John the son of James Proud was baptized the 14 of June 1736.

Mary Metcalfe baptised April the 5 in the year 1738.

Jane daughter of Joseph Medcalf baptized the 5th of April 1738.

Elizabeth Trewhit daughter of Tho. Trewhit baptized [blank] May 1739.

Marriages for the year 1737 from March the 25th.

July the 22 James Kendale & Margery Buttery married in the Chappel of East Rounton by vertue of a Licence granted by Mr Coocke.

Marriages for the Year 1738.

April the 24 John Waller & Ann Hall were maried by vertue of a Licence granted by Mr Hopkinson.

Baptisms.

Averel daughter of Joseph Chapman baptised November 7th 1738.

Hanah daughter of Joseph Chapman baptized March 18, 1739.

Mary daughter of James Proud baptized the 19th of May 1740.

John Foster son of Daniel Foster baptized January 14th day 1738.

Mary Metcalfe daughter of Joseph Metcalfe baptized 7th April 1740.

Ann Trewhit daughter of Tho : Trewhit baptized November 25th.

Elizabeth daughter of Leonard Edon baptized January the 4th 1740.

Thomas Groves, Yeoman, and Ann Hall, Spinster, were maried May the 30th by vertue of a Licence granted by Mr Coocke May the 3.

Sarah daughter of Daniel Foster was baptized January the 7, 1741.

Sarah the daughter of James Proud, Yeoman, was baptized the 10th of July, 1742.

James the son of Leonard Edon, Yeoman, baptized May 15, 1743.

Joseph Metcalf the son of Joseph Metcalf was baptized July 7 day 1743.

Margaret daughter of Joseph Chapman the younger was born the thirtieth day of June and baptized the 27 day of September.

Thomas son of Thomas Trewhit was baptized August the 15, 1744.

Margaret daughter of Daniel Foster was baptized January 28.

Baptisms.

David son of James Proud, Yeoman, was baptized May 18th 1745.

John son of Marmaduke Gill was baptized June the 29.

Joseph son of Joseph Chapman, householder, was baptized the 16 day of March in the year 1746.

Marmaduke Gill, widower, and Sarah Edon, spinster, were married by vertue of banns in the Chappel of East Rounton the 7th day of May 1746.

Baptisms for the Year 1746.

Nathaniel son of Thomas Trewhit was baptized September 7th 1746.

Thomas son of Joseph Medcalf was baptized February the 1st 1746.

Bernard son of William Robinson was baptized February 1st 1746.

Mary daughter of Tho : & Jane Trewhitt was born ye 9th Novr 1748 & baptized ye 21 December.

Thomas son of Tho : & Margrett Preston was born the 1st November and baptized 26th 1748.

Funeral for the Year 1748.

Thomas son of Thomas Trewhit, Yeoman, was buried the 30th day of March.

Baptisms.

Dianah Chapman daughter of Joseph Chapman baptized July 8th 1749.

John Metcalf son of Joseph Metcalf baptized 9th of September 1749.

Mary daughter of Jane Lowther baptized the 8 day of July 1750.

Thomas son of Marmaduke Gill was baptized [blank] December 1750.

Jonathan son of Thomas & Margrett Preston baptized 24th February 1750.

Thomas son of Thomas Trewhit, Yeoman, baptized August 5th 1750.

Katharine daughter of William Hauxwell, Yeoman, baptized the 10th November 1751.

Hellen daughter of John Smith, Yeoman, baptized 2d of December 1751.

Sarah daughter of Marmaduke Gill was born & baptized 1st February 1753.

Ann daughter of John Sanderson was born & baptized 5th February 1753.

Mary daughter of Joseph Metcalfe was born & baptized 10th February 1753.

Margt daughter of Tho : Preston was born 10th January & baptized 4th March 1753.

William Jackson, Batchelor, and Mary Rimer, Spinster, were married by virtue of a licence granted by Mr Thwaites the 28th January 1750.

One Marriage 1752. N.S.

Edward Cressop, Batchelor, and Ann Walton, Spinster, were married by virtue of a Licence granted by Mr Hopkinson the 16th day March.

One Baptism for the year 1752.

William son of Thomas Trewhit, Yeoman, baptized the 21 September.

Elizabeth daughter of John Smith, Yeoman, baptized 7 of December 1753.

Benjamin son of Marmaduke Gill, Yeo : & Sarah born 5 Jan : & baptized 1754.

Jane daughter of Joseph Metcalf & Martha his wife was born 6th & baptized 11th June 1754.

John son of John Sanderson, Yeoman, and Susanna his wife was born the 3d day and baptized the 5th of January in the year 1755.

Margaret Daughter of Thomas & Jane Trewhitt was born the 20th day of November and baptized the 7th of December 1755.

Joseph son of Thomas Preston was baptized the 22 day of November 1756.

John son of James & Mary Proud was born the 15th and baptized the 16th April.

Thomas son of Ralf Brackon, householder, was baptized 2nd of May.

John son of John Smith, Yeoman, was baptized the 14th day of March.

Elizabeth Daughter of John Barnet, Yeoman, baptized 13th of March 1757.

Elizabeth Daughter of George Wood, Yeoman, baptized the 13th of March 1757.

George Son of John Smith, Yeoman, was baptized the 22d of April 1758.

Jemimah Daughter of George Harrison, Yeoman, baptized September 24th.

Mary Daughter of Ralf Breckon, householder, baptized the 30th of September.

Margaret Daughter of George Wood, Yeoman, baptized 10th day of January 1759.

Joseph son of Thomas Preston baptized the 22 of November 1759.

Sicily daughter of William Robinson baptized the 6th day of September 1759.

Jane daughter of Thomas Trewhit, Yeoman, was baptized the 14 of August 1757.

Baptisms.

Dinah Daughter of John Barnet, Yeoman, baptized 27th of Jany 1760.

Thomas son of John Proud, yeoman, was baptized the 6th day of June 1760.

Matthew son of William Robinson, householder, baptized 11th day of June 1760.

George son of George Wood, yeoman, was baptized the 9th of January 1761.

Michael son of George Harrison, householder, baptized 20th of Novembr 1761.

William son of George Wood, Yeoman, baptized the 5th day of April 1763.

Elizabeth Daughter of John Proud, yeoman, baptized the 11th of September 1763.

Mary Daughter of Nicholas Robinson, yeoman, baptized 8th of Jany 1764.

John son of Nicholas Robinson, yeoman, baptized the 16th day of June 1765.

Jane Daughter of Richard Car, householder, baptized the 9th of September 1765.

Catharine Daughter of John Proud, yeoman, baptized 22nd of December 1765.

David son of George Wood, yeoman, was baptized the 31 day of March 1766.

Baptisms 1766.

Jane daughter of Tho : Leckonby and Jane Robinson was born 15th & baptized ye 18th of May 1766.

Baptisms continued, transcribed from the marriage Register of East Rounton.

1767. None.

1768.

February 7th John son of John & Catharine Proud.

March 31st Joseph son of William & Ann Robinson.

June 10th Jane daughter of Nicholas Robinson.

September 10th John son of Thos Proud.

1769.

January 27. Ann daughter of Ann Appleton, a bastard.

February 2d Ann daughter of Thomas Raper.

August 13th Barbara daughter of Ralph Bracken.

1770.

May 5th William son of John Proud.

August 26th Elizabeth daughter of Nicholas Robinson.

1771. July 28th William son of William Robinson.

August 4th Isaac son of Thos Proud.

1772. August 29. William son of William Mettle.

December 3rd James son of John Proud.

1773. May 24th Robert son of Mary Lowther, Single woman.

1774. May 8th Susannah daughter of Nicholas Robinson, Farmer.

May 8th David son of Thos Elcote, Labourer.

The above is a true Copy extracted & compared by me,

F. Blackburne, Curate.

MARRIAGES in the Chapel of East Rounton.

(The following are abstracts. All Marriages were by banns and by J. Grice, curate, from here to 1819, unless otherwise stated.)

1765. Aug. 18. Thomas Duck of Whitby and Elizabeth Robinson of the Chapelry of East Rounton, by Geo : Stainthorp, Curate of East Rounton. Licence. Witnesses, Nich : Robinson, John Bentley.

1770. May 21. Thomas Elcoat of the par. of Etton and Ann Appletion of East Rounton in the parish of Rudby, by J. Grenside vice Mr Grant. Licence. Witns., Nich : Robinson & Thomas Rymer.

1770. Nov. 27. William Kilvington of Yafforth, batchelour, & Ann Sanderson of East Rounton, spinster, by D. Grant, curate. Licence. Witns., Dor : Kilvington, Ann Smith.

1772. March 3. John Thompson of Ingleby & Barbara Bracken of E. Rounton, by D. Grant, curate. Witns., George Wood, junior, Nathaniel Truhit.

1774. May 13. John Crossick and Jane Robinson, by F. Blackburne, curate. Witns., John Proud, Nicholas Allen, Nich. Robinson.

1772. May 14. Ralph Wetheral of Stockton & Ann Parkin of East Rounton, by D. Grant. Witns., Jonathan Appelton, Ann Bateman.

1776. Feb. 12. David Mitchel & Jane Duck, both of this Chapelry, by F. Blackburne. Witns., Nich. Robinson, Geo. Wood, junior, Saml Robinson.

1781. Dec. 28. James Sanderson, bachelor, of the township of Hutton and Helen Carr, spinster, of this Chapelry, by J. Grice, curate. Witns., John Sanderson, Jonathan Appelton.

1782. Feb. 12. Joseph Jefferson, bachelor, of Kirby Sigston and Rachel Tompson of this Chapelry, spr. Witns., Robert Thompson father of the above Rachel, Joseph Dobinson, George Wood, John Heslop.

1784. Dec. 7. William Appleby, bachelor, and Sarah Dent, spr., both of this chapelry. Witns., Thomas Appleby, William Wood.

1785. Nov. 28. William Breckin of this chapelry, widr., and Margaret Herring of Kirby Fleetham, spr. Witns., Geo. Wood, Henry Preston.

1791. May 9. Mark Spurrs, bach., and Isabella Hood, spr., both of this chapelry. Witns., Edward Harrison, John Heslop, John Kilvington.

1794. Nov. 27. Jacob Dowson of Ayton, bachelor, and Mary Hathwaite of this chapelry, spr. Witns., John Heslop, John Huthwaite.

1795. May 3. John Johnson of East Harlsey, bach., and Mary Temple of this chapelry, spinster. Witns., Wm Mohun, John Sanderson, John Kilvington.

[*A leaf is here missing, having been cut out.*—W.T.R.]

1797. Nov. 18. Ralph Bruce of Ingleby Arncliffe, bach., and Ann Wright of East Rounton, spr. Witns., John Kilvington, James Smith, William Wilson.

1796. July 6th. Benjamin Smith of East Rounton, yeoman and bach., and Jane Raper of Whorlton, spr. Licence. Witns., Sarah Smith, William Raper.

1798. April 14. Francis Stainthorpe, widr., and Hannah Waring, spr., both of Rudby. Licence. Witns., Geo : Kingston, John Sanderson.

1799. Nov. 26. William Elders of Stokesley, bach., and Mary Wilson of East Rounton, spr. Licence. Witns., Ann Burdon, William Wilson.

1799. Nov. 27. Richard Richardson of Hutton in Rudby par., bach., and Harriot Winn of East Rounton, spr. Witns., John Jowsey, Wm Wood, John Sanderson, John Kilvington, Wm Garbutt, Nathaniel Jackson.

1801. Nov. 26. Thomas Smith, bach., and Jane Pyburn, spr., both of this chapelry. Witns., James Pyburn, James Smith, William Orton, Mary Leckonby, Jane Wake.

1803. Nov. 24. William Michal, bach., and Eleanor Watson, spr., both of this chapelry, by Jerh Grice. Witns., Edward Herrison, John Kilvington, Edward Middelmass, George Humble, William Hildreth.

1806. April 7. Robert Balier of East Rounton, farmer, and Elizabeth Passman of Rudby, spr. Licence. Witns., William Wood, Matthew Appleton, Eliza Kay, Hary Passman.

1806. Aug. 31. John Passman, labourer, and Arabella Cust, spr., both of Rudby. Licence. Witns., Wm Passman, Nichs Reed, William Hildreth.

1807. Nov. 28. John Pattison of Hutton Rudby, bach., and Isabella Mankin of East Rounton, spr. Witns., Ann Atkinson, John Pattinson, William Elders.

1808. Aug. 29. Charles Maclane of Whorlton, bach., and Frances Smith of this chapelry, spr., by William Deason, asst. curate. Witns., Ann Hunton, John Raby.

1810. July 21. Matthew Appleton, junior, bach., and Ann Robinson, spr., both of Rudby. Licence. Witns., Ann Scarlet, William Elders, Robert Story, Jacob Allison.

1811. March 7. John Wailes, esquire, bachelor, and Hannah Dixon, spr., both of East Rounton. Licence. Witns., Peter Rigg, James Smith.

1811. May 23. Matthew Wilkinson, bach., and Ann Atkinson, spr., both of East Rounton. Witns., Anne Wailes, John Smith, Simon Wilkinson.

1811. Nov. 26. Anthony Swan, bach., and Jane Robinson, spr., both of this chapelry. Witns., Robert Garbutt, Thomas Swan, Ann Garbutt.

1811. Nov. 29. Joseph Dinsley, bach., and Hannah Scarlet, spr., both of Rudby par. Witns., Francis Heugh, Jacob Allison.

1812. Jan. 20. John Busby, widr., and Susannah Hugill, spr., both of this chapelry. Witns., William Hildreth, Ann Busby.

1812. May 12. Joshua Emmerson, bach., and Elizabeth Christall, spr., both of Rudby par. Licence. Witns., George Christall, James Smith.

1813. Feb. 15. William Hammond and Mary Hobson both of Rudby par. Witns., Robert Balier, James Smith.

1813. Oct. 4. James Elliot of East Rounton and Mary How of Rudby, by Richard Garnett, asst. curate. Witns., Robert Balier, Elizabeth How.

1814. May 19. John Routledge of Welbury and Margaret Wilkinson by Rd. Garnett, curate. Witns., David Atkinson, R. Routledge, George Humble.

1817. June 1. Ralph Bell of Thornteny Beans, Leek, bach., and Hannah Kingston of this par., spr., by Robert Fawcitt, officiating minr. Licence. Witns., John Kilvington, James Flintoff.

1817. Aug. 27. James Fowler of Boston in co. of Lincoln, bach., and Ann Ridley of this par., spr. Licence. Witns., John Armstrong, Henry Storey.

1817. Oct. 19. Thomas Appleton, widr., and Margaret Hodgson, wid., both of this par. Witns., John Kilvington, George Humble.

1819. Jan. 3. George Foggins of Ripon, bach., and Hannah Raper of this par., spr. Licence. Witns., John Foggins, William Hildreth.

1820. May 22. William Carnegie and Thomasin Wilkinson both of this par., by R. Shepherd. Witns., Robert Wilkinson, Thomas Carnegie, George Humble.

1820. Dec. 26. Thomas Wailes of Welbury and Elizabeth Ayton of this par., by Rd. Shepherd. Witns., Robert Elwood, Ann Ayton, Isaac Peacock.

1821. March 1. George Scales and Ann Gedling, widow, both of Hutton Rudby, by Robt. Fawcitt, off. minr. Witns., Mich. Todd, James Grimston, George Humble.

1822. May 21. Robert Wilkinson and Mary Flintoff both of this chapelry, by Rd Shepherd. Witns., Richard Todd, Jane Atkinson, Thomas Carnegie.

1824. March 2. Thomas Hood of Thirsk and Ann Smith of this chapelry, by R. Shepherd. Witns., Jno Smith, Thomas Mawlam, Thomas Carnegie, Jane Atkinson.

1824. July 25. Thomas Pearson of this par. and Mary Richardson of this chapelry, by Rob. Fawcitt, offi. min. Witns., William Wall, George Humble.

1827. July 26. John Hugill of Nunthorpe and Maria Jackson of this chapelry, by R. Shepherd. Licence. Witns., Martin Smith, Ann Scarth, Jane Jackson, Ralph Jackson, John Scarth, Elizh Jackson.

1827. Oct. 17. The Rev. Henry Stocken of Ripley and Charlotte Pullan of this par., by R. Shepherd. Licence. Witns., Thos Myles, Sarah Pullan, Edward Pullan, Mary Walker, Richd A. Pullan.

1832. Nov. 17. John Smith, bach., of Billingham and Mary Stonehouse of East Rounton, spr., by R. J. Barlow, curate. Licence. Witns., William Smith, Ann Stonehouse.

1834. June 2. William Lincoln, bach., of Rudby, labourer, and Alice Fidler, spr., of East Rounton, by R. J. Barlow. Licence. Witns., Wm Chapman, Ann Fidler.

1834. June 2. William Render, bach., of the par. of [blank], countryman, and Ann Smith of East Rounton, by R. J. Barlow. Witns., Thos Smith, George Humble.

1836. Feb. 15. William Bayford, widr., of Myton, farmer, and Sophia Eleanor Kendall of this par., spr., by R. J. Barlow. Licence. Witns., Robert Kendall, Charles Park.

1837. April 15. Thomas Smith, bach., farmer, and Jane Kilvington, spr., both of this par., by R. J. Barlow. Licence. Witn., William Moore.

BAPTISMS.

1775. August 26th David son of John Proud, Farmer.

Sep : 10th James son of John Crossick alias Crookshanks.

1776. March 9th John son of William Metal, Labourer.

August 6th William son of David Mitchel, Labourer.

Baptisms 1777 None.

1778. March 4th Ann Daughter of Ralph Jackson, Farmer.

November 15th Mary Daughter of Magdalen Humphrey, by Robert Bell, reputed Father.

1779. February 22d Hannah Daughter of David Mitchel.

March 23d Thomas Son of William Metal.

April 11th Diana Daughter of Aaron Reid of Pickton in the Parish of Kirklevington.

September 12th William Son of John Crookshanks, Labourer.

December 7th Jane Daughter of James Davidson, Farmer.

1780. March 15th Robert son of Ann Bennison, Single Woman.

April 1st Ralph the son of John Wiley, Butcher.

1781. Dec. 23. Frances Daughter of James Smith, labourer.

1782. Jan. 5th Ann Daughter of James Davidson, Farmer.

Jan. 13th David son of David Mitchell, Labourer.

April 1. Jane Daughter of James Sanderson, labourer.

Oct. 26. Magdalen Daughter of Magdalen Humphrey, Spinster.

1783. April 21. Jemima Daughter of John Hugill, labourer.

June 19. Christiana Daughter of William & Elizabeth Medd.

1784. May 9th Elizabeth Daughter of Ann Bennison, Spinster.

July 4. John son of Magdalen Humphrey, Spinster.

1785. May 22. Thomas son of David Mitchel.

August 14. Elizabeth daughter of William Medd, farmer.

Magdalen Humphrey & Ann Bennison of this Chapelry are excommunicated.

Aug. 30. Ann daughter of W^m & Sarah Appleby born August 29.

1786. Apr. 17. Jemima daughter of John and Ann Hugill.

Apr. 30. Elizabeth daughter of Isaac & Margaret Walker, flax dresser, born April 20, 1786.

Apr. 10. Mary daughter of Robert & Mary Dawson.

Aug. 27. William son of Magdalen Humphrey, natus in fornicatione.

1787. March 11. Ralph son of William Breckin.

Sep. 30. Uriah son of Eleanor Wilkinson, natus in fornicatione a Pauper

Oct. 14. John son of Sarah & William Appleby.

Nov. 6. William son of William and Elizabeth Medd.

1788. March 9. John son of David Mitchell.

May 25. I read an excommunication against Thomas Appleby.

1789. April 5. William son of William and Margaret Breckin.

June 7. Richard son of William & Elizabeth Medd.

July 5. John son of Ann Bennison (natus in fornicatione).

Sep. 18. Elizabeth daughter of Mr John Jefferson born Sep. 18.

Oct. 25. Elizabeth daughter of William & Sarah Appleby.

1790. Jan. 1. Catherine daughter of Ann Elcoat, et ut fertur of Wm Lazenby.

1791. April 25. Aney daughter of Anne Bennison, pauper.

May 22. Richard son of William & Elizabeth Medd.

July 17. Jane daughter of David & Jane Mitchell.

Aug: 21. Mary daughter of Edward & Sarah Harrison.

Sep. 25. Ann daughter of William & Margaret Lazenby.

Oct. 23. Isaac son of Isaac & Catharine Peacock.

1792. Jan. 1. Thomas son of William and Sarah Appleby.

Mar. 11. Mary daughter of Anthony and Sarah Carlton, pauper.

Apr. 1. Isabella daughter of Mark and Isabella Spurrs, pauper.

1793. Apr. 1. Appleton son of Ann Bennison, Spinster.

July 28. Elizabeth daughter of Edward Harrison.

Aug. 19. Christiana daughter of William & Elizabeth Medd.

1794. Jan. 5. Faith daughter of William and Margaret Lazenby.
July 27. Isabella daughter of William and Sarah Appleby.
Nov. 2. Elizabeth daughter of Anthony and Sarah Carlton.
1795. Jan. 25. Mark son of Mark & Isabella Spurs.
Jan. 25. John son of Ann Bennison.
Feb. 8. Sarah daughter of Edward and Sarah Harrison.
7. George son of David and Jane Mitchel.
June 22. Elizabeth daughter of Mr James Ward and Mrs Bridget Ward.
Aug. 23. Ann daughter of William and Elizabeth Medd.
Dec. 27. Elizabeth daughter of William & Margaret Lazenby.
1796. Mar. 20. Jacob son of Martha Baker.
Sep. 18. Sarah daughter of William and Sarah Appleby.
1797. Mar. 4. Thomas son of William Medd.
Apr. 17. Ann daughter of Edward & Sarah Harrison.
May 14. John son of Benjamin & Jane Smith.
Aug. 13. Thomas son of Ann Bennison.
Oct. 25. Deborah daughter of James & Bridget Ward born Oct. 11.
1798. Mar. 11. Mary daughter of Sarah Calvert.
Feb. 25. George son of John & Hannah Brigham.
July 8. Margaret daughter of Margaret Minto, Spinster.
1799. Jan. 9. Elizabeth daughter of Benjamin & Jane Smith.
Jan. 27. Jane daughter of Ann Bennison.
27. Ann daughter of Ann Bennison.
July 28. Jane daughter of David and Jane Mitchel.
Nov. 26. Margaret daughter of Thomas and Margaret Brignal.
1800. June 22. John son of Margaret Minto.
Sep. 14. Thomas son of William and Mary Elders born Sep. 13, 1800.
1801. Mar. 15. Thomas son of Thomas & Margaret Brignal.
Mar. 15. Catharine daughter of Edward & Sarah Harrison.
May 13. Elizabeth daughter of John and Hannah Brigham.
Sep. 23. Christopher son of Benjamin and Jane Smith born Sep. 20
Dec. 30. Mary daughter of William & Mary Elders.
1802. Jan. 31. Margaret daughter of James and Ann Grimson.
Sep. 22. Margaret daughter of Edward Harrison.
1803. Feb. 1. Christopher son of Benjamin and Jane Smith Born Jan.31.
April 11. Thomas son of John & Hannah Brigham.
23. Elizabeth daughter of John & Mary Elders.
Aug. 28. Sarah daughter of Margaret Minto.
1804. March 18. Robert son of James & Ann Grimshaw.
March 26. Ann daughter of William and Mary Elders.
1805. May 3. Mary daughter of Benjamin & Jane Smith.
Aug. 11. William son of John Brigham.
Nov. 13. Mary daughter of John & Jane Robinson.
Dec. 21. Jane daughter of William & Mary Elders.
1806. Mar. 30. Sarah Wailes daughter of Hannah Dixon and John Wailes, Esq., born March 1st 1806.
June 9. Francis son of Francis & Ann Hugill.
Aug. 31. Tomlinson daughter of Thomas Medley.
1807. Feb. 17. Margaret daughter of Benjamin & Jane Smith.
Feb. 22. William son of William & Mary Elders.
May 17. Mary daughter of James & Ann Grimstone.

Nov. 28. John son of Francis & Ann Heugh.

1808. Aug. 18. Hannah Wailes daughter of Hannah Dixon and John Wailes, Esq., both of Rounton Grange.

1809. Jan. 20. Margaret daughter of William & Mary Shaw.

June 5. Mary daughter of Benjamin and Jane Smith.

Oct. 7. Margaret daughter of William & Mary Elders born Oct. 4th.

   30. Abraham son of Francis Heugh.

Nov. 26. Ann daughter of James Grimston.

1810. Aug. 6. Jane Wailes daughter of Hannah Dixon and John Wailes, Esq., Rounton Grange, born July 12, 1810.

Sep. 18. Ann daughter of Benjamin & Jane Smith.

   24. Elizabeth daughter of Francis and Ann Heugh.

1811. Aug. 4. Thomas son of James & Jane Ridley.

1812. Feb. 3. John son of John Wailes, Esq., and of M[rs] Hannah Wailes of Rounton Grange.

June 21. Jane daughter of John Kilvington, farmer, and Ann his wife, late Grimston, was born June 17, 1812.

July 3. Thomas son of William & Mary Elders born July 2, 1812.

1813. Jan. 1. William son of James & Ann Grimstone, East Rounton Town, Labourer. The ceremonary was performed by Jer[h] Grice, Curate.

Feb. 8. Margaret daughter of John & Susannah Busby, East Rounton, Haygarth Hill, Farmer.   J. Grice.

   11. Sarah daughter of Benjamin & Jane Smith, Haygarth Hill, Farmer.   J. Grice.

   1. Mary daughter of Anthony & Jane Swan, East Rounton Town, Labourer.   Robert Fawcitt, Off. Min.

Ap. 25. Mary daughter of John and Sophia Tiplady, East Rounton, Weaver.

Aug. 20. Ann daughter of Francis and Ann Heugh, East Rounton, Farmer.   Jer[h] Grice.

Sep. 12. John son of John & Ann Kilvington, East Rounton, Farmer. By the Rev. Richard Garnett, Assistant Curate.

Nov. 29. Elizabeth daughter of John and Hannah Wailes, East Rounton Grange, Gentleman.   By Jer[h] Grice.

1814. March 27. George son of James & Margaret Tompson, East Rounton, Labourer. By Richard Garnett, Assistant Curate.

Sep. 25. Charlotte daughter of James and Jane Robinson, East Rounton, Labourer.   Jer[h] Grice.

Oct. 9. Anthony son of Anthony and Jane Swan, East Rounton, Labourer.   Jer[h] Grice.

Nov. 16. Jane daughter of John and Margaret Routledge, East Rounton, Labourer.   Robert Fawcitt.

Dec. 4. James son of James and Jane Ridley, East Rounton, Labourer.   J.G.

   13. John son of William and Mary Elders, East Rounton, Farmer.   J.G.

1815. Jan. 11. Benjamin son of Benjamin and Jane Smith, East Rounton, Farmer.   Jer[h] Grice.

Feb. 12. George son of William and Mary Carnegie, East Rounton, Gardener.   Jer[h] Grice.

March 17. Matthew son of Matthew and Ann Ingledew, Haggit Hill in
East Rounton, Farmer.   Jer^h Grice.

Dec. 10. Caroline daughter of John and Hannah Wailes, Rounton
Grange in East Rounton, Gentleman.   Jer^h Grice.

1816. Jan. 20. John son of John and Seythey Tiplady, East Rounton,
weaver.   J.G.

Feb. 4. Robert Robinson son of Anthony and Jane Swan, East
Rounton, labourer.   Robert Fawcitt.

June 12. Mary daughter of William and Jane Smith, Haggit Hill,
farmer.   J.G.

Octr 7. Jane daughter of Francis & Ann Heugh, East Rounton,
farmer.   James Wilcock.

1817. Feb. 28. Susannah daughter of John & Ann Kilvington, East
Rounton, farmer.   Robert Fawcitt.

April 4. John son of Matthew and Ann Ingledew, Haggit Hill in East
Rounton, Farmer.   Robert Fawcitt.

January 17. Nathaniel son of James and Jane Ridley, East Rounton,
labourer.   Robert Fawcitt.

Sepr 30. Martha daughter of John and Hannah Wailes, Esqr, Rounton
Grange, Gentleman.   Jer^h Grice.

1818. May 31. Christopher son of William and Hannah Smith, Haggit
Hill, Farmer.   Jer^h Grice.

Sep. 6. Mary daughter of Thomas and Jane Smith, East Rounton,
Tailor.   Jer^h Grice.

Oct. 26. Mary Ann daughter of Eleanor and James Garnett, East
Rounton Barr, Blacksmith.   Jer^h Grice.

Nov. 1. William son of Francis and Ann Heugh, East Rounton,
Farmer.   Jer^h Grice.

Nov. 6. John son of Mary Jackson, East Rounton, Spinster. W^mGray.

Dec. 15. Martha daughter of William and Mary Hammond, East
Rounton Barr, Toll Bar Keeper.   Jer^h Grice.

1819. January 17. Ann daughter of Ann and Matthew Ingledew, Haggit
Hill, Farmer.   Jerem. Grice, curate.

March 8. Jane daughter of James and Jane Ridley, East Rounton,
Labourer.   Richard Shepherd, curate.

July 23. Penelope daughter of John and Hannah Wailes, Esq., Rounton Grange, Gentleman.   Jerem. Grice.

1820. Jan. 9. John son of William and Jane Mawer, East Rounton,
Labourer.   Richard Shepherd, Curate.

April 30. John Sanderson son of John and Ann Kilvington, Yeoman,
East Rounton.   Richard Shepherd, Curate.

June 25. William son of William & Jane Smith, Haggit Hill, Farmer.
                                         Richard Shepherd, Curate.

28. Jane daughter of Mary Wilson, East Rounton, Spinster.
                                         William Gray, Rector of W^t Rounton.

1821. Jany 21st Mariah daughter of William & Mary Hammond, East
Rounton Bar, Toll Bar Keeper. R^d Shepherd, Curate.

Feby 4th Richard son of Thomas & Jane Foster, East Rounton,
Labourer.   R^d Shepherd, Curate.

April 8. William son of William & Thominson Carnegie, East Rounton,
Gardener.   William Gray, Rector of W^t Rounton.

23. William son of John & Hannah Wailes, East Rounton Grange, Gent.   Richd Shepherd, Curate.

23. Jane daughter of William & Eleanor Mitchell, East Rounton, Labourer.   Richd Shepherd, Curate.

Novr 4th Elizabeth daughter of James & Jane Ridley, East Rounton, Labourer.   R^d Shepherd, Curate.

1822. Feby 24. Anne daughter of John & Ann Kilvington, East Rounton, Farmer.   R^d Shepherd, Curate.

May 21st Elizabeth daughter of William & Jane Smith, Haggit Hill, Farmer.   R. Shepherd, Curate.

Oct. 6. Christopher son of Thomas & Jane Smith, East Rounton, Tailor.   R. Shepherd, Curate.

Decr 8. James son of James & Eleanor Garnitt, Trenholme Bar, Blacksmith.   R. Shepherd, Curate.

1823. March 31st. Ann daughter of Robert & Mary Wilkinson, East Rounton, Farmer.   R. Shepherd, Curate.

ı June 21st Mary daughter of Thomas & Jane Foster, East Rounton, Labourer.   R. Shepherd, Curate.

August 31st Thomas son of James & Jane Ridley, East Rounton, Labourer.   R. Shepherd, Curate.

1824. Jany 18th Eleanor daughter of Isabella Mitchel, East Rounton, Spinster.   Benjn Richardson, Int of Glaisdale.

April 27th Sarah daughter of William & Jane Smith, Haggit Hill, Farmer.   Edm^d Goldsmith, Curate of West Rounton.

1825. Feb. 27. Hannah daughter of William & Eleanor Mitchel, East Rounton, Labourer.   Robert Fawcitt, Curate of Hilton.

March 13th John son of Robert & Mary Wilkinson, East Rounton, Farmer.   Andrew Gatenby, Ass^t Curate of Egton.

Septr 11th Nancy daughter of James & Eleanor Garnett, Rounton Barr, Blacksmith.   R. Shepherd, Curate.

Decr 4th Benjamin son of James & Jane Ridley, East Rounton, Labourer.   R.S.

1826. Jany 15th Mary daughter of Thomas & Jane Forster, East Rounton, Labourer.   R.S.

Jany 29th John son of William & Thomasin Carnegie, East Rounton, Gardener.   R.S.

Feby 28th John son of William & Jane Smith, Haggit Hill, Farmer. R.S.

May 22nd Hannah daughter of Thomas & Mary Pearson, East Rounton, Labourer.   R.S.

Decr 17th Simon son of Robert & Mary Wilkinson, East Rounton, Farmer.   R.S.

1827. Feby 11th Thomas son of Isabella Mitchel, East Rounton, Spinster.   R.S.

July 1st Joseph son of William & Ann Armstrong, Haggit Hill, Blacksmith.   R. Shepherd, Curate.

Octr 7th Margaret daughter of John & Elizabeth Meynell, Haggit Hill, Joiner.   R.S.

1828. March 10th Benjamin son of William & Jane Smith, Haggit Hill, Farmer.   Robt. Fawcitt, Curate of Hilton.

June 1st Ann daughter of James & Jane Ridley, East Rounton, Labourer.   R.S.

Decr 26th Sarah daughter of Thomas & Jane Foster, East Rounton, Labourer.   R.S.

1829. March 22nd James son of James & Eleanor Garnitt, Rounton Bar, Blacksmith. The Revd R. Grenside, Rector of Crathorne.

May 17th James son of William & Ann Armstrong, Haggit Hill, Blacksmith.   R.S.

18th Robert son of Thomas & Jane Pick, Haggit Hill, Schoolmaster.   Robert Fawcitt, Curate of Hilton.

Oct. 13th Hannah daughter of Richard & Maria Scarth, Hollings, Farmer.   R. Shepherd, Curate.

1830. May 19th John Simpson son of William & Ann Armstrong, Haggit Hill, Blacksmith.   Robt Fawcitt, Curate of Hilton.

Decr 12th Mary Ann daughter of Thomas & Mary Pearson, East Rounton, Labourer.   T. Hartley, Off^g Minister.

27th Thomas son of William & Jane Smith, Haggit Hill, Farmer.   T. Hartley, Off^g Minister.

1831. March 18. Sarah daughter of Matthew & Hannah Ailey, Potto, Farmer.   R.J.B.

Septr 18. Thomas son of Thomas & Ann Smyth, East Rounton, Farmer.   R.J.B.

Octr 30. Thomas son of William & Mary Forster, East Rounton, Labourer.   R.J.B.

Novr 13th Maria daughter of Richard & Maria Scarth, Hollings, East Rounton, Farmer.   R. J. Barlow, Curate.

Decr 25. Marianne daughter of John & Jesse Atkinson, East Rounton, Labourer.   R. J. Barlow, Curate.

1832. Feby 15th John son of James & Jane Ridley, East Rounton, Labourer.

June 24th Mary daughter of Elizabeth Wilkinson, Harlsey.

1833. August 18. William son of John & Jane Bulmer, Oxgang House, Hutton, Farmer.   R. J. Barlow, Curate.

August 18. Jane daughter of John & Jane Bulmer, Oxgang House, Hutton, Farmer.   R.J.B.

1834. Feby 28th Jane Anne daughter of William & Jane Smith, Haggit Hill, East Rounton, Farmer.   R.J.B.

Novr 10. Robert son of John & Jessy Atkinson, East Rounton, Labourer.

27. Jane daughter of Richard & Maria Scarth, Hollands, East Rounton, Farmer.   R.J.B.

1835. August 1st Thomas William son of Robert & Elizabeth Bailey, Hutton, Farmer.   R.J.B.

Sepr 27. Henrietta Bathurst daughter of George Henry & Lydia Fothergill, East Rounton, Clerk, Curate of West Rounton.   R. J. Barlow, Curate.

1836. Jany 31. Jannet daughter of John & Jessy Atkinson, Labourer, East Rounton.   R.J.B.

March 27. John son of John & Mary Smith, East Rounton, Labourer.   R.J.B.

1837. Feby 11th William son of William & Anne Mitchell, East Rounton, Labourer.   R. J. Barlow, Curate.

GENERAL INDEX.

Ailey, Han., 34 ; Matt., 34 ; Sarah, 34.

Akland, West, 2.

Allan, Alice, 1 ; Eliz., 22 ; Geo., 22 ; Kath., 3 ; Jane, 7 ; Margy., 7 ; Nich., 26 ; Will., 1, 5.

Allison, Jacob, 27* ; Jane, 22.

Appleby, Alice, 11 ; Ann, 29 ; Eliz., 3, 8, 10, 13, 29 ; Giles, 13, 14 ; Isab., 30 ; Jno., 29 ; Margt., 3*, 4* ; Rob., 1 ; Sar., 26, 29*, 30* ; Tho., 26, 29* ; Wid., 9 ; Will., 14, 26, 29*, 30*.

Appleton, Ann, 25*-27 ; Jon., 26* ; Margt., 2, 27 ; Matt., 27* ; Tho., 27.

Armstrong, Ann, 10, 11, 33, 34* ; Barth., 10-12 ; Geo., 9 ; Jas., 34 ; Jane, 12 ; Jno., 27 ; Jno. Simpson, 34 ; Josh., 33 ; Will., 8*-10, 33, 34*

Athie, Gilian, 6 ; Jane, 4 ; Jno., 4.

Atkinson, Ann, 4, 27* ; Dav., 27 ; Hen., 2 ; ane, 28* ; Jannet, 34 ; Jesse, 34*; Jno., 34* ; Marianne, 34 ; Orpah, 20 ; Peter, 20* ; Rob., 34 ; Seitha, 2.

Ayton, 26 ; Ann, 28 ; Eliz., 28.

Bailey, Eliz., 34 ; Rob., 34 ; Tho. Will., 34.

Baine, Eliz., 9.

Baker, Eliz., 22 ; Jacob, 30 ; Martha, 30.

Balier, Eliz., 27 ; Rob., 27*.

Bardrum, Jo., 21*.

Barlow, R. J., 28*, 34*.

Barnet, Dinah, 25 ; Eliz., 24 ; Jno., 24, 25.

Bateman, Ann, 26.

Bayford, Sophia Eleanor, 28 ; Will., 28.

Bell, Han., 27 ; Ralph, 27 ; Rob., 28.

Bennison, Aney, 29 ; Ann, 29*, 30* ; Appleton, 29 ; Eliz., 29 ; Jane, 30 ; Jno., 29, 30 ; Rob., 29 ; Tho., 30

Bentley, Jno., 26.

Best, Manda, 2.

Billingham, 28.

Blackburn, F., 25, 26.

Blades, Chris., 14, 17 ; Eliz., 17, 19 ; Jane, 16* ; Joan, 15 ; Jno., 18 ; Leon., 13*-16, 18 ; Margt., 18 ; Rob., 13, 16-19 ; Tho., 13, 15, 16* ; Wid., 15, 19 ; Will., 15.

Bonwell, Ann, 3, 5*.

Boomer, Gilian, 2 ; Hen., 2.

Boons, Ann, 14 ; Will., 14.

Boston, 17.

Bowes, Eliz., 19 ; Jas., 15 ; Tho., 17.

Bracken, Barb., 25, 26 ; Margt., 26, 29 ; Mary, 24 ; Ralf, 24*, 25, 29 ; Tho., 24 ; Will., 26, 29*.

Bradford, Sar., 5.

Bradsonne, Sar., 5.

Brigham, Eliz., 30 ; Geo., 30 ; Han., 30* ; Jno., 30* ; Tho., 30 ; Will., 30.

Brignal, Margt., 30* ; Tho., 30*.

Brown, Geo., 19 ; Mary, 19 ; Will., 19.

Bruce, Ann, 26 ; Ralph, 26.

Brunton, 2.

Bulmer, Jane, 34* ; Jno., 34* ; Will., 34.

Burdon, Ann, 26.

Burnholme, 3*.

Burton, Margt., 2.

Busby, Ann, 27 ; Jno., 27, 31 ; Margt., 31 ; Sush., 27, 31.

Buttry, Alice, 5, 6 ; Ann, 1*, 3, 5 ; Chris., 3 ; Giles, 5 ; Hen., 6 ; Jo., 3 ; Margt., 2 ; Margy., 23 ; Ric., 1, 2, 5, 8 ; Rob., 1*, 2, 4*-6*, 8 ; Seitha, 2 ; Symon, 6 ; Tho., 5, 12 ; Tomasin, 5* ; Will., 3*-5*, 8.

Byrd, Mary, 6.

Calvert, Mary, 30 ; Sar., 30.

Campershine, Bar., 10, 11 ; Eliz., 11 ; Margt., 12, 21 ; Tho., 10, 11*, 12.

Campion, Ann, 1 ; Eliz., 3 ; Flo., 8 ; Jane, 9 ; Margy., 5, 6 ; Robt., 1*, 3, 5, 6 ; Will., 1*.

Car, Helen, 26 ; Jane, 25 ; Ric., 25.

Carlton, Ant., 29, 30 ; Eliz., 30 ; Mary, 29 ; Sar., 29, 30.

Carnegie, Geo., 31 ; Jno., 33 ; Mary, 31 ; Tho., 28* ; Thomasin, 28, 32, 33 ; Will., 28, 31-33.

The Publications of
The Yorkshire Parish Register Society.

VOL. LIV.

Issued to Subscribers for the year 1916.

The Register

OF THE

CHURCH OF ALL SAINTS,

WESTON,

NEAR OTLEY.

1639-1812.

TRANSCRIBED, EDITED AND INDEXED BY

JAMES SINGLETON.

PRIVATELY PRINTED FOR
THE YORKSHIRE PARISH REGISTER SOCIETY.
1916.

J. WHITEHEAD AND SON, LEEDS AND LONDON.

PREFACE.

This volume contains the entries in the Weston Parish Registers extending from the year 1639 to the year 1812—including the transcripts from York, which have been copied by Mr. R. B. Cook.

The first book measures 8 by 13¼ inches, and contains 7½ leaves of parchment. The entries are now very faint, and many of them illegible. Mr. G. D. Lumb rendered much assistance in the copying of this book.

The second book is 14¼ by 8 inches, bound in parchment with a metal clasp, and contains 16½ leaves of parchment, one page blank, and many blank spaces throughout the book.

The third book, bound in skin, measures 14¼ by 9½ inches. About one-third of the book has been used. The leaves are of paper. The entries from 1790 to 1812 are in different handwritings. This accounts for the varied spelling " Asquith " and " Askwith " on the same pages. These entries are recopied on subsequent pages, and additional information occasionally given, which has been incorporated in the print in square brackets.

The fourth book, which contains marriages only, is bound in stout cardboard, 11 by 17 inches, and contains printed forms filled in with the pen. About half the book is used.

Weston Church, situate at the back of the Hall, and within a short distance of the river Wharfe, is an interesting old edifice in the Norman and Early English styles, consisting of nave, chancel, south porch, and a western turret containing a bell. In the church-yard is an ancient sun dial, and the following is a copy of an inscription on one of the old tombs: " Hoaping for the riserection

heare lieth the bodie of William Crooke, of Askwith, who departed
this life Avgvst the 15, Anno Domini 1698, in the 71 yeare of his
aidge."

Weston is two miles north-west of Otley, and the parish com-
prises, in addition to Weston, the village of Askwith, the small,
peaceful hamlet of Snowden, and Dob Park.   In 1811 the popula-
tion of Weston was 128; that of Askwith, 306.

In Speight's *Upper Wharfedale*, (1900), there is a chapter on
" The Parish of Weston " (pp. 163–171), in which much interesting
information is given about the manorial history of Weston, the
Norman church, and the Vavasour, Asquith, and Kendall families.

To the Rev. C. L. Tweedale, the Vicar, are due the thanks of
the Society for permission to print and affording facilities for
copying the registers.

                                JAMES SINGLETON.

DELPH MOUNT,
    HYDE PARK, LEEDS.

REGISTERS

OF THE

CHURCH OF ALL SAINTS, WESTON,

NEAR OTLEY.

TRANSCRIPTS FROM YORK.

The Christenings, Weddings, and Burialls in Weston, Anno Dñi 1639.

CHRISTENINGS.

Anne Hunt, the daughter of Robert Hunt & Anne his wife, was baptized March 28th

Anne Barlow, ye dau. of George Barlow & Anne his wife, Septem. 29th

Thomas Aufeild, ye sonne of Thomas Aufeild & Jane his wife, Oct. 5th

Sarah Hunt, ye dau. of Will. Hunt & Alce his wife, Decemb. 2

Henry Hanson, ye sonne of Phillip Hanson & Anne his wife, Decemb. 15th

Katherine Storks, ye dau. of Ottowell Storks & Elizabeth, Jan. 19th

Francis Manners, ye dau. of Richard Manners & Ellin, Feb. 6th

Margaret Rose, ye dau. of Francis Rose & Elizabeth, March 8th

WEDDINGS.

Thomas Marshall & Elizabeth Mechinor married July 2th

Robert Walker & Katherine Marshall, July 30th

John Bee & Elizabeth Urry, November 14th

Thomas Gaskoine & Millesant Marshall, January 30th

BURIALLS.

Katherine Smith was buried May 30th

Anne Hunt, ye wife of Robert Hunt, June 7th

Will. Walker, September 9th

Izot Urry, widow, September 10th

Anne Barlow, ye wife of George Barlow, Octob. 5th

Thomas Smith, Octob. 14th

Katherine Parnell, Octob. 23th

Izot Wells, ye wife of Richard Wells, January 15th

Katherine Storkes, ye daughter of Ottowell, Jan. 23th

Sarah Hunt, ye daughter of Will. Hunt, Jan 23th

Elizabeth Skinner, ye daughter of Will. Skinner, Feb. 12th

Richard Wells, Feb. 19th

Anne Skelton, widow, March 22th

John Lewerton, Phillip Hanson, Churchwardens.

A Catalogue of the Christninges, Burialls, & Marriages for the present yeare in the Parish Church of Weston.

CHRISTENINGES 1640

Cudbert, the sonne of James Hodshon, baptized May ye 3

Mary, the daughter of William Robberts, May ye 16th

Elizabeth, the daughter of Thomas Foster, June ye 14th

A

Constantine, the sonne of Constantine Bayneton, July ye 19th
Mary, the daughter of Thomas Butler, August ye 30th
Elizabeth, the daughter of William Pickarde, August ye 30th
Anne, the daughter of Josias Bellwoode, Septemb. ye 27th
Thomas, the sonne of William Richardson, Octob. 18th
John, the sonne of John Newsome, Novemb. 12th
Isabel, the daughter of Thomas Ratcleife, Novemb. 22
Mary, the daughter of William Warde, Decemb. 13th
Bridgett, the daughter of Henry Harper, March ye 7th
Henry, the sonne of Henry Thompson, March ye 14th

BURIALLS 1640.

William Bradley ye younger,	buried April xvth
Ralphe Shutt,	,, Apr. 28th
Roger Hyrde,	,, May ye 13th
John Bradley,	,, June ye 8th
Elizabeth Illingeworth	,, July ye 10th
Isabell, ye wife of Constantine Bayneton,	,, Augus. ye 5th
Jennett Townend, widdowe,	,, Novemb. 22
Elizabeth Rawcleife,	,, Octob. 25th
Elizabeth Pickarde,	,, Decemb. 14th
Thomas Lambert,	,, Decemb. 17th
Elizabeth Brayshay,	,, Decemb. 27th
Elizabeth Hill, widdowe,	:: Jan. 11th
Margrett, ye wife of John Watter,	,, March 15th
Thomas Foster, of ye West end in Asquith,	,, March 19th

MARRIAGES 1640.

Christopher Warde and Margarett Laycocke,
    married with a Lycence,   Aprill 26th
Mr Thomas Croft and Mrs Olive Dyneley,
    married with a Lycence,   May 26th
John Richardson and Mary Warde,
    married with a Lycence,   June 23
John Clapham and Joyce Ratcleife, married   Novemb. 12
Thomas Kendall and Elizabeth Lambert,   Jan. 20th
Guilbert Dawson and Francis Laycock, widdow,
    married with a Lycence,   March 6th

Josias Bellwood, ibid. Vicarius.

PAROCHIA DE WESTON.

A trew Catalogue of Xtninges, Marriages, and Burialls
this last yeare 1641.

XTNINGES.

Anne, ye daughter of Francis Gamblin, baptized the 18th of Aprill 1641
Ralphe, ye sonne of William Shutt of Asquith, ye 2 of May
John, ye sonne of John Courteise, baptiz. ye 10th of June
Mary, ye daughter of John Richardson of Snawden, ye 20th of June
Isabell, ye daughter of John Crooke of Asquith, ye 4th of July
John, ye sonne of Robbert Blacey, baptized ye 12th of Octob.
James, ye sonne of James Steade, baptized ye 17th of Octob.
Thomas, ye sonne of Martin Bowlin of Asquith, ye 24th of Octob.
Marmaduke, ye sonne of John Mawson of Asquith, ye last of Octob.

James, yᵉ sonne of William **Pickarde**, baptiz. yᵉ 14ᵗʰ of Novemb.
Mary, yᵉ daughter of George Mawson of Asquith, yᵉ 16ᵗʰ of Novemb.
Margarett, yᵉ daughter of William Watter of Asquith, yᵉ 2 of Jan.
Francis, yᵉ sonne of Thomas Kendall of Asquith, yᵉ 16ᵗʰ of Jan.
Eden, yᵉ daughter of Thomas Illinworth of Snawden, yᵉ 20ᵗʰ of March

BURIALLS.

Myles Smyth, buried yᵉ 3 of Apr. 1641, beinge of Asquith
Jane, yᵉ daughter of Thomas Foster of Asquith, yᵉ 28 of Aprill
Mary, yᵉ daughter of Thomas Butler of Weston, yᵉ 22 of June
Francis Robberts of Snawden, buried yᵉ 7ᵗʰ of August
John Hargreave, son of Will. Hargreave of Asquith, yᶜ 22 of Septemb.
Thomas Marshall of Asquith, buried yᵉ 27 of Septemb.
Francis, yᵉ wife of George Mawson of Asquith, yᵉ 16ᵗʰ of Novemb.
John Brooke, buried yᵉ 6ᵗʰ of March 1641
Dorathy, yᵉ wife of Thomas Smyth, buried yᵉ 11ᵗʰ of March 1641
Jonas, yᵉ sonne of Thomas Butler of Weston, yᵉ 11ᵗʰ of March
Jane, yᵉ wife of John Netherwood of Asquith, yᵉ 20ᵗʰ of March

MARRIAGES.

Richard Ballarde and Elizabeth Browne, married yᵉ 3 of August 1641
William Gilliote and Ellen Bradley, the 7ᵗʰ of September
Francis Lambert and Jane Harper, the 26 of Octob.
Henry Wright and Ellen Lupton, yᵉ ii of Novemb.
Mʳ Ralph Phyncham and Mʳˢ Katherine Bateson, yᵉ 14 of Decemb.
Richard Watter and Anne Pickarde, yᵉ 27ᵗʰ of January 1641

Josias Bellwoode, ibid. Vicarius.
Churchwardens: William Smyth ju., Thomas Illinworth.

A Coppie out of oʳ Register at Weston for yᵉ last yeare (1669).

BAPTISMES.

John Hodgson, sonne of John Hodgson, yᵉ 24ᵗʰ June (69)
John Muschampe & Margrett, the Children of William Muschampe, the
20ᵗʰ November (69)
Willm Horner, the sonne of Jonath. Horner, the 4ᵗʰ March
Mary Watter, Daug. of Wᵐ Watter, yᵉ 10 Febru.

BURIALLS.

Willm Ward, yᵉ 4ᵗʰ December 1669.
Willm Mawson, 10 December
Christ. Kendell, yᵉ 14ᵗʰ December
Thomas Muschampe, the 16ᵗʰ December
Thomas Stead, the 18 December
James Smith, yᵉ 31 January (69)
Margrett Snell, yᵉ 10 February
Willm Watter, yᵉ 20 February

Wᵐ Hudson, Vic. de Weston.
George Whittacre, Wᵐ Mauson, Churchwardens.

N.B.—No Transcript remaining for 1668.—R. B. C.

[BOOK I.]

[Only about two inches from the binding of the first leaf is left, the rest being cut off.]

CHRISTENINGS 1671. [Transcript from York.]

William Brown, son of Will Brown, bapt. the 2nd of July
Grace Lathome, daughter of Thomas Lathome, the 16th of July
George Mauson, son of John Mauson, the 27 of August
Margaret Dale, daughter of John Dale, the 1st day of October
James Pickard, son of Will. Pickard, the 23 of October
Ellin Shutt daughter of Will. Shutt junior, the 26 of Oct.
Will. Bowling, son of Richard Bowling, the 10 of March
Dorothy, daughter of Thomas Richardson, the 15 of Aprill, 1672

MARRIAGES 1671.

John Richardson and Sarah Martiall, married the 17 of August
Richard Robertts and Anne Robinson, the 15 of January
Marmaduke Mauson and Isabell Stowe, the 13 of January

BURIALLS 1671 AND PART OF 1672.

Will. Smith buried the 13 of June 1671
Ester Butler, daughter of Thomas Butler, the 29 of June 1671
Elizabeth Blakey, the wife of Thomas Blakey, the 13 of September
James Hodgson buried the 26 of September
Will. Butler, the son of Thomas Butler, the 7th of January 1671
Alice Harper, the wife of Henery Harper, the 22 of February
John, the son of Thomas Lathome, buried the 4 of March
Alice Hargreaves, the wife of Will. Hargreaves, the 22 of March
Major Vavasour buried the ninth day of Aprill 1672
Jane Blakey, the wife of Walter Blakey, the 11 of April 1672

CHRISTENINGS 167⅔. [Transcript.]

Sarah Wardman, Daughter of John Wardman, bapt. the 25 of May
Isabel Roberts, Daughter of Lawrence Roberts, bapt. the 14 of July
Cuthbert and Dorothy, children of Will Muschamps, the 21 of July
Susanna Richardsonne, Daughter of John Richardsonne, the 25th June
Alice, the Daughter of Will Colter, baptized the 28 of July
Ann, the Daughter of Will Mausonne, bapt. the 18 of November
Thomas, the son of Thomas Latham, bapt. the 29 of September
Elizabeth, the Daughter of William Thackrey, the 27 of Decem.
Mary, the Daughter of Thomas Smith, the 5th of Jan. 167⅔
Anne, the Daughter of Richard Roberts, the 18th of Jan. 167⅔
Grace, the Daughter of Will Watter junior, the 19 of Jan. 167⅔

MARRIAGES IN THE YEAR 1672.

Christopher Staintonne and Elizabeth Hodgson, the 2d of May 1672
Thomas Kidde and Jane Whitfield, the 26th of Julii 1672
Thomas Pousonne and Elizabeth Crooke, the 29 of Novemb.

BURIALS IN THE YEAR 1672.

A Child of Stephen Braithwaits, still borne, the 4th of August
Three Children of Thomas Scotts buried the 20th of August

Antho. Fell, Marma. Richardson, Churchwardens.

CHRISTENINGS 1673. [Completed from Transcript.]

[Caleb son of John Pauson of Weston] baptized [the first of May] 1673

[Samuell] son of John [Harper] baptized the 30th [of June] 1673
[James the son] of Thomas [Kidde bapt.] the 27th [of July] 1673
[Robert the] son of George [Whittecar] baptized the [23^d Augu]st 1673
[William the] son of Richard [Kendall] baptized the 7th [Septemb]er 1673
[Elizabeth] the doughter [of Stephen] Braithwaite [bapt.] the 13th of Septem'
[Thomas] the son of John [Pauson of Asquith] baptized the 26th [of O]ctober 1673
[Richa]rd the son of Thomas [Latho]m baptized the 16th [of] November 1673
[Eliza]beth the daughter of [James] Hodgson baptized [the 2]3^d of November 1673
[Mary] the daughter of Will [Thac]k[ray] of Asquith bapt. [26] of Decem. 1673
[Thomas] the son of William [Mouson] of Asquith baptized [21] of February 1673
[Jane and] Elizabeth [Children] daughter[s] of Anthony [Snell] baptized the 8th of [Mar]ch 1673
[Richard] the son of John [Wat]ter baptized the [15th] of March 1673
[Susanna the Daughter of William Pickard bapt. the 18th of March 1673]

MARRIAGES [1673].

[James Hodgson and Mary Bolton maried the first of May 1673]
[Richard Whitfield and Frances Teale maried the 12 of Novem. 1673]

BURIALS [1673].

[John Smith of Weston buried] the 1[8]th of April 1673
Mary the wife of John Crook buried the 20th of April 1673
Elizabeth the wife of Cuthbirtt Adkinson buried the 21st of Aprill
William Nuttman buried the 23^d of May 1673
John Townend buried the second of August 1673
[Michaell Smith buried the second of September 1673]
[Dorothy Muschamps buried the 21th of October 1673]
[Frances Stead buried the 24th of October 1673]
Lyonell Snell buried the 16th of December 1673
Cuthbirt Muschamp[s] buried the first of January 1673

George Emsley and George Newsome, Churchwardens, 1673

CHRISTENINGS 1674

John the son of John Richardsonne baptized the 28th of May
Elizabeth the daughter of Richard Bowling baptized the 7th of June
Mary the daughter of Willm Maud baptiz: the 28th of June
Margarett the doughter of Will Foster baptized the 7th of January
Mary the doughter of Thomas Cookson baptized the 7th of March
William the son of John Harper bapt. the 25th September [see 1675]

MARRIAGES 1674.

William England and Mary Bridge married the . . . of August
Thomas Stead and Isabell Fell married the first of Novem.
William Clapham and Anne Sowden married the 6th of Aprill 1674
Thomas Cook and Isabell Foster married the 25th of May 1674

BURIALS 1674.

A Child of George Emsleys buried the 3^d of May 1674
Jane Lambert buried the 29th of May

Mary the wife of William Richardson buried the 29th of May
Elizabeth Browne buried the 18th of January
? Richard Brathwate buried the 27th of February
[*An entry illegible*]
. . . . Kendall . . . .
Mary Blakky . . .
John Browne bur^d . . . .

CHRISTENINGS 1675.

James the son of Thomas Stead . . . .
William the son of John Harper baptized the 25th of September 1675
John the son of Richard Whitfield baptized the 16th of January 1675
John Hodgson baptiz: the 26th of March 1676
Christopher the son of Robert Smith baptized the 27th of March 1676

MARRIAGES 1675.

James Adkinson, Richard Waddington, Churchwardens
Marmaduke Bramley and Grace Richardson married the first of July
John Robinson and Isabell Smith married the 22nd of July
William Milner and Annes Foster married the 31th January

BURIALS 1675.

Elizabeth Nutman buried the 24th of May
Jane the daughter of John Kendall buried the 24th of May
A Child of George Emsleys still born buried the 13th of June
John Bradley buried the 24th July
A Child of Charles Walmsleys buried the 14th of September
Mrs. Williamson buried the 17th of Nov:
Margarett Kendall buried the 24th of November
William Mouson of Weston buried the 12th of December
Thomas Radcliffe buried the 14th of December
Frances Smith the wife of William Smith buried the 17th of December
A Child of Thomas Latham buried 8th of January
Anne the wife of Thomas Radcliffe buried the first of February
The wife of William Smith of . . . . was buried the 2 . . . .
A Child of . . . .

CHRISTENINGS 1676.

Annamaria Adkinson bapt. the 18th of May 1676
John the son of Cuthbirt Hodgson baptiz: the 15th July
John the son of Will England baptiz: the 23d of July
Dorothy the daughter of Will Maud bapt: 28th of Sept.
John the son of Will Watter junior bapt. the 28th of October
John the son of Will: Thackray of Weston bapt: the 15th October
Stephen the son of Stephen Braithwaite bapt: 3d October
Thomas the son of Will Thackray of Asquith bapt. 30th Octob.
Elizabeth the daughter of John Pawson of Asquith bapt. ye 5th Novem.
Mary the daughter of John Robinson bapt. the 19th of November
Peter the son of Richard Bowling baptized the 28th of January
John the son of John Mowson of Weston bapt. ye 18th of February
Elizabeth the doughter of Richard Waddington baptized the 31st of
    March 1677

MARRIAGES 1676.

Richard Smith and Elizabeth Fowler married the 6th of . . .

BURIALS 1676.

Elizabeth Smith the wife of John Smith of Asquith buried the 23d of May

James the son of James Adkinson buried the 24th of May

John . . . of Asquith buried the . . . of June

George Stead of Norwood buried the 28th of June

Jane the doughter of Anthony [? Snell] buried the 30th of September

Mary the daughter of . . . . Thakray of Weston buried 30th of October

Thomas Browne senior buried the 8th of November

Henry Thackray buried the 12th of November

Jane Beane buried the 20th of November

Margarett the daughter of John Curtis buried 2nd of January

Margaret the wife of John Curtis buried the 6th of January

Anne the wife of John Mawson buried the 15th of January

A Child of George Emsley stillborn buried the first of February

James the son of Thomas Stead buried the same day

Will Hudson vicar of Weston buried the 5th Febr.

John the son of Cuthbirtt Hodgeon buried ye 21st Febru.

Mary the wife of Will England buried ye 12th of March

Christopher Radclife buried the 20th of March

Will Stead of Weston buried the 27th of March 1677

Elizabeth the wife of Richard Waddington buried the 31st of March 1677

Finis Hujus Anñ 1676 Anthony Snell, Willm Hardcastle, Churchwardens.

CHRISTENINGS 1677.

Thomas the son of Thomas Stead bapt: the 9th May

Jane Smith the daughter of Richard Smith baptized the 23d of June

Anthony the son of Anthony Snell bapt. the 23^d August

Anna Kidd baptized the 16th of September

Ellen the daughter of Thomas Lathom baptized the 23d of September

John the son of John Watter baptiz. the 30th of September

John Beane baptiz: the 30th of September

Will the son of John Robinson baptiz: the 18th of November

Will the son of Thomas Vavasour bapt: the 25th of December

John the son of Cuthbirt Hodgeon bapt: the 10th Februa.

Miles the son of Thomas Browne baptiz. 10th March

Anne the doughter of Matthew Wharton baptized the 14th of Aprill 1678

MARRIAGES 1677.

Christopher Aumon and Elizabeth Smith married the 23^d of September

Will England and Ann Whittiker married the 27th January

Richard Waddington and Mary Banks married the 30th of March 1678

BURIALLS 1677.

Mary the daughter of James Stead buried the 12th June

Maudlen the daughter of Thomas Vavasour buried the 30th of June

Will. Shutt senior buried the 30th day of July

A Child of Charles Walmesley still borne buried the 11th of July

John the son of James Hodgeon bur. the 29th of September

John the son of John Watter buried the first of October

Charles Walmesley buried the 26 of November

Ellen the wife of Thomas de hilltopp buried the 6th of December

Ellen the daughter of Thomas Lathom buried the 13th of December

Will Mouson the son of Edmund Mouson buried the 9th of January
Margarett the wife of Edmund Greenwood buried the 7th of February
Thomas Vavasour buried the 10th of February
Will the son of John Harper buried the 25th of February
 Finis Huius Anni 1677 John Mauson and Richard Bowling, Church-
wardens

REGISTER OF WESTON PARISH FOR THE YEAR 1678 AND PART OF THE
YEAR 1679. [*Transcript*]

Ellen the dau. of Will. Mouson senior bapt. yᵉ 28 of Aprill
John the son of John Dale bapt. yᵉ 19 of May
Eliz. the dau. of Will. Smith bapt. yᵉ 19 of May
Susanna the dau. of James Hodgson bapt. yᵉ 19 of May
Anne the dau. of John Harper bapt. yᵉ 9 of June
Robert the son of Richard Whitfield bapt. yᵉ 18 of August
Will. the son of Will. Shutt junʳ bapt. yᵉ 27 of October
Mary the dau. of Richard Smith bapt. yᵉ 4 of January
Alice the dau. of Richard Kendall bapt. yᵉ 6 of January
Anne the dau. of John Richardson bapt. yᵉ 16 of February
Mary the dau. of Richard Waddington bapt. yᵉ 18 of February
James the son of James Adkinson bapt. yᵉ 1ˢᵗ of March
Will. the son of Will. England bapt. yᵉ 2ⁿᵈ of March
George the son of George Whitiker bapt. yᵉ 5ᵗʰ of Aprill 1679
John the son of Stephen Braithwaite bapt. yᵉ 5ᵗʰ of May

MARRIAGES 1678.

John Waite and Anne Risworth of Ighley ye 14ᵗʰ of July 1678
Chris. Holmes of Middleton and Rebecca Thompson of Asquith, 24 Nov.
Thomas Mouson & Mary Stead married 24ᵗʰ of November

BURIALLS 1678.

Annis the wife of [*blank*] Sowden buried the 9ᵗʰ of May
Grace yᵉ dau. of Thomas Ackman buried the 19ᵗʰ of May
Will. yᵉ son of Thomas Vavasour buried the 19 of May
A child of Geo. Emsleys still born buried 13 of July
Margaret Silson buried 26 of Novʳ
Benjamin Shutt buried 18 of Janʸ
Anne Roberts buried 9 May 1679
Frances Midgley & Beatrice Day married Novʳ 14ᵗʰ 1678
George the son of George Whitiker baptized the 5ᵗʰ of Aprill 1679
John the son of Stephen Braithwaite bapt. the 5ᵗʰ of May 1679

CHRISTENINGS 1679.

. . . . doughter of Thomas . . . 22th of May
. . . . son of Robert W . . . of July
. . . . Will Tho . . . yᵉ 13th . . .
. . . . yᵉ doughter of Thomas . . . 20th of September
. . . . son of John Mouson . . . November
. . . . Richard [? Bowers] . . .
. . . . 24th of December

[BURIALS 1679]

Grace Holland buried . . . of August 1679
A Child of George Emsley . . . of October
Matthew . . . . buried yᵉ 19 of November 1679

. . . . Holmes spurius bapt: Febru. 8ᵛᵒ die
Maria filia Will Pickard de Askwith jun: bapt: Feb. 23
Willielmus Pulleine de Timble et Maria Mauson de Askwith nupt. Feb. 19
Will. Stead et Alicia England nupt. Feb. 24
Thomas Thwaite vic. Westoniensis et Sarah Fowler de Healey nupt.
    12 die Octobris.
Elizabetha fillia Johannis Pauson de Askwith sepulta Feb. 25
Jane vidua Martini Bowlin de Askwith sepulta 26 die Febr:
Thomas fillius Will Thackry de Askwith sepultus 6 die Martij
Margreta filia Will Mauson de Askwith bapt: 7 die Martij
    Finis hujus Anni 1679 Roberto Walker et Joseph' Hargraves deonomis
Ecclesia

Baptiz. 1680.

Thomas filius Roberti Muschamps bapt. undecimo die Julij
Thomas filius Tho: Thwaites vicarii bapt. 25 die Julij
Jane filia Richardi Waddington bapt: eodem die
Jo: filius Thomæ Brown bapt: Sept. 25
Charolus Latham filius Thomæ Latham bapt. Sept. 26
Jo: filia Johannes [sic] Robinson Octobris 17 die
Georgius filius Georgius Booth bapt. Novembris 16 die
Gulielmus filius Thomæ Stead bapt: Martij 13 die

Sepulturæ hujus Anni 1680.

Maria filia Thomæ Foster de ul'mo sepulta fuit 11 die Maij
Maria filia Willielmi Walter sep: 28 die Maij
Antonius Whitfield sep: 25 die Junij
Maria uxor Thomæ Bowlin Septembris 28 die
Margreta uxor Thomæ Bradley sep: Octobris 3tio die
Cecilia Gilyate Novembris primo die
Wilielmus Brown de Weston Novembris 14 die
Puella (filia Johannis Kendale junior) in baptizata sepulta est Nov. 16
Wilielmus Gilyate sep: Decembris 22 die
Ellena Shutt sep: Februarij 3tio die
Johanna Kendale d . . . . Maria Kendale 16 die
Radulphus Ashlea de . . . . comitatu Lancastrie duxit in uxorem
    Dominam Mariam Vavasour unicam filiam et hered' Thomæ
    [Vava]sour de Spaldington . . . .
    Finis hujus anni Thomas Thwaites vicarius, meæ anno quarto
Georgius Booth et Robertus Pattison, Guard' Ecclesiæ.

1681 Baptiz.

Maugerus filius Richardi Smith Martij 26 die
Willielmus filius Matthei Wharton Martij 26
Johanes filius Johannis Curtoise Maij 10 die
Robertus filius Roberti Walker Junij 4
Johanes filius Jacobi Hodgshon Junij 12
Thomas filius Willielmi England Augusti 7
Jane filia Johannis Kendale Novembris 23
Wilielmus filius Wilielmi Thackery de Weston Augusti 2 die
Jacobus filius Thomæ Latham Decembris 18
Thomas filius Thomæ Crooke, Elizebetha filia Wilielmi Thackray de
    Askwith Decembris 27

Jacobus filius Thomæ Thwaites vicarij Febr. 5to die
Carolus filius Georgij Booth Febru: 20
Wilielmus filius Wilielmi Crooke jun^r Martij 5to die

SEPULTORUM.

Alicia Ward vidua Apr. 3to
[*Probably 2 entries indecipherable.*]
. . . . Richardi Smith . . . . Julij 2do
. . . . Stead de Weston 9bris 19
. . . . filius Richardi Whitfield de Askwith 9bris 7
. . . . Hardcastle de . . . . Januarij 22 die
. . . . Brown vidua Jan. 30
. . . . Booth uxor . . . . Booth [de Askw]ith Februarij 29

NUPTIÆ.

. . . . son et Anna . . . . de Snowden Jan: 31
    [Finis huijus] Anni per me [Thoma'] Thwaites vicarium.
. . . . [? Hudson] et Richardo . . . .

1682 BAPTIZ.

. . . .
. . . . filius Richardi . . . . Maij 16
. . . . filius . . . . wait de Carr house vicessimo die
. . . . tha filia Richardi . . . . de laund houses . . . . [sec]undo die
. . . . filius Thomæ Curtoise . . . . die
. . . . Johannis Curtoise . . . . 21 die
. . . . filius Richardi . . . . bapt. 24 die
. . . . die
. . . . Roberti Muschamp . . . . 12 die
. . . . Pauson bapt. 18 die Novembris
Willielmus filius Wilielmi M . . . . son de Askwith bapt. decimo die
    Decembris
Edwardus filius Wilielmi . . . . de Askwith bapt: vi[cessimo] die 10bris
Anthonius filius . . . . 28 die

SEPULTURÆ.

Johannes Stead Septembris 8vo
Joshua Lowcock sept: quarto die
Will Brown de Askwith 10bris primo
Abrahamus Coates, Martij secundo

NUPTIÆ.

Robertus Standish & Elizabethe . . . . Jan. 21 die
Johannes King et Margritta Smith Jan: 22 die
Thomas Kendale et Maria Brown Febr. tertio die
    Finis hujus anni pr. me Thoma' Thwaits vicarium inductionis meæ
sexto anno Will: Stead et Josepho Hargraves æadituis.

WESTON.
[From back of Transcript for 1689.]
Anno 168⅔.
CATECHUMENI, Martii 4to die.

Malgerus Snell, Will. Thackray, Malgerus Greenwood, Will. Horner,
    Johannes Thackray de Weston, Will. Hardcastle, Tho. Thwaits, Antonius
    Snell. 8

Martii 11mo die.

Johannes Thackeray de Ask., Antonius Pauson, Henricus Atkinson, Richardus Sowden.   4

Martii 18vo die.

Chr. Bowlin, Chr. Kendall, Will. Kendall, Tho. Latham.   4

BAPTIZ. 1683. [*Transcripts in brackets*]

Anna filia Thomæ Brown bapt. Aprilis 28 die
Willielmus filius Johannis Mauson Maij 28 die
Johannes filius Johannis Cryer eodem die
Josephus filius Johannis Robinson Junij nono
Sarah filia Johannis Richinson Junij 30 die
[Anne filia] Jacobi Hod[gshon] de Askwith bapt . . . .
Margreta filia Johannis . . . . mer de Grassgarth [Aug.] 19 die
Maria filia Johannis Atkinson baptized Sept. 22mo die
Laurentius filius Thomæ Thwaitҽ baptiz: Octobris quarto decimo die
Benjamin spurius Mariæ Walter[s] vidua de Askwith baptiz. decimo octavo die Novembris
Frances Walker filia Robert Walker baptizata fuit 12mo die Januarij
Ellen filia Cuthberti Hodgson baptizata Febru: 24 die
Johannes filius Georgij Whitaker Martij 9no die
Wilielmus filius Thomæ Mauson baptizatus 22 die Martij
   Totalis numerus 14.

SEPULTORUM NOMINA 1683.

Laurentius Kendale 26 die Martij
Dominus Henricus Hudson amicus mihi charissimus 16 die Maij
Jane filia Richardi Smith 21 die Maij
E[d]en Illingworth Junij 5to die
Josephus filius Johannis [Robinson] Junij 16to die
Elizabetha Walter Septembris die 22do
Margarita filia Johannis Harper die 7mo Octobris
[Isabell Jubbs Decem. 25]
[Thomas Muschamps January ye 11th]
[Samuel Harper Jan. 14th]
[John] Wardma[n] . . . . cus mihi . . . . [20th] die Martij
   Noe Marriages this year in our parish.

Finis hujus annị per me Thoma' Thwaits vic' Johannes Nichols, Josephus Hargreaves ædituis.

BAPTIZ' ANNO 1684.

Anna filia Thomæ . . . .
Thomas filius Johannis . . . .
Hanna filia Johannis . . . . baptizata fuit . . . . 17 annos . . . .
Anna filia . . . .
Maria Mauson filia Thomæ de Askwith baptizata May ye 25
Elizabetha filia Johannis . . . . de Askwith baptizata Junij . .
Francisca filia Thomæ . . . . 9no die
Thomas filius Johannis . . . . die Junij
Jane filia Johannis Curt . . . . secundo die
Margrita filia Thomæ . . . . 14 die
Thomas filius Willielmi . . . . ray de Askwith Febr. . . . .
Margrita filia . . . . de Askwith Febru. 15

Richardus filius . . . . thwaite Febru. . . . . die
Nicholas et Johannes filij Nicholai . . . . son de Snawden Martij primo
die

SEPULTURÆ 1684.
Abrahamus filius Johannis Nicholls Maij 18 die
Johannes filius Georgij Whitaker Junij primo die
Eliz: Stead de Sicklinghall Julij 21
Anna Beaumont de Skipton in Craven 11 die
Franciscus Kendale Anabaptista of Fremebundus Sept: 23
Johannes Mauson de Askwith Octob' octavo die
Sarah Hargraves October yᵉ 9th
Isabella Pauson vidua Novʳ 19 die
Jenetta Latham vidua Nov: 29
Tho: Foster de monte Januarij 8vo
Maria Mauson de Weston vidua Januar: 30
Eliz: Thornton pauper puella Febr: 6to die
Jana Horner de Askwith Mar: 14
    Finis hujus anni per me Tho: Thwaits vic: Roberto Hardcastle,
Christofero Wharton ædituis.

BAPTIZATORU' NOMINA 1685.
Richardus filius quartus Tho: Thwaits vicarij Aprillis 7mo die . . . . fillia
    Willielmi England baptizata Maij 10 die
Anna Wharton filia Christoferi . . . . Maij 16 die
Robertus filius Mariæ Illingworth et . . . . baptizat: Maij 26 die
Franciscus filius Thomæ [Ken]dale baptiz: Augusti nono die
Thomas filius Johannis Cry[er] Octobris die 26to
Maria filia Jacobi Hodgshon de Askwith 19 die Novembris
Malgerus fillius Richardi Smith Decembris 16ᵗᵒ die
Marmaducus filius Marmaduci Roundale Decembris 21mo die
Malgerus filius Johannis Mauson 31 die Januarij
Georgius filius Josephi Hargreaves octavo die Februarij
Jane filia Thomæ Latham baptizata Martij 21ᵐᵒ die
Joana filia Roberti Walker baptiz: Martij 22do die

SEPULTURÆ 1685.
Anna England Apr: secundo die
Jane Latham Maij 28vo die
Christoferus Harrison Aug: 19 die
Wilielmus Hardcastle Aug: 23 die
Maria England Octobris 13 die
Johannes Roundall Novem: 20 die, uxor ejus eodem die
Jane Lowcock Decem: 17 die
Johannes Atkinson 24to die Januarij
Maria Brown   Martij 14to die

NUPTIÆ 1685.
Johannes Robinson et Maria Lane Octobris 13 die
Anthonius Raycroft & Frances Snell . . . . lis vicessimo primo die
Wilielmus Clifton de Clifton et Anna Nelson Aprilis vicessimo tertio die
Malgerus Pickard et Margerita Mauson Febr. undecimo die
    Finis hujus Anni per me Thomam Thwaits vicarium, Johanne Curtis
et Johanne Richinson ædituis.

BAPTIZ: NOMINA 1686.

Henricus Rycroft Julij primo die
Anthonius Curtis filius Thomæ Curtis Augusti 3tio die
Maria filia Symonis Pott Sept. quinto die
Wilielmus filius Johannis Maud Sept: 19 die
Johannes spurius Hanah Gill eodem die
Johannes filius Johannis Curtoise 28 die Sept:
Willielmus filius Thomæ Thwaits Octobris 26 die
Johanes filius Richardi Houseman Novembris quarto die
Jane filia Johannis Nichols Novembris 17 die
Elizabetha filia Thomæ England junr. Decembris quinto die

SEPULTORUM 1686.

Eliz. Shutt Maij 10
Joana Walker Aug: 23
Jo: Pauson Sept: 1mo
Ric: Bowlin Octo: 22
Jo: England Jan: 2do
Anna Usherwood Jan: die 15
[blank] Kendale Jan: 30
Maria Roberts Febr: die 11
       Finis hujus Anni per me Tho: Thwaites vic. de Weston.

NOMINA BAPTIZ: 1687.

Will filius Stephane Brathwaite Apr:
Christopher filius Christoferi Wharton Aprilis 25
Will filius Johanis Richinson Apr: 30
Maria filia Johannis Harrison Maij 7mo die
Willielmus filius Elizabethæ Kendale viduæ Augusti 27 die
Ellena fillia Lawrentij Preston Novembris 27 die
Georgius filius Johannis Kendall Novembris 29no die
Willielmus filius Josephi Hargraves [sic]
Elizabetha filia Johannis Cryer Martij 15 die
Johannes filius Roberti Walker Novembris 27 die

NUPTIÆ 1687.

Jonathanus Nicholls et Mariæ Jowett Octobris 23 die
Johannes Battie de Warmsworth et Susanna Vavasour de Weston Novembris 6to die
Johannes Kendale et Ruth Waite Octobris 23 die

SEPULTURE 1687.

Willielmus filius Stephane Brathwaite Aprilis 21 die
Elizabetha filia Richardi Smith Aprilis 29 die
Willielmus Kendale primo die Maij
Infans Johannis Robinson de Snowden May 31 die
George Hargraves filius Josephi Hargraves Junij 16 die
Elizabetha Hodgshon 19 die Junij
Nathan Atkinson Junij 22 die
Elizabetha Crook Junij 27
Maria Hudson Novembris 14 die
    Finis hujus Anni per me Tho: Thwaits vic: Edw: Ackman, Williel. Smith ædituis.

BAPTIZ: NOMINA 1688 MIRABILIS ANNUS.

Johannes Hetton filius peregrinæ cujusdam Aprilis tertio die
Rachell England filia Willelmi Aprilis octavo
Wilielmus filius Willielmi Foster Aprilis 19 die
Jacobus filius Jacobi Hodgshon Aprilis 21ᵐᵒ die
Marmaduke filius Marmaduci Roundale Aprilis vigessimo quarto die
Lawrentius et Elizabetha gemelli Johannis et Elizabethe Kendale Aprilis
   28 die
Robertus filius Georgij Whitaker Julij 29no die
Katherina fillia Thomæ England eodem die
Elizabeth fillia Will Smith Sept: nono die
Antony fillius Nichole Pauson Oct: 14 die
[blank] fillius Stephane Braithwaite Novembris 5to die
Maria filia Josias Baune Decembris 3tio die
Willielmus filius Johannis Kendall de Askwith Decembris vicessimo
   secundo die
Anna filia Christopheri Loftas Januarij 13 die
Jacobus filius Radulphi Gill de Newhall Carr Jan: vicessimo quarto die
Anna fillia Richardi Houseman Febr: 16to die
Frances fillia Thomæ Latham Mar: 11 die

NUPTIÆ 1688.

Robert Emsley et Eliz. Kendale Febru: 4to
Will Watson et [blank] Martij 10 die
Will Hudleston et Eliz. Mauson, Apr: 11 die

SEPULTURÆ 1688.

Tho: fillius Johannis Cryer Maij 18mo die
Infans Willie[l]mi Blakey de Denton Junij 10 die
Infans Johannis Robinson Junij 17
Ma . . . . Marmaduci Nove'b. . .
[About 6 entries illegible.]

A True Copy of yᵉ Register of yᵉ Parish of Weston containing all Christenings, Marriages, and Burialls
   for the year of our Lord 1689. [Transcript.]

CHRISTENINGS.

Hester yᵉ daughter of John Thackeray Sept. yᵉ 13ᵗʰ
Tho. son of Lawrence Preston October yᵉ 9ᵗʰ
Will. son of Jonas Atkinson October yᵉ 10ᵗʰ
Sarah dau. of Thomas Thwaites October yᵉ 22
Geo. son of George Booth December yᵉ 3ᵈ
Dorathy dau. of Ric. Smith May yᵉ 26ᵗʰ
Marmaduke son of John Mauson June yᵉ 2ᵈ
John son of Tho. Curtoise December 22ᵈ
Will. son of Tho. Kendall Febr. the ninth

Noe Marriages.

BURIALLS.

John son of Will. Foster July yᵉ 29ᵗʰ
Eliz. dau. of John Kendall October yᵉ 15ᵗʰ
John son of Tho. Curtoise January yᵉ 8ᵗʰ

By us, Tho. Thwaits Vic. ibid.

BAPTIZ. [1690].

[About two entries illegible.]

. . . . filius Willelmi . . . .
Christopherus fillius Johannis Rhodes de Askwith 11mo die Maij
Maria fillia Georgij Raley de Grimstown 25to die Maij
Marmaducus fillius Willielmi Foster de Askwith Maij 31mo die
Gulielmus Hodgshon fillius Jacobi Hodgshon de Askwith 17 die Augusti
Maria fillia Johannis Robinson de Snowden Augusti 24to
Jane fillia Johannis Maude de Scales 29to die Octobris
Georgius fillius Timothei Medcalf Novembris 13 die 1690
Sarah fillia Josephi Hargrave 1obris 12mo die 1690
Anna fillia Johannis Cryer de Scales 23tio die 1obris
Sarah fillia Thome England de Snowden Feb: 9no die
Sarah fillia Georgij Booth de Askwith Feb: 12mo die
Elizabetha fillia Christopheri Wharton de Westonia Mar . . . .

NUPTIE 1690.

Tho: Hudson & Frances Bradford Maij 26to die
Henricus Ley de Hamp . . . . & . . . . July 25
. . . . Mar . . . .

[One or two entries illegible.]

SEPULTURÆ 1690.

Frances filia Tho: Latham . . . .
Maria filia Richardi Smith . . . .
Thomas Atkinson . . . .
. . . . primo die
Johannes Kendale vicessimo secundo die Ju . . . .
. . . . Smith de Weston decimo die Augusti
. . . . Hodshon filius Jacobi Hodshon decimo septimo die Augusti
Maria filia Johannis . . . . Septembris septimo die
. . . . Septembris die decimo
Petrus . . . . vicessimo die Septembris
Maria . . . . kering decimo octavo . . . .
. . . . filia Tho: England . . . . Januarij
Eliz. Kendale uxor Tho: Kendale . . . . quarto die Februarij
. . . . uxor Simonis . . . . vicessimo sexto die Februarij
Ge . . . . Newsom primo die Martij
Nathanielus filius J$_0$: Maude . . . . die
. . . . Aediles . . . . per Thoma' Thwaites vic'

WESTON REGISTER. BAPTIZED 1691. [Transcript.]

Tho. fillius Tho. Hudson Maii 3^{tlo} die
Hester fillia Christopheri Loftas 10mo die Maii
Margaretta fillia Gulielmi Foster 28to die Junii
Tho. fillius Nicholæ Pauson 16to die Julii
Anna filia Edwardi Greenwood Octobris 12mo die
J$_0$. filius Tho. Mauson Octobris 17mo die
Johannes fillius J$_0$. Thackeray 18vo die Octobris
Maria filia Marmaduci Pauson primo die Novembris
Sarah filia Gulielmi England Novembris 30mo die
Jane filia Jacobi Hodshon primo die Januarii
Maria filia J$_0$. Kendall 17mo die Februarii

Law. filius Lawrentii Preston sexto die Martii
NUPTIÆ 1691.
Nicholas Waddington & Frances Clapham [de Bethemsley] Septembris 27mo die
SEPULTURÆ 1691.
Margaretta Stead 19mo die Aprilis
Jo. Crooke [calebs] quarto die Julii
Cuthbertus Hodshon 16to die Julii
Isabella Beane 27mo die Augusti
Margaretta filia Gulielmi Foster Septembris 18to die
Will. Sowden Septembris 19mo die
Will. filius Jo. Robinson 24to die Septembris
Gracia filia Thomæ Latham 27° die Octobris
Maria Dale 20mo die Novembris
Elizabeth Standish [de Weston] 13^{tio} die Decembris
Deborah Smith 27mo Februarii

Tho. Thwaits.
BAPTIZ. 1692.
Anna filia Thomæ Thwaites pastoris huius ecclesiæ Maij vicessimo primo
[? Maria] filia Willmi Foster Julij vig . . . . quarto die
W'mus filius Will'mi Leeson ho . . . iolæ . . ejus . . . . vicessimo die Julij
. . . . filia Jacobi Dade vicessimo . . . die Augusti
. . . . filius Tho: Hudson . . . . die Octobris
. . . . filius Geo: Booth primo die Decembris
Joħes filius Thomæ England nono die Januarij
[? Maria] filia Joħis Rhodes Martij decimo die
NUPTIÆ Año 1692.
Joħes Thackeray de Otley & Maria Wardman de Snowden Aprilis decimo octavo die
Joħes Heartley & Sarah Wardman Maij vicessimo sexto die
Joħes Calverd & Frances [? Lawcock] Augusti vicessimo nono die
[? Malgerus] Shutt & [? Frances] . . . . Decembris primo die
Johannes Harper et Maria . . . . Februarij . . . .
FUNERA 1692.
[? Anna] uxor Johannis Harper . . . . die Augusti
. . . . [? Robinson] Augusti primo die
Joħes Pawson de Askwith Septembris undecimo die
Johannes Robinson duodecimo die Septembris
Marmaducus Richinson die duodecimo Novembris
Jana uxor Antonii Fell die quinto Januarij
Estera fillia Joħis Thakeray Januarij septimo die
Infans Joħis Heartley quarto die Februarij
Josephus Greenwood cælebs vigessimo secundo Februarij
Sarah puellula Josephi [? Hargrave] Martij undecimo die

Finis huius Anni, Anthonio Snell & Johanne Rhodes æditibus. Scriptum per me Thomam Thwaites, juniorem.
BAPTIZ. Año Dom'i 1693.
Anna filia Josephi Marshall Aprilis secundo die
Ellena filia Joħis Mawd . . . . Aprilis decimo quarto die
Frances filia Willmi Vavasour Armigeri Aprilis vicessimo die

Willmus filius Christopheri Wharton Maij decimo quarto
Willmus filius Timothei Medcalf de Grass-garths May vicessimo quinto
  die
Thomas et Georgius gemini Joñis Crier de Scales Junij vigessimo séptimo
  die
Thomas filius naturalis Susannæ Sowdon de Askwith Julij xxijdo die
Anna filia Marmaduci Pawson de Askwith die xxiijº Julij
Christopherus filius Edwardi Greenwood Novembris 14to die
Eliz: infans abortiva Joñis Mawson die 10 Nov'bris
[*An entry illegible.*]
Anna . . . .
. . . . Kendall . . . .
Elizabetha . . . .

NUPTIÆ Año D'ni 1693.

Joñes Cat . . . . & Gracia Maude Maij 22do die
Joñes Shutt & Eliz: Ratcliff Septembris 14 die

BAPTIZ. Anno 1693.

Will . . . . tricessimo die [*rest illegible*].

B

[BOOK II.]

[*On fly leaf*] 1693. Baptiz: Frances the daughter of Wm Vavasour Esq. of Weston, April ye 20th.

W^m ye Son of Wm Vavasour Esqr Baptiz: Augt 26/1698.

BAPTISMATA 1694.

Anna filia Johannis Harper de Grassgarths die 12mo Aprilis.
Maria filia Thomæ Mauson de Scales, Aprilis 22do.
Johannes filius Johannis Foster de Askwith, Aprilis 20.
Franciscus filius Johannis Thackeray de Askwith die 12mo May.
Johannes filius Jacobi Dade de Askwith Junij vicissimo nono die.
Malgerus filius Guillielmi Vavasour Armigeri die vicessimo sexto Septembris.
Williemus filius Nicholæ Pauson de Snowden vicessimo octavo die Octobris.
Henricus filius Johannis Robinson de Snowden eodem die.
Thomas filius Georgius Booth de Askwith die 8vo Decembris.
Euphemia filia Thomæ Thwaits vicarij Westoniensis die vicessimo primo Aprilis.
Anthonius filius Richardi Smith de Weston Aprilis 23^tio die.
Maria filia Johannis Foster de Weston 2.
Christopherus filius Christopheri Loftas die 3^tio Junii.
Anna filia Georgij Marshall de Weston Decembris 10 die.
Margrita filia Lawrentij Preston Decembris 27mo die.

NUPTIÆ 1694.

Samuelis Marshall et Margrita Muschamps Julij 4to die.
Georgius Muschamps et Susanna Richardson Julij 25 die.
Jacobus Patricke et Gratia Wardman Octobris primo die.

SEPULTURÆ 1694.

Anna filia Jonathani Horner Februarij decimo septimo die.
Franciscus filius Johannis Thackeray de Askwith Jumÿ 15to die.
Elizabetha filia Christopheri Wharton de Weston Julii 31mo die.
Susanna Pauson de Askwith Augusti vecessimo sexto die.
Elizabetha Brown de Askwith Octobris tricessimo primo die.
Thomas filius Georgij Booth de Askwith die 13 Decembris.
Gratia Uxor Jacobi Patricke de Hawksworth Februarij 3^tio.
Johannes filius R. . . . . Manton [?] de Askwith Februarij 12 die.

BAPTIZAT. ANNO 1695.

Johannes fillius Will Foster de Askwith Aprilis 7mo die.
Josephus filius Johannis Harrison 21mo Aprilis.
Georgius filius Tho: Hudson eodem die.
Johanes filius Johannis Kendale Julij 14to die.
Will fillius Willielmi Moss Julij 22do die.
Sarah filia Georgij Muschamps Sept: 27mo die.
Margrita filia Anthonij Pauson Oct: 12mo die.
Will filius Johannis Thackray Oct: 19no die.
Georgius fillius Johannis Darraine Oct: 27mo die.
Jo: filius Marmaduci Pawson Novemb: 2do die.
Mattheus fillius Timothei Medcalfe Novemb: 17 die.
Jane filia Jos: Hargraves Decemb: 14mo die

Wiłł filius Edwardi Greenwood Decemb: 15to die.
[*blank*] filia Johannis Maude Decemb: 18vo die.

SEPULT. 1695.

Thomas Snell Julij 28vo die.
Martha filia Wiłł Vavasour Decembris ultimo die.

NUPTIÆ 1695.

Johannes Thackray de Burleigh et Frances Ryley die ultimo Septembris.

Tho: Thwaits, vic. de Weston.

BAPTIZAT. ANNO 1696.

Wiłł: filius Georgij Marshall Maij 29no die.
Wiłł: spurius Hannæ Gill Junij 14to die.
Maria fillia Johannis Harper Junij 27mo die.
Wiłł: fillius Jacobi Dade Augusti 9no die.
Malgerus fillius Malgeri Shutt Oct: 18vo die.
Antonius fillius Antonij Foster Novemb: 17mo die.
Mickaell fillius Johannis Lamb Decemb: 27mo die.
Tho: fillius Tho: Mauson Jan: 24to die.
Wiłł: fillius Symonis Pott Febr. 7mo die.
Eliz: filia Johannis Roades Febr. 28vo die.

SEPULTURÆ 1696.

Margrita Harrison Martij ultimo die.
Johanes Shutt Maij 5to die.
James Atkinson Junij primo die.
Wiłł Spurius Secundus Hannæ Gill Junij 29no die.
Tho: Stead Julij 26 die.
Joanna Crooke Septembris 25to die.
Willielmus Thwaits fillius meus præcharissimus objt die decimoquinto
   Octobris, inhumatus autem decimo septimo die cujus animulæ blandulæ
   miserere deus Amen Amen.
Antonius fillius Antonij Foster Decemb: 23^{tio}.
Anna Seatree Feb^r 4to die.
Wiłł: Mauson Febr. 24to die.

NUPTIÆ 1696.

Malgerus Snell et Ellen Marshall Junij 28 die.
Jo: Holmes et Rebeccha Kendale Julij 2do die.
Jo: Seatree et Anna Roberts Novemb: 17mo die.
Jo: Ratcliff et Susanna Souden Novembris 13^{tio} die.

BAPTIZAT: 1697.

Maria fillia Wiłł: Foster Aprill 25to die.
Maria Vavasour Maij 28vo die.
Antonius Pauson Maij 30 die.
Wiłł: Snell Junij 22do die.
Jo. Scaubert Julij 13^{tio} die.
Bernard Cryer Novemb: 15to die.
Maria Foster Novemb: 16 die.
Maria Darraine Decemb: 27mo die.
Henricus Pauson Febr: 28 die.

SEPULTURÆ 1697.

Jacobus Pickard Maij ij^{mo} die.
Malgerus Vavasour Maij 24to die.

Will: Muschamps Junij 10 die.
Jo: Harper Augusti 5to die.
Maria Vavasour Oct: 23^{tio} die.
Zephanas Brathwaite Decemb: 15to die.

NUPTIÆ.

Robertus Knapton et Eliz: Shutt, Mertij 9no die.

Tho: Thwaits. Anno Institutionis meæ vigessimo primo.

1698.

BAPTIZ: Johannes filius Antonij Pauson Octobris 9no die.
Francis filius Johannis Thackeray Novr 7mo die.
Jane uxor Jacobj Pickard November ye 12 die sepulta.
W^m the son of Wm Vavasour Esqr Baptiz: Aug. 26, 1698.
NUPTIÆ. Georgius Mauson et Elizabetha Snell Octobris die primo.

November the 15th anno 98. Mr. Thwaite (of Papist: Princip:) ejected the Vicarage of Weston & April the 12, 99, J. R. Barker was presented to it.

1699.

NUPTIÆ. Henry Adkinson & Isabell Stead, June ye 5th day.
Richard Sowden & Isabell Bowling, 7tember ye 17th day.
BAPTIZ: Major the Son of George Mawson, August ye 23^d day.
George the Son of John Newsom, September ye 13 day.
[blank] the Son of Will. Moss.
Ann ye Daughter of Will. Kendall, October ye 14 day.
Rebecka ye Daughter of John Kendall, October ye 15 day.
Will. ye Son John Mashans [?], October ye 19 day.
Sarah Daughter of William Vavasor Esqr, October ye 26.
Timothy son of Timothy Medcalf ye 4th of November.
SEPULT. John Hudson, June ye 3^d day.
Will: Crook, Gent., August ye 21 day.
Will. Foster, August ye 27.
Major Pickard, November 3^d.
John Kendall, November 10.
John Robinson, December 12th.
Antony Rycroft, December 25.
Antony Whitfeild, December 25.

1700.

BAPTIZ. Ellen Ratclif, March 25.
John Adkinson, March 28.
Major Snell, Aprill 14.
Henry Rycroft, August 7.
SEPULT. Joseph Hargraves, January 3^d.
Mary Pattison, january 16.
Elis Smith, March 28.
Elis Darraine, June 7.
a daughter of Lawrence Preston.
NUPTIÆ. Robert Pattison, Mary Mawson, June ye 3^d.

1701.

BAPTIZ: Richard Cowell, May ye 3^d.
John Maud, June ye 30th.

Susanna Vavasour, September 11th, of Weston.
Sepult.   Richard Smith, March 3[d].
Chris: Foster, July 27.
Major Shutt, September 20.
Mary Mawde, December 8.
Eliz. [?] Mawson, December 10.
Nuptiæ.   John Mawson & Eliz: Adkinson, July 23.
Rob: Pattison & Eliz: Sted, wit D[r] Turner.

1702.

Baptiz.   Elizabeth Newsom, Jan: 5th.
Ric. Lofthouse, Aprill 8.
Willm. Ratclif, Aprill 30.
Sepult.   John Stead, Aprill 30th.
John Hudson, March 26.
Baptiz.   Ann Pawson, Aprill y[e] 3[d].
Ric. Newsom, june y[e] 12th.
Sarah Kendall, june y[e] 2[d].
Elis Greenwood, August y[e] 5.
Tho : Vavasour the Decem: 21 son of W[m] Vavasour Esq[r].
Buried.   Sarah Curtis, Feb: 8th.
Will. Shutt, March 22.
Joh. Smith, March 29.
John Foster, August 15.
Married.   John Vavasour, Ester Turner, June 22.

1703.

[Buried.]   Lydia Greenwood, Feb. 16.
Sarah Muschamps, March 4th.
John Newsom, March 8.
Martha Cowell, June 7th.
July the 8th 1703, Mr. Barker resigned and July the 29th I W[m] Croft was
   presented.
Married.   John Smith, Ann Smith, September 4th.
Miles Brown, Alice Kendall, Ap[r] 4[o] p[r] M[r] Willson de Scotton.
Bap.   Henry the son of James Pickard, December 18.
Ann y[e] Daughter of Miles Brown, Jan: 8th 170¾.
Major the son of Anthony Foster, Jan: 23[d] 170¾.
Joseph Smith.
Buried.   Rob[t] Knapton, Feb. 29.
Bapt: Margett y[e] Daughter of Christopher Kendall, Feb. 24.
Anthony the son of Anthony Pawson, March y[e] 18th.
Timothy the son of W[m] Moss, March y[e] 20th.

1704.

Bap: Elizabeth y[e] daughter of M[r] Robert Walker, March y[e] 29th.
Mary y[e] daughter of John Maud, Aprill y[e] 8th.
Buried.   Joseph Smith, Aprill 30th.
Bap.   W[m] the son of W[m] Hodghon, May y[e] 14th.
Mary the Daughter of John Thackery, June y[e] 3[d].
George the son of M-Duke Pawson, July y[e] 17th.
William the son of Richard Sowden, 7ber 9th.
Elizabeth y[e] Daughter of John Lamb, July y[e] 6th.

MARRIED. Willm Crook, Catherine Currer, August ye 10th.

Christopher Lofthouse, Sarah Knapton, August ye 20th.

John Green, Ann Lister, October ye 3^d.

BURIED. Mary Muschamp, Octob^r ye 20th.

Mary Wardman, December ye 12th 1704.

Mem: That I John Hartley do ask leave of Willm Vavasour Esq: to bring the Corps of Mary Wardman afores^d my mother over his pasturing ground and doe allow him a recompence for the same. Witness my hand, John Hartley.

John the son of Tho: Brown, Decem^br 23.

BAP. Margett ye Daughter of Tho: Procter, Nov. 10.

Mary ye Daughter of John Ratcliff, Nov. 18.

Ellin ye Daughter of Major Snell, Jany 1st.

Elizabeth ye Daughter of Isack Hudleston Feb: 11th.

1705.

BAP. John the son of Wm Crook, July ye 3^d 1705.

Richard Brown.

Theadosia Walker, Octob^r ye 18.

Jane Pickerd, Decemb^r 9th.

BURIED. Elizabeth Brown.

Margett Dale, March ye 3^d.

MARRIED. Joseph Rhodes, Margett Shutt.

Año d^ni 1706.

BURIED. Mrs. Susaña Vavasour, Aprill ye 1st.

M^dam Frances Vavasour, Aprill ye 6st.

BAP: Tho: the son of Geo. Mawson, May 1st.

James the son of Tho: Stead, June 1st.

Elizabeth the Daughter of Hen: Atkinson, June 6st.

Mary the Daughter of Tho: Cowell, August 3^d.

Margett the Daughter of Wm Vavasour Esqr born Baptiz^d and Buried June ye 18th 1706.

BURIED. Anthony Pawson, Decemb^r 30th.

John Vavasour, Jan. 15th 170⁶⁄₇.

Wm Thackrey, March 2^d 170⁶⁄₇.

BAP. Major the son of John Thackrey, Jan: 6, 170⁶⁄₇.

Richard the son of Chris: Kendall, Jan. 19th 170⁶⁄₇.

Anno D^ni 1707.

BURIED. John Mawson, March 26st.

Elizabeth Atkinson, March 29th.

Ann Brown, March 30th.

Robt Pattison, August 21st.

BAP. Easter the Dau: of J^no Mawson, May 11th.

W^m the son of Wm Waker, May 13th.

Sairah the Daughter of Robt Walker, Septemb^r 17th.

James the son of James Pickard, Septemb^r 29th.

John Thackrey, Decemb^r 20.

MARRIED. Wm Tidswell, Allixe Thackwray, Novemb^r 2^d.

John Cryer, Elizabeth Thackwray, Novemb^r 4th.

BURIED. Anthony Fell, Decemb^r 30.

Tho: Buttler, Jan: 1st.

1708.

Buried. John Robinson, May 24.

Easter Mawson, 7^{br} 2^d.

Eliz: Bowling, Novemb^r 3^d.

Eliz. Hardcastle, Decemb^r 21st.

John Foster, Jan: 27th.

Wm Watter, Jan: 29th.

Margett Sowden, Feb: 16.

John the Son of Wm Vavasour Esqr born att York Aug. —— Bap:
22^d Aug: Dyed 22^d Buried 23^d of 7^{br} 1708 in Belffreys [St. Michael-le-
Belfrey] Church.

Bap: W^m the son of John Cryer, October 12th.

Richard the son of Ric: Wadington, Dec. 26.

Tho: the son of Miles Brown, Feb: 12th.

Robt the son of Wm Walker, March 24th.

1709.

George the son of Chris: Kendall, April 17th 1709.

Jane the Daughter of Tho: Stead, May 15th.

Henry the Son of John Thacray, May 23^d.

Frances the Daughter of Robt Walker, June 25th.

Geo. & Eliz. children of Geo. Mawson, June 26th.

Tho: Son of Thomas Procter, July 2^d.

Año Dni. 1710.

Bap. John the son of Wm Walker, June 26st.

Thomas son of John Thackray, mason, bap: 28 Mar:

Ric. the son of Ric: Sowden, Jan: 6st.

Edward the son of Geo. Wharton, March 4.

Mary the Dau: of John Mawson, March 5th.

Buried. Mary Cowell, Aprill 27th.

Sarah Walker, May 10th.

Major Pickard, Decemb^r 10th.

Frances Walker, 10^{br} 24th.

John Foster, Feb: 9th.

Mary Bramley, Feb: 13th.

Tho: Laytham, March 19th.

Married. Caleb Pawson, Mary Berry, May 17th.

Geo: Whittaker, An Richardson, for Mr Wilson de Scotton, July 18.

Wm Ryley, Mary Brown, p^r Mr Wilson.

Mr. Tho: Cocshott, Mrs. Sairah Booth, Feb:

1711.

Bap: John the Son of J_o: Ratcliff, Aprill 3^d.

Mary the Daughter of Geo. Whittaker, March 12th.

Septemb^r 29 Ann the Daughter of Tho: Procter.

Joⁿ Son of Tho: Bramley, Octob^r 7th.

Willm Son of Willm Hardcastle, Novem: 13.

Eliz: Daughter of John Dale, Feb: 9th.

Jane Daughter of Miles Brown, Feb: 17.

Martha Daughter of Willm Moss, Feb: 25th.

Jane Daughter of Geor. Mawson, March 23.

Buried. Mary Mawson, Aprill 5th.

Ann Whittaker, Aprill 14th.

Chris: Son of Xtopher Kendall, Octob: 12th.

Richard son of Rich. Sowden, November 5th.

Robt Son of Robt Walker Jun: Decemb^r 9th.

John Son of Robt Walker, gen^t, Jan: 7th.

Mary Daughter of John Mawson, Jan: 14th.

Mathew Son of Tim: Medcalf, Jan: 22^d

Sarah Wife of Mr Geo. Booth, Feb: 8th.

Ellin Daughter of Major Snell, March ye 5.

MARRIED. Tho: Cowell & Margret Dale, November 5.

Edward Robinson & Mary Rhodes, Feb. 5.

Chris: Holt, Vic. de Weston.

1712.

BAPTIZ'D. Elizabeth Daughter of Martin Bowlin, May 21st.

Joseph Son of James Pickard, May ye 24th.

Ann Daughter of Richd Waddington, June ye 9th.

Susannah Daughter of Tho: Hougate, June 22.

John Son of Major Snell, June ye 28th.

Rich. Son of Rich: Brown, December ye 24th.

Sarah Daughter of Willm Walker, Jan: 17th.

Elizabeth Daughter of Richd Sowden, Jan: 24th.

Margaret Daughter of Tho: Stead, Feb: 21st.

Joseph Son of Edmund Greenwood, March ye 22.

Arathusa Daughter of Willm Vavasour Esqr Born at London Feb: 1st
   & Buried at St. Andrew's in Howborn.

BURIED. George Son of Stephen Braithwit, Apr: 17th.

James Son of Tho: Stead, Apr. 19th.

Theodosea Wife of Robt. Walker, Junr, June 2^d.

Martha Kendall of Asquith, Wid^w, Augst 22^d.

Mary ye Daughter of Tho: Hudson, November 19th.

Richard Roberts of Snowden, Jan: 11th.

John Jeffery of Weston, Jan: 24th.

Elizabeth Wife of Xtopher Wharton, Feb: 28th.

MARRIED. Tho: Foster of Asquith & Ails Lambert, May ye 2^d.

John Flesher & Frances Teal of Asquith, June ye 9th.

Willm Smith & Elizabeth Pawson of Weston, Augst 9th.

Robt Procter of Leathley & Jane Billinson of Laund houses, Sep. 18th.

Willm Stubs of Ripley & Mary Foster of Asquith, Jan: 31st.

Willm Mawson of Harwood & Mary Clepham of Scales, Feb: 2^d.

1713.

BAPTIZ'D. Willm Son of Willm Ryley, March ye 27th.

Catherine Daughter of Joⁿ Flesher of Asquith, Augst ye 1st.

Thomas Son of George Mushcams of Asq: Husband, Sep^{tr} 5th.

Major Son of John Thackray of Asquith, Husband, Sep^{tr} 19.

Margaret Daughter of Tho: Cowel of Weston, Husband, Sep^{tr} 19.

Martin Son of Martin Bowlin of Asquith, Mason, Sep^{tr} 21st.

John son of Caleb Pawson of Weston, Taylor, October ye 25th.

Thomas Son of Robt Whitaker of Snowden, Husband, October ye 29th.

Joseph Son of Joⁿ Thackeray of Grass Garth, Mason, Nov. ye 29th.

Willm Son of George Hardesty of Asquith, Lin. Webster, Dec^{br} 28th.

John Son of John Dale, Husb: of Snowden, Jan: ye 30th.
Peter Son of Tho: Procter of Laund houses, Skinner, Feb: 27th.
Charles Son of Willm Vavasour Esqr Born & Bap^t March ye 23^d.
BURIED. Judith Wife of Richard Brown of Weston, April ye 12.
Robt Leatham of Asquith, April ye 23^d.
Elizabeth Dickson of Snowdon, Widow, May ye 8th.
Alice Wife of Tho: Foster of Asquith, Taylor, July ye 2^d.
Mr. George Booth of Asquith, October ye 28th.
Mary Pickard of Asquith, Spinster, March ye 8th.
MARRIED. Edward Rhodes of Wetherby & Frances Walker of Weston,
    Ap. 6th.
Willm Roberts & Sarah Richardson of Snowden, May 26th.
Robt Walker of Weston, Yeo', & Mary England, Widow, July 10th.
Tho: Ward & Rachel England of Snowden, September ye 6th.
Tho: Ellis of Hawksworth & Mercy Stead of Baildon, Sepe^{br} ye 29th.
Tho: Lister of Burley & Ann Hirst of Asquith, Octob^r ye 19th.
Willm Fairbanck, Maltster, and Hanna England, Sp^r, both of Otley,
    Feb: 23^d.   1714.
BAPTIZ: Susanna daughter of Robt Illingworth of Asquith, May ye 1st.
Easter Daughter of Tho: Mawson of Snowden, Husb: May ye 5th.
Willm Son of Willm Roberts of Snowden, Whitesmith, &c. May ye 23.
Sarah Daughter of Geo: Whitaker of Snowden, Husbⁿ, July ye 19th.
Joseph Son of Francis Kendill of Asquith, Mason, October ye 9th.
John Son of Miles Brown, Shomaker, Dec^{br} ye 29th.
William Son of John Ouldfield, Husbⁿ, Jan: ye 1st.
Ann Daughter of John Flesher of Asquith, Husb^d, Jan: ye 3^d.
Thomas Son of Tho: Bramley of Asquith, Pauper, Feb: 20th.
Ann Daughter of Willm Pawson of Weston, Meltster, Feb: 22^d.
BURIED. Mary Wife of Tho: England of Snowden, Hush: May ye 21st.
Thomas Cowel of Weston, husbandman, June ye 12th.
Mrs Elsley of Asquith, wid: June ye 13th.
Willm Son of Major Snell of Weston, Husbⁿ, June ye 20th.
Tho. Foster of Asquith, Scool-master, June ye 30th.
Marmaduke Pawson of Asquith, Mason, Augst 20th.
Willm Rycroft alias Airton Son of Widow Rycroft, October ye 2^d.
Thomas Hudson of Snowden, Husbandman, October ye 14th.
Mary Walker of Asquith, Widow, December ye 2^d.
Jane Wife of Antony Snell of Weston, Jan: ye 6th.
John Son of Miles Brown, Shomaker, Jan: ye 12th.
Joseph Son of Francis Kendal of Asquith, Mason, Jan: ye 31st.
Anthony Snell of Weston, Husbandman, February ye 15th.
Ann Daughter of Jane Oxley of Scales, Spins: Feb: 26th.
John Calvert of Weston, Husband: March ye 10th.
MARRIED. John Oldfield & Ann Crooke, L: Willm Wilson Ap: 2^d.
Willm Long of Horsforth, Clothier, & Eliz: Kendill of Asqth, Spin: May
    ye 4th.
Roger Clark of Harrogate, Yeo: & Grace Foster of Asquith, Spins: Octo^{br}
    ye 26th.
John Smith of Weston, Husband, & Sarah Hargrave of Asquith, Spinster,
    Nove^{br} ye 1st.

Tho: Foster of Asquith, Taylor, & Mary Stephenson of Knaresborough,
Spin: Jan: 6th.

Willm Kendall of Asquith, Mason, & Mary Lawson, Spin: of Helmsley,
Jan: 23^d.

Isaack Stot of Knaresborough, Husb: & Mary Foster of Asquith, Spin:
Jan. 29th.

1715.

BAPTIZ: Isaack Son of James Pickard of Laund houses, Hushⁿ, April 23^d.

Xtopher Son of Martin Boulin of Asquith, Mason, May ye 7th.

Frances Daughter of Major Snell of Weston, Husba: July ye 3^d.

Mary Daughter of Tho: Stead of Weston, Husb, July ye 31st.

John Son of John Ratlife of Scales, Husbandⁿ, Augst ye 22^d.

Mary Daughter of Robt Walker of Weston, Junr, Novemb^r ye 25th.

William Son of Tho: Foster of Asquith, Taylor, December 3^d.

Ann Daughter of John Jennings of Asquith, Husbandⁿ, December ye 17th.

Martha Daughter of Miles Brown of Weston, Shoemaker, Jan: ye 7th.

George Son of Robt Whtiker of Snowden, Husbⁿ, Feb: ye 4th.

Francis Son of Willm Roberts of Snowden, Whitesmith, Feb: 4th.

BURIED. Isabel Wife of Richd Waddington of Scales, Serge Weaver,
Ap. 13th.

Sarah Pickard of Dog Park, Spinster, May ye 29th.

Christo^r Son of Martin Boulin of Asquith, Mason, July ye 18th.

Margaret Foster of Asquith, Widow, October ye 19th.

MARRIED. Willm Mawson & Sarah Bro: of Weston, April 23. L. Will:
Wilson.

Thomas Thackeray of Kythorp, Mason, & Margret Lamb of Asquith,
Spins: Jan: 17th.

1716.

BAPTIZ'D. Henry son of John Thackeray, Mason, Ap: ye 15th.

Susanna Daughter of John Richardson of Snowden, May 22^d.

Mary Daughter of John Olfield of Weston, Husbⁿ, July 22^d.

Margaret Daughter of Tho: Kilner of Asquith, Husbⁿ, Augst ye 5th.

Margaret Daughter of Chris: Greenwood of Scales, Yeo: Augst ye 21st.

Joanne Daughter of John Smith of Weston, Woollen Webster, Septr 9th.

Mary Daughter of Caleb Pawson of Weston, Taylor, October ye 14th.

Robert Son of Willm Hardcastle of Weston, Lastmaker, December 2^d.

Sarah Daughter of Moses Crabtree of Heaton, Dec^{br} ye 2^d.

Mary Daughter of Martin Bowlin of Asquith, Mason, Dec^{br} ye 20th.

John Son of John Pawson of Dog-park, Husbandⁿ, January ye 6th.

Ails Daughter of Miles Brown of Weston, Shoe-maker, Jan: ye 20th.

Elizabeth Daughter of Edward Smith of Asquith, Husbⁿ, January ye 27th.

BURIED. George Wharton of Asquith, Husbⁿ, April ye 7th.

Margarett Water of Asquith, Widow, April ye 13th.

Margaret Daughter of Edmund Greenwood of Asquith, May ye 6th.

John Varlay of Weston, Miller, May the 17th.

William Thackeray of Weston, Parish Clark, May ye 20th.

Elizabeth Foster of Asquith, Widow, June ye 13th.

Issabel Vavasour of Dog Park, Widow, June 26th.

Thomas Son of Tho: Kendill of Asquith, Mason, July ye 31st.

Thomas Son of Tho: Bramley of Asquith, Pauper, Augst ye 10th.

Ails Wife of Martin Bowlin of Asquith, Mason, Dec^{br} ye 29th.

Ann Shutt of Asquith, Spinster, January ye 29th.

Elizabeth & A sister still born Daughter of Edward Smith of Asq: Hush^n, Jan. 30th.

MARRIAGE.   Richd Wadding[ton] of Scales, Serge Weaver, & Eliz: Cryer, Spinster, Nove^{br} 22^d.

1717.

BAPTIZ'D.   Thomas Son of Tho: Stead of Weston, May ye 18th.

John Son of Jhon Flesher of Asquith, Husb^n, June ye 22^d.

Ann Daughter of Major Snell of Weston, Husb^n, July ye 4th.

Elizabeth Daughter of Geo. Hardisty of Grassgarth, Lin. Webster, Augst ye 18th.

Tho: Son of John Dale of Snowden, Husband: September ye 7th.

George Son of Willm Cryer of Snowden, Mason, October ye 12th.

George Son of James Pickard of Snowden, Husb: October ye 7th.

Sarah Daughter of Jo^n Thackeray of Asquith, Husb^n, Dece^{br} ye 7th.

John Son of Tho: Foster of Asquith, Taylor, Jan: ye 11th.

Ann Daughter of John Shires of Snowden, Husb^n, Jan: 11th.

Hellen Daughter of John Jennings of Asquith, Husbandman, Jan: ye 28th.

John Son of Tho: Kilner of Asquith, Husband^n, February ye 9th.

Elizabeth Daughter of Richd Waddington of Scales, Searge Weaver, Feb: 22^d.

Robert Son of Robt Walker of Weston, Junr, Maltster, March ye 12th.

BURIED.   Margaret Wife of Tho: Thackeray of Kaythorp, Mason, March ye 26th.

Thomas Curtis of Weston, Husband: May ye 8th.

Frances Daughter of Major Snell of Weston, Husb^n, July 1st.

Stephen Brathwait of Carr-house, Husband: August ye 21st.

Mary Wife of Willm Moss of Snowden, Husb^n: Augst ye 22^d.

Susanna Daughter of Jo^n Richardson of Snowden, Husb^n, October ye 22^d.

Mary Wilson of Asquith, Spinster, November ye ninth.

X^{to} Son of X^{to} Wharton of Weston, Husban^n, Janu: ye 22^d.

Mary Daughter of Caleb Pauson of Weston, Taylor, Feby ye 13th.

John Son of John Dale of Snowden, Husb^n, February ye 24th.

Robert Son of Robt Walker, Junr, of Weston, Maltster, March ye 14th.

John Son of Widow Calvert of Weston, March ye 18th.

MARRIAGES.   Edward Thompson of Asqth, Shomaker, & Eliz: Kendall, Spinster, Sept. 10th.

Thomas Kendall of Asquith, Skinner, & Jane Wilson, Spinster, Octo^r 15th.

Tho: England & Jane Wate of Snowden, Nove'ber ye 30th.

Walter Wade of Leeds Parish, Gent., & Beatrix Killingbeck, Spins: Dec^{br} ye 2^d, by Licence Hen. Humphry Sur:

John Asquith of Asqth, Husb^n, & Ann Harper of Girs Gar: [Grass Garth] Spins: Febru: ye 17th.

1718.

BAPTIZ'D.   Catherine Daughter of Geo. Whitaker of Snowden, Hush^n, Apr. ye 14th.

Margaret Daughter of Miles Brown of Weston, Sho-maker, Apr. ye 14th.

Sarah Daughter of John Ouldfield of West: Husb^n, June ye 15th.

Mary Daughter of John Asquith of Asquith, Husb^n, July the 13th.

John Son of Edward Smith of Asquith, Husb^n, August ye 9th.

Thomas Son of Tho: Mawson of Snowden, Husbⁿ, Augth ye 31st.

John Son of Robt Whitiker of Snowden, Hushⁿ, Septem^{br} ye 6th.

Deborah Daughter of Joⁿ Smith of Weston, Clothier, September ye 21st.

Elizabeth Daughter of Thomas Kendall of Asquith, Skinner, Nov^{br} ye 1st.

John Son of Robt Harrison of Carrhouse, Carpinter, November ye 23^d.

Willm Son of Willm Mawson of Weston, Husbañ: Dec^{br} ye 20th.

Sarah Daughter of Edward Thompson of Asquith, Sho-maker, Feb: ye 1st.

Francis Son of Robt Walker of Weston, Junr, Meltster, Feb^r ye 2^d.

Mary Daughter of Tho: England of Snowden, Husbandⁿ, Feb. 15th.

Anthony Son of Caleb Pawson of Weston, Taylor, March ye 1st.

John Son of John Dale of Snowden, Husbandⁿ, March ye 21st.

BURIED.   Thomas Son of Miles Brown of Weston, Sho-maker, March ye 27th.

Sarah Daughter of John Oldfield of Weston, Husbⁿ, July ye 20th.

John Son of John Flesher of Asquith, Hushⁿ, July ye 22^d.

Frances Daughter of John Lamb of Asquith, Yeoman, Augst ye 6th.

John Son of Tho: Kilner of Asqth, Husbⁿ, Augst ye 8th.

Margret Daughter of X^{to} Kendall of Asquith, Carpenter, Jan: 16th.

Mary the Wife of Willm Stead of Weston, Husbandⁿ, Feb. ye 21st.

MARRIAGE.   Tho: Win of Ilkley, Taylor, & Ellin Preston of Asqth, Spinster, Apr. ye 15th.

1719.

MARRIAGES.   Marmaduke Foster of Askwith, Husbⁿ, & Judith Watson of Weston, Spin^r, 9^{br}: 23^d.

John Foster & Mary Voking both of Askwith, December ye 20th.

Isaack Simpson of Bramham, Taylor, & Mary Brogden of Weston, Spin^r, Jan. ye 5th.

Robt Whitaker of ye Par. of Leeds & Sarah Ingland of Snowden, Jan: ye 31st.

Lawrance Preston of Asqth, Mason, & Mary Bradley of Weston, Spinster, March ye 1st.

BAPTIZ'D.   Major Son of John Thackray of Weston, Par: Clark, April ye 4th.

Thomas Son of Francis Kendall of Askwith, Mason, May 19th.

Mary Daughter of Tho: Kilner of Laund houses, Husbⁿ, May 24th.

John son of John Eltoft of Askwith, Husbandman, July ye 5th.

Elizabeth Daughter of Major Snell of Weston, Husbⁿ, Augst ye 10th.

Frances Daughter of John Flesher of Asquith, Husbⁿ, October ye 11th.

Christopher Son of Chris: Greenwood of Scales, Husbⁿ, Nove^{br} ye 21st.

Henry Son of John Pawson of Snowden, Cloth-maker, Nove^{br} ye 27th.

Jane Daughter of Geo. Hardesty of Girs Gar: Lin. Webster, Dece^{br} ye 26th.

Lawrance Son of Geo: Lowcock of Dog Park, Husbⁿ, Dece^{br} ye 26th.

Miles Son of Miles Brown of Weston, Shoe-maker, March ye 20th.

BURIED.   Rachel ye wife of Law: Preston of Askwith, Mason, April ye 25th.

John Ratlif of Scales, Husbandman, May ye 7th.

Jane Brown of Askwith, Spinster, May 16th.

Robt Son of Willm Hardcastle of West: Lastmaker, May ye 27th.

Thomas Mawson of Askwith, Husbañⁿ, May ye 28th.

Francis Son of Robt Walker of Weston, Maltster, May 29th.

Elizabeth Wife of John Mawson of Weston, Shomaker, Augst 13th.

Elizabeth Wife of John Curtis of Weston, Husbⁿ, Augst ye 30th.
William Hardcastle of Weston, Lastmaker, Septe^{br} ye 7th.
Ann Daug^r of Richd Sowden of Asquith, Blacksmith, Nove^{br} ye 3^d.
Henry Son of John Pawson of Snowden, Cloath-maker, December ye 24th.
Barbara Scafe of Snowden, Widow, December ye 27th.

1720.

Baptiz'd.   John Son of John Oldfield of West: Husbⁿ, April ye 3^d.
Sarah a base born child of Mary Pickard of Weston, May ye 8th.
Jane Daughter of Richd Waddington of Scales, Serge Weaver, May ye 9th.
Mary Daughter of John Jennings of Ask: Husbⁿ, June ye 12th.
Isabel Daughter of Tho: Stead of Weston, Hushⁿ, June ye 12th.
Ann Daug^r of Tho: Foster of Askwith, Taylor, July ye 23^d.
Sarah Daug^{er} of Robt. Walker of West: Junr, Augst ye 5th.
Willm Son of John Foster of Scales, Husbⁿ, Septe^{br} ye 24th.
Sarah Daug^r of Ezekiel Thompson of Ask: Serg: Weaver, Octo: ye 23^d.
Mary Daug^r of Robt Whitaker of Snowden, Trunk Maker, Nove'ber ye 4th.
Elizabeth Daughter of Tho: Atkinson of Ask: Blacksmith, Dece^{br} 4th.
Sarah Daug^r of John Smith of Weston, Wool: Webster, Dece^{br} ye 14th.
Simon Son of Edward Smith of Askwith, Hushⁿ, Jan: ye 2^d.
Anthony Son of Jam: Pickard of Snowden, Husbⁿ, Feb: 18th.
Joseph Son of Tho. England of Snowden, Junr, Husbⁿ, Feb: 18.
Buried.   Robt Hardcastle of Weston, Husbⁿ, May ye 13th.
Christo: Son of X^{to} Loftas of Ask: Lin: Webster, Augst 5th.
A still born Child of John Richardson of Snowden, Septe^{br} ye 11th.
Elizabeth Curtis of Weston, Widow, September ye 20th.
James Hodshon of Askwith, Pauper, February ye 3^d.
Gervast Son of Tho: Mawson of Scales, Husbⁿ, Feb: 10th.
Frances Whitfield of Askwith, Widow, Feb: 18th.
Henry Thackray of Snowden, Hatter, Feb. ye 21st.
Marriages.   Tho: Nailer of West: Husbⁿ, & Eliz: Barrit of West: Spinst:
    May ye 19th.
Willm Wharton of West: Husbⁿ, & Ann Tenant of West: Spins^r, June y^e
    24th.   1721.
Baptized.   Isabel the daughter of Tho: Nailor Baptizd Aprel the 23.
Robart Son of Rob: Whitker Baptisd Aprel the 23.
Dauid the Son of Will: Cryer Baptisd Sep: the 4.
Isabel the daughter of Tho: Mowsan Baptisd Sep. 17.
Ann the daughter of John Dall, September the 23.
John the Son of John Ingland, october the 8.
Elizabeth the daughter of george thorp, october the 15.
John the Son of Tho: Kendel, Nouvember the 26.
Mary the daughter of Will. Kendel, December 31.
Mary the daughter of John Thackwray, march 10.
Jann the daughter of John Eltoft, march the 11.
Marriages.   Richard Parson & mary Kendell, June the 12.
Oliuour Spenc & mary Thackwray, nouem: the 12.
Tho: Skora & Elizabeth Mawson, Desember the 24.
Michael Lamb & Elizabeth Hird, desember the 26.
Martin Bowlin of Askwith, Mason, & Ellin Hadcastle of Weston, Spin^r,
    Jan. 20 [an insertion].

BURIED.   Isabel the daughter of Tho. Naller, Aprel the 26.

Elen Mawson, Widdow, May the 18.

1722.

BAPTIZED.   John the Son of John Richardson of Snowden, labourer, Baptiz'd april the first.

Elizabeth the Daughter of John Fletcher of Askquith, labourer, Baptiz'd april 15th.

John the Son of Tho: Naylor of Weston, labourer, baptisd June ye 17th.

David the Son of Francis Gouthwaite of York, Linnen Weaver, bap. June the 27.

Hannah the Daughter of Richd Waddington of Scales, Woolen weaver, baptiz'd Septr 6to.

Jane the Daughter of martin Bowling of Askwith, Mason, baptiz'd January 24to.

Anne the Daughter of Robt Harrison of Car-house, baptizid Jan: 27to.

Mary the Daughter of John Dale of Snowden, Husbandman, baptiz'd March 2°.

MARRY'D.   Roger Flecher of Leeds parish & Elizabeth England of Snowden, December the first.

William Coulton of Denton & Ellen Maud of Scales ma'rryd December 11.

BURIED.   John Curtis of Weston, Weaver, bury'd April 8th.

Jane Brown of Weston, Widdow, bury'd April 22^d.

Elizabeth the wife of Chris: Kendall of Askwith, Wright, bury'd April the 29.

Mary Ratcliffe of Scales, spinster, bury'd May ye 6th.

David the son of Wm Cryer of Snowden, mason, bury'd June 17th.

Isabel ye Daughter of Tho: Stead of Weston, Husbandman, bury'd July the . . . . . .

Elizabeth the Daughter of John Fletcher of Asquith, labourer, bury'd Aug. . . . . . .

Elizabeth the Daughter of Frances Rhodes of Collingham, Widdow, bury'd Augst 13to.

Martha Cowell of Weston, Spinster, bury'd Dec. 20to.

Tho: Kendall of Askwith Town-head, labourer, bury'd Decem. 23.

William the Son of Richard Brown of Weston, Husbandman, bury'd Jan: 24to.

Mary the Daughter of John Jennings of Askwith, labourer, bury'd Jan: 29to.

Mary Thackwray of Nuell [Newhall], Widdow, bury'd Feb: 28.

Nathanael Drake of Askwith, Woollen-Weaver, bury'd March 6to.

Anne the Daughter of Miles Brown of Weston, Shoe-maker, bury'd March 23to.   1723.

BAPTIZD.   Elizabeth Daughter of Tho: Stead of Weston, Husbandman, baptiz'd April 23to.

Elleanor Daughter of Edwd Smyth of Askwith, Husbandman, baptiz'd April 28to.

Mary Daughter of John Foster of Scales, Labourer, bap: May 5to.

Mary Daughter of Tho: Skerrah of Clifton, Wright, baptiz'd July 1to.

Edwd son of Edwd Thompson of Askwith, Shoemaker, baptiz'd Augst 24to.

Robt Son of John Smyth of Weston, Woolen Weaver, bap: Sept: 8to.

Martha Daughter of Robt Walker, Junr, of Weston, Yeoman, bap: Sept: 17to.

John Son of Richd Brown alias Lofthouse of Weston, Gardener, bap: Octob^r 18to.

Allice Daughter of John Askwith of Askwith, Labourer, bap: Oct^{br} 27.

Isaac Son of Tho: Foster of Askwith, Taylor, bap: Nouemb^r 23.

John Son of John Jennings of Askwith, Labourer, bap: December 2to.

Tho: Son of Tho: Kilner of Askwith, Labourer, bap: March 1to.

MARRIAGES. Tho: Johnson and Allice Hudson marry'd May 26to.

Jonas Mann & Anne Wharton marry'd June 6to.

Tho: Holme & Sarah Pawson marry'd Novr 5to.

William Collingwood Esqr and Sarah Vavasour of Weston, Spinster, marry'd February 18to by Richd Haighton, by vertue of License granted by John Audley, Leg: Doc: Rog^l Mitton Cõmissar: in Ecclesiâ parochiali de Weston.

BURY'D. Elizabeth Daughter of Tho: Stead of Weston bury'd April 2to.

A still born Child of Wm Moss of Snowden bury'd April 3to.

Jane Jackson of Askwith, Widdow, bury'd June 10to.

Major Walter of Askwith bury'd Decemb^r 22to.

Margret Pickard of Askwith, Widdow, buryd Jan: 19to.

John Richardson of Snowden bury'd Jan: 25to.

Martha Braithwaite of Otley, Widdow, bury'd Jan: 30to.

Richard^m Haighton, Vicarium Westoniensem.

Chris: Kendall, Tho: Stead, Æcelsiæ Occonomis.

1724.

BAPTIZ'D. Willm Son of Major Snell of Weston bap: May 10to.

Mary Daughter of Jonas Mann of Askwith, husbandman, bap: Augst 4to.

Ann Daughter of Caleb Pawson of Weston, Labourer, bap: Augst 30to.

Martha Daughter of John Eltoft of Askwith, Husbandman, bap: Novemb^r 3to.

Thomas Son of Tho: Naylor of Weston, Labourer, bap: Novemb^r 30to.

Sarah Daughter of Francis Pullan of Scales, Labourer, bap: Novemb^r 22to.

William Son of Tho: England of Snowden, Labourer, bap: Feb: 20to.

John the Son of Tho: Brumfit of Ilkley, Spurius, bap: June 30.

BURY'D. Esther the Daughter of John Thackwray of Askwith, Husbandman, May 24to.

A still-born Child of Wm Moss of Snowden, Junr, June 19to.

George Teale of Askwith, Mason, July 6to.

Margret Pawson of Askwith, Widdow, July 21to.

Grace Smith of Weston, Spinster, Augst 14to.

Ellin [?] Hodgson of Askwith, Widdow, Septemb^r 15to.

James Hodgson of Askwith, Labourer, Novemb^r 15to.

A still-born Child of James Hodgson of Askwith, Mason, Novr 25.

Tho: Son of Tho: Kilner of Askwith, Labourer, Dec^{br} 18to.

John Son of Tho: Kilner of Askwith, Labourer, Dec^{br} 30to.

MARRY'D. John Hargreaves of Farnley, husbandm^n, & Mary Askwith of Askwith, Spinster, April 7to.

Anthony Ward of Weston, Tobacconist, & Elizabeth Walker of Weston, Spinster, Sept: 1to.

John Powell in the Parish of Leeds & Elizabeth Foster of Askwith, Spinster, Sep: 29to.

Stephen Watmoth of Weston, Labourer, & Ann Cowell, Spinster, Octob^r 19to.

Tho: Powell in the Parish of Leeds, Taylor, and Ellin Foster of Askwith,
Spinster, Nov[r] 8[to].

1725.

BAPTIZ'D. John y[e] Son of Richard Parret of Askwith, Husbandman,
March 27[to].

Mary y[e] Daughter of Stephen Wathmoth of Askwith, Labourer, Apr. 18.

Sarah the Daughter of Will[m] Kendall of Askwith, Mason, Apr. 18.

Peter Son of John Dale of Snowden, Husbandman, July 11[to].

Geo: Son of Tho: England of Snowden, Labourer, July 25[to].

Sarah Daught[r] of Rich[d] Waddington of Scales, Weaver, Octob[r] 10[to].

Ann Daughter of Tho: Kilner of Askwith, Labourer, Octob: 10.

Mary Daughter of Tho: Powell, Taylor, December 5[to].

MARRY'D. Sam[l] Craven of Ilkley, Labourer, to Grace Darwen of Askwith,
Spinster, who was baptiz'd Aug[st] 12[o] & marry'd Aug. 19.

Tho. Ledgard of Weston, Husbandman, & Ann Powell of Otley, Spinster,
Sept[r] 8[to].

John Bramley near Fewston, Husbandm[n], & Margret Pawson of Snowden,
Spinster, Feb: 14[to].

BURY'D. Major Snell of Weston, Husbandman, Sep: 8[to].

Jno. Dale, Sen[r], of Snowden, Husbandm[n], Nov: 20[to].

W[m] Smyth of Askwith, Husbandman, Jan: 19[to].

Margret Smyth of Weston, Spinster, Feb: 14.

Will[m] Vavasour, Sen[r], Dy'd at Bath & Bury'd at Weston Dec[r] 4[to], 1729.

Mrs. Mary Vavasour Daughter of W[m] Vavasour, Jun[r], Esq[r], Born March
the 8th 1732, Baptiz[d] at y[e] Church of St. Andrew's, Holborn, London.

Sam[ll] Son of W[m] Vavasour Esq[r] Born Aug[st] 11[to] and Baptiz'd Sept[r] 3[to]
1733 & Bury'd May the 10th 1737.

Walter Son of W[m] Vavasour Esq. Born August 13[to] and Baptiz'd Aug[st] 31[to]
1734.

John Son of Will[m] Vavasour Esq[r] Born Feb[ry] 14, Bapt. March 22, 1745.

[YORK TRANSCRIPTS from here to 1739.]
WESTON. BAPTIZ'D 1726.

Margret the Daughter of Edward Smith of Askwith, husbandman, June 17

Anne the Daughter of John Richardson of Snowden, labourer, Septembr.
11[to]

Francis the son of Francis Pullan of Scales, labourer, July 24

Henry the son of Will[m] Pawson of Askwith, wright, Sept[r] 25

Mary the Daughter of W[m] Moss of Snowden, labourer, Novemb. 6th

Mary the Daughter of Thomas Bolton, Novemb. 27th

Christopher the son of W[m] Muschamps of Askwith, labourer, Dec[r] 20

Susanna the Daughter of John Jennings of Askwith, labourer, Jan[y] 18

Elizabeth the Daughter of John Askwith of Askwith, labourer, Feb. 12

MARRY'D 1726.

William Muschamps of Askwith, labourer, & Jane Greenwood of Askwith,
spinster, by vertue of Banns,   June 10th

William Andrew of Hamsthwaite, husbandman, & Catherine Pawson of
Snowden, spinster, by vertue of Banns,   Feb. 13[to]

John Smailes of Otley, Ironmonger, & Elizabeth Smith of Burley, spinster,

by vertue of Licence granted by Jo. Audley, Leg. Doct^r, & Benj. Ken-
net, Sur.,   Febry. the seventh
Bury'd 1726.
Margret the Daughter of Edward Smith of Askwith, labourer,   July first
John Harrisson of Askwith, husbandman,   Augst 2to
John the son of Thomas Foster of Askwith, taylor,   Sept. 17to
Richard Hudson of Weston, labourer,   December 14to
Thomas the son of Francis Kendall of Askwith, mason,   Decr 19to
Richd Haighton, Vic. of Weston.
Robt Walker Junr, John Lamb, Churchwardens.
Weston. Baptiz'd 1727.
Marmaduke the son of Marmaduke Foster of Askwith, husbandman,
March 10
Ann the daughter of John Foster of Askwith, husbandman,   March 20
Theodosia the Daughter of Anthony Ward of Weston, Tobacconist,
August 9th
William the son of Major Snell of Weston, clogger,   August 10th
Susanna the Daughter of Robert Whittaker of Snowden, husbandman,
October 18
Elizabeth the Daughter of Thomas Kilner of Askwith, husbandman,
November 5
Marry'd 1727.
William Moon of Newell, Linnen weaver, and Mary Tod, Weston, spinster,
  by vertue of Banns,   November the 18
Bury'd 1727.
Frances Hudson of Dob Park, widdow,   May the 21to
John the son of Major Snell of Weston, clogger,   June 12to
Ann the wife of John Askwith of Askwith, labourer,   July ye 27to
Ann the Daughter of John Foster of Askwith, husbandman,   July 27to
Elizabeth ye Daughter of John Flesher of Askwith, labourer,   June 30
Elizabeth Harrison of Askwith, widdow,   August ye 1st
Jane the Daughter of Martin Bowling of Askwith, Innkeeper, August 5to
Alice the Daughter of John Askwith of Askwith, lab^r,   August 16
Barbara the Daughter of Thomas Proctor of Snowden, skinner, August 20
Catherine Whittaker of Snowden, widdow,   August 27
Edward the son of Edward Thompson of Askwith, shoemaker,   August 27
Jane the Daughter of Thomas Stead of Weston, Innkeeper, Septemb^r 8
Francis the son of Nathaniel Drake, woollen weaver,   Septemb^r 13
Martha the Daughter of John Eltoft of Askwith, husbandman,   Oct. 1st
Mary the Daughter of Henry Atkinson of Weston, husbandman, Oct. 17to
Tryphene Crooke of Askwith, widdow,   November the 12to
Margret Silson of Askwith, widdow,   December the 20
James the son of John Mawson of Weston, shoemaker,   Jan. 31
Thomas Mawson of Scales, Householder,   February 8
Hannah Gill of Askwith, spinster,   February 25
Susanna Ratcliffe of Scales, widdow,   March 19to
Richard Haighton, Vic. of Weston.
Christopher Greenwood, John Atkinson, Churchwardens.
Weston 1728. Baptiz'd.
William the son of John Dale of Snowden, labourer,   April 17

c

John the son of John Atkinson of Weston, husbandman,   May 18
Mary the daughter of Willm Bramley of Askwith, labourer,   Octob. 27
Christopher the son of Stephen Watmoth of Askwith, labourer, Octob. 27
Margret the Daughter of Willm Muschamps of Weston, labourer, Novr 3to
John the son of John Hargreave of Scales, husbandman,   Feb. 16
Elizabeth daughter of Edward Thompson of Askwith, shoemaker, Mar. 2

BURY'D 1728.

Thomas England of Snowden, labourer,   April 3to
Thomas Kilner of Askwith, labourer,   June 6to
Peter son of Thomas Proctor of Snowden, skinner,   June 15
Margret the Daughter of John Newsham of Snowden, husbandman, Dec. 1st
Mary wife of Willm Pawson of Askwith, wright,   Dec. 2
Samuel Overand, sojourner,   Dec. 5
Jane wife of Thomas Kendall of Askwith, skinner,   Dec. 18

MARRY'D 1728.

John Askwith of Askwith, labourer, & Catherine Green, spinster, by
   vertue of Banns published at Weston church,   May ye sixth

Richard Haighton, Vic. of Weston.

Willm Crooke, Major Snell, Churchwardens.

WESTON Anno Dñi 1729. BAPTIZ'D.

Thomas the son of John Jennings of Askwith, labourer,   Oct. 5
William the son of Richd Parret of Askwith, husbandman, Jan. 18
Jane the Daughter of Charles Swire of Askwith, labourer, Jan. 18

MARRY'D 1729.

Sampson Walker of Leathley, labourer, and Judith Brown of Weston, by
   vertue of Banns pubd at Weston,   Feb. the 10th

BURY'D 1729.

John Hargreaves of Scales, husbandman,   Sep. 25to
Robt Walker of Weston, husbandman,   Octob. 27to
Rebecca Pawson of Askwith, widdow,   November 6to
Susan Muschamps of Askwith, spinster,   February 26to

Richd Haighton, Vic. ibdm.

Robt Walker, Wm Crooke, Churchwardens.

THE REGISTER OF WESTON 1730. BAPTIZ'D.

Margaret the Daughter of Christo. Greenwood of Askwith, husbandman,
                                                          July the 26to
John the son of Thomas Skirrow of Askwith, husbandman,   Novr 18to
Samll son of Marmaduke Foster of Askwith,   Novr 22
John son of John Smart, Traveller,   Janry 3to
Abraham son of John Moon of Askwith, Linnen weaver,   Janry 3to
Willm son of John Atkinson of Weston, husbandman,   Janry 24to

MARRY'D 1730.

Thos Hudson of Addingham, Carrier, and Mary Pickard of Askwith,
   by vertue of Banns published at Weston church,   Novr 24to
Thos Teal in the parish of Ilkley, Blacksmith, & Rebeckah Kendall of
   Askwith, spinster, by vertue of Banns,   Feb. 2to

BURY'D 1730.

Alice the wife of John Mawd of Askwith, tayler,   July 28to
George son of Geo. Newsom of Weston, husbandman,   Augst 17to
Willm son of John Dale of Snowden, husbandman,   Augst 18

Wiłłm Moss of Snowden, housholder,	Octob^r 1st
Anne the wife of Thomas Proctor of Snowden, skinner,	Octob^r 17to
John Richardson of Snowden, labourer, and Anne his wife,	Decemb. 3to
John Nicholson of Askwith, husbandman,	Decemb. 27
Joseph Watmough of Askwith, sojourner,	Decemb. 31
Thos Rawson, quondam Schoolmaster of Otley,	Janr^y 19to
Emanuell Teal of Snowden, labourer,	Feb. 13to
Margaret wife of Joseph Rhodes of Askwith, husbandman,	March 3to
Frances Daughter of Michael Lamb of Askwith, husbandman,	March 21to

Richd Haighton, Vic.

Robt Walker, Wm Crooke, Churchwardens.

WESTON REGISTER 1731.   BAPTIZ'D.

Catherine Daughter of John Topham of Asquith, Officer on the Excise,	Augst 29
Sarah Daughter of Thomas Robinson of Asquith, labourer,	Septem^r 5
John ye son of John Bean of Asquith, labourer,	October 10
John ye son of John Smith of Weston, labourer,	October 10
Mary ye Daughter of Major Brown of Weston, husbandman,	Novemb^r 7
Susannah ye Daughter of Charles Swire of Asquith, labourer,	Decemb^r 5
William ye son of William Bramley of Asquith, shoemaker,	Decemb^r 12
Elizabeth ye Daughter of Elizabeth Milner of Asquith, widow,	March 19

BURY'D 1731.

Anne ye Daughter of Thomas Bradley of Farnley, husbandman,	Oct. 10
Frances the wife of John Harper of Weston, husbandman,	Janr^y 17to
Mary the Daughter of George Hardisty of Weston, Linnen weaver,	March 5to

Richd Haighton, Vic^r.

Robt Walker, Christo. Greenwood, Churchwardens.

WESTON REGISTER 1732.   BAPTIZ'D.

Alice daughter of Joseph Harrison of Askwith, Dish-turner,	Apr^l 9to
Anthony son of Anthony Ward, yeoman,	April 15
Mary daughter of Caleb Pawson, labourer,	April 23
Mary daughter of John Shires, labourer,	July 16
Elizabeth daughter of Samuel Walker, husbandman,	Septem^r 3
John son of Robert Harrison, husbandman,	Septemb. 10
Sarah Daughter of John Newsham, husbandman,	October 8
Mary Daughter of Edward Thompson, Cordwainer,	October 15
John son of Joshua Calvert, labourer,	Novr 26
Rachel Daughter of Thomas Askwith, husbandman,	Dec. 4
John son of John Wilson, milner,	Febr^y 5to
John son of John Moon, weaver,	March 18to

BURRY'D.

Joan Sowden of Askwith,	April 7to
Jane Ratcliffe of Weston,	June 19
Mary ye wife of John Wilson,	Febr^y 5to

MARRY'D 1732.

Thomas Wray of Weston, labourer, & Mary Stead of Burley Woodhead, by vertue of Banns,	May 30
Timothy Thorp of Fewston, labourer, & Anne Teale, widdow, by vertue of Banns,	June 28

William Tidswell, labourer, & Jane Beecroft, spinster, by vertue of
   Banns,   Decemb. 4
John Snowden of Eldwick, cordwainer, & Mary Pawson, spinster, by
   vertue of Banns,   Decemb. 14to

Richd Haighton, Vic^r.

Robt Walker, Christo. Greenwood, Churchwardens.

WESTON REGISTER 1733. BAPTIZ'D.

Anne the daughter of Thomas Robinson of Askwith, mason,   April 8
Elizabeth the daughter of William Muschamps, labourer,   July 29
George the son of George Whittaker of Snowden, husbandman, Aug. 12
Anne the dau. of John Bean of Askwith, labourer,   Aug. 26
Richard the son of John Atkinson of Weston, husbandman,   Sep. 2
Samuel the son of William Vavasour of Weston, Esqr,   Sep. 10
Sarah the dau^r of William Mawd, husbandman,   Sep. 15
Lydia the dau. of Stephen Watmoth of Askwith, labourer,   Sep. 23
Joseph the son of Richd Brown Junr of Weston, husbandman, Oct. 7to
John the son of Anthony Lycroft of Dobb Park, milner,   Oct. 7to
Gervase, the son of Lydia Greenwood of Askwith,   Oct. 14to
Christopher the son of Richd Kendall of Askwith, wright,   Oct. 21to
Sarah the dau^r of Willm Tidswell of Askwith, labourer,   Dec. 9to
Mary the dau. of Willm Howard, husbandman,   Jany 27to
John the son of Charles Swire of Askwith, labourer,   Feb. 3
Michael the son of Michael Lamb of Askwith, husbandman,   Feb. 24

MARRY'D 1733.

William Sowden of Askwith, Blacksmith, & Sarah Fawcet, spinster, by
   vertue of Banns,   Octob. 29
Thomas Colton of Denton, labourer, & Elizabeth Hargreaves of Weston,
   spinster, by vertue of Banns,   Novr 4th

BURY'D 1733.

Allice the wife of John Dale of Snowden, husbandman,   June 21
Willm the son of William Hodgson of Askwith, labourer,   Nov. 3
Jane Mawson of Scales, widdow,   Nov. 30to
Henry Atkinson of Weston, husbandman,   Feb. 20th

Richd Haighton, Vic.

William Walker, Thomas Skirrow, Churchwardens.

WESTON REGISTER 1734. BAPTIZ'D.

Richard the son of Willm Sowden of Askwith, blacksmith,   June 23
John son of Thomas Colton of Askwith, labourer,   August 18th
Walter son of Willm Vavasour of Weston, Esqr,   August 31
Willm son of Andrew Moss of Snowden, husbandman,   Oct. 6th
John son of Richd Kendall of Askwith, wright,   Decr 25
Elizabeth daughter of Willm Bramley of Askwith, shoemaker, Jan. 19
Margret, daughter of George Rhodes of Askwith, wright,   March 15

BURY'D 1734.

William Stead of Weston, husbandman,   Apr. 15to
George Dixon of Grass garths, husbandman,   July 7th
Mary Mortimer of Weston, widdow,   Oct. 12th
Judith Whitfield of Askwith, spinster,   Nov. 26
Ellen Snell of Weston, widdow,   Dec. 10
George Muschamps of Askwith, labourer,   March 14

MARRY'D 1734.

Richard Holliday of Bayldon, Roper, & Margret Lyster of Bayldon, spinster, Nov[r] 12th, by vertue of Banns
Rich[d] Haighton, Vicar.
William Walker, Thomas Skirrow, Churchwardens 1734.

WESTON REGISTER. BAPTIZ'D A.D. 1735.

William y[e] son of William Tidswel of Weston, husbandman,	April y[e] 6
James y[e] son of Robert Harrison of Weston, husbandman,	April y[e] 15
Alice y[e] dau. of Thomas Askwith of Weston, husbandman,	April y[e] 27
Joseph y[e] son of John Overend of Weston, husbandman,	May y[e] 11
Leonard y[e] son of John Shires of Weston, husbandman,	May y[e] 11
Sarah y[e] dau[r] of Anthony Ward, husbandman, of Weston,	June y[e] 11
Mary y[e] dau[r] of John Moon of Weston, Linnen weaver,	June y[e] 15
Charles y[e] son of Charles Swier of Weston, husbandman,	Oct. y[e] 26
John y[e] son of John Bean of Weston, husbandman,	Nov. y[e] 2
Joseph y[e] son of Thomas Robinson of Weston, mason,	Nov. y[e] 16
Mary y[e] dau. of William Musham of Weston, labourer,	Dec. y[e] 25
Mary y[e] dau. of John Atkinson of Weston, husbandman,	Jan. y[e] 18
Mary y[e] dau. of Joseph Farmer of Weston, mason,	Feb. y[e] 14

BURY'D 1735.

Mary y[e] wife of Robert Harrison of Weston, husbandman,	April y[e] 15
Christopher Lofthouse of Weston, labourer,	April y[e] 22
Priscilla Hargreave of Weston,	May y[e] 6
Hellen y[e] wife of Robert Illingworth of Weston, labourer,	June y[e] 12
John Kendall of Askwith, labourer,	November 2
Miles Brown of Weston, shoemaker,	January y[e] 30
George Hodgson of Dob Park, husbandman,	Febr[y] y[e] 13
Jonas Mann of Weston, husbandman,	Febr[y] y[e] 16
Frances Lamb of Askwith, widdow,	March y[e] 3

MARRY'D 1735.

Robert Illingworth of Askwith, labourer, & Jane Mawd, of Askwith, spinster, by vertue of Banns,   Octob. 6
John Simpson of Askwith, husbandman, & Lydia Greenwood of Askwith, spinster, by vertue of Banns,   Novemb. 2
John Brogden of Weston, labourer, & Mary Leach of Weston, spinster, by vertue of Banns,   November 25
Richard Haighton, Vic. ibđm.
William Walker, Thomas Skirrow, Churchwardens.

WESTON REGISTER, 1736. BAPTIZ'D.

Margret the daughter of Stephen Watmoth of Askwith, labourer, July 18
John the son of John Mawd of Scales, Linnen weaver,   Sept[r] 27th
Margret the daughter of John Simpson of Scales, husbandman,   Oct[r] 3
Jane the daughter of Nicholas Grunnell of Weston, husbandman, Oct[r] 9
Nathan the son of John Overand of Dob Park, milner,   Febr[y] 13[to]

BURY'D 1736.

Allice the daughter of Willm Pawson of Askwith, labourer,   March 27
Catherine the wife of W[m] Crooke of Askwith, Innkeeper,   Apr. 3[d]
Margret the daughter of George Rhodes of Askwith, wright,   Apr. 11th
Richard son of John Atkinson of Weston, husbandman,   Apr. 18th
Sarah the daughter of Anthony Ward of Weston, husbandman, Apr. 23[to]

John Mawson of Askwith, husbandman,   May 23
Robert Whittaker of Snawden, husbandman,   Sep. 2
John Whitfield of Askwith, Blacksmith,   Nov. 18
Joseph Rhodes of Askwith, husbandman,   Nov. 19
Isabell Whitfield of Askwith, Widdow,   Dec. 11
Richd Sowden of Askwith, Blacksmith,   Jany 15
Edward Hall of Askwith, husbandman,   Feby 6
Jane the daughter of Wm Howorth, husbandman,   March 20

MARRY'D 1736.

William Pickard of Askwith, husbandman, and Mary Mawd of Askwith,
    spinster, by vertue of Banns,   Dec. 22to
George Smith of Askwith, wright, and Rebekah Pawson of Askwith,
    spinster, by vertue of Banns,   Janr^y 26to
Marmaduke Foster of Askwith, labourer, & Mary Nicholson of Askwith,
    widdow, by vertue of Banns,   Feb. 21to

Richd Haighton, Vicar.
William Walker, Thomas Skirrow, Churchwardens 1736.

WESTON REGISTER FOR THE YEAR 1737. BAPTIZ'D.

Joseph the son of George Teal of Askwith, labourer, April the 3^d
Margret the Daughter of Richard Kendall of Askwith, wright, May 1st
Johanna the Daughter of William Sowden of Askwith, blacksmith,
    May 8th
Rachel the Daughter of Joseph Farmer of Weston, mason, June 7th
John the son of William Bradley of Askwith, labourer, October 9th
Isabel the Daughter of George Whittaker of Snowden, husbandman,
    Nov. 14
Samuel the son of Michael Lamb of Askwith, husbandman, Decr 27
John the son of George Smith of Askwith, wright, December ye 27th
Andrew the son of Robert Proctor of Snowden, tawer, December ye 29th
Ellen the Daughter of Thomas Askwith of Askwith, husbandman, Jan. 29th
Wilfred the son of Thomas Skirrow of Askwith, husbandman, Feb. 12th
William the son of Charles Swire of Askwith, labourer, Feb. the 19th
Mary the Daughter of Anthony Ward of Weston, yeoman, Feb. the 26th

BURIALS AT WESTON 1737.

William the son of John Shires of Askwith, labourer, May the 1st
Samuel the son of William Vavasour of Weston, Esq., May the 10th
Mary the Daughter of William Muschamps of Weston, labourer, Aug.
    the 20th
William Walsh of Weston, bachelor, September the 23
William Thackwray of Newhall, Dish turner, November the 1st
Robert Askwith of Askwith, widdower, November the 17th
Ruth Kendall of Askwith, widdow, November the 20th
John Thackwray of Weston, mason, December the 3^d
Margret Hewit of Weston, sojourner, December the 30th
Thomas the son of Thomas Stead of Weston, bachelour, Jan. the 23^d
William Pawson of Askwith, labourer, February the 17th

MARRIAGES 1737.

Joseph Brimham of Leedes, bucher, & Margret Hudson of Dob Park,
    widdow, by vertue of Banns, April the 11th

John Darby of Askwith, Tassell planter, & Frances Whitfield, spinster,
  by vertue of Banns, May the 16th
John Sudal of Dob Park, husbandman, & Elizabeth Harrison of Askwith,
  spinster, by vertue of Banns, September 29th
Joseph Thackwray of Hampsthwait, husbandman, & Jane Teal of Askwith,
  spinster, by vertue of Banns, February 13th
Richard Haighton, Vicar.
William Walker, Thomas Skirrow, Churchwardens.

Weston Register. Baptiz'd 1738.

Catherine ye Daughter of William Crook of Askwith, Inkeeper, April 9th
Willm the son of Willm Muschamp of Weston, labourer, May 14
Robert the son of William Mawd of Scales, Linen weaver, June 4
Willm the son of John Bean of Askwith, labourer, June ye 4
Isabel the Daughter of John Darby of Askwith, husbandman, June 25
Sarah the Daughter of John Moon of Askwith, Linen weaver, June 25
John the son of Henry Harper of Askwith, labourer, July the 2^d
Elizabeth Daughter of John Walter of Askwith, labourer, Aug. the 13th
Anne the Daughter of Robert Hemsley of Askwith, labourer, Aug. 13
Sarah the Daughter of William Sowden of Askwith, blacksmith, Nov. 19
Joseph the son of John Mawd of Askwith, taylor, Feb. the 10
Anne the Daughter of Richard Brown of Weston, husbandman, March 18

Bury'd 1738.

Sarah the Daughter of Hannah Lee of Askwith, July the 19
Isabel the wife of Emanuell Teal of Snowden, October ye 24
Frances Scaubert of Weston, widdow, December the 21st
Thomas Stead of Weston, Inkeeper, February the fourteenth

Marriages 1738.

John Pawson of Snowden, labourer, & Mary Marston, spinster, by vertue
  of Banns, April the 11th
Anthony Pawson of Snowden, husbandman, & Sarah Whittaker, spinster,
  by vertue of Banns, June ye 14
Thomas West in the parish of Skipton, husbandman, & Mary Stead of
  Weston, spinster, by Banns certified by Roger Mitton, Nov. 13
James Pickard of Snowden, husbandman, & Margret Dale, spinster, by
  vertue of Banns, January the 24
Richard Haighton, Vicar of Weston.
William Walker, Thomas Skirrow, Churchwardens.

The Register of Weston 1739. Baptiz'd.

Richard the son of Richard Kendal of Askwith, wright, June 29
Anne the Daughter of Thomas West of Weston, husbandman, Septr 9
Mary the Daughter of Joseph Thackwray of Snowden, labourer, Dec. 9
John the son of John Darby of Askwith, husbandman, Dec. 29
Joshua the son of John Overand of Dob Park, milner, Dec. 29
James the son of Charles Swire of Askwith, labourer, January 6
Richard the son of Mary Bolling of Askwith, spinster, January 6
Sarah the Daughter of Moses Pawson of Askwith, labourer, Jan. 6
Thomas the son of John Newsom of Snowden, husbandman, Feb. 24

Bury'd 1739.

William Greenwood of Askwith, mason, March the 29th

Theodosia the wife of Isaac Hudleston of Lawnd House, husbandman,
　　April the 2
Anne England of Snowden, widdow, May the 6th
Ellen the wife of Edward Smith of Askwith, labourer, May 9th
Mary the wife of Marmaduke Foster of Askwith, Linnen weaver, Sept^r
　　the 1st
Mary Kendall of Askwith, widdow, October the 25th
Robert Walker of Weston, husbandman, November the 11th
Allice Brown of Askwith, widdow, March the 2^d
Thomas the son of Joseph Farmer of Weston, mason, March 16th

MARRY'D 1739.

Stephen Buck, blacksmith, & Catherine Flesher, spinster, both of Ask-
　　with, by vertue of Banns, September the 10th
Thomas Mason, within the parish of Bolton, husbandman, and Margret
　　Greenwood of Scales, spinster, by Banns, Sept. 27
　　　　　　　　Richard Haighton, Vicar.
　　　　　　Wm Walker, John Dale, Churchwardens, 1739.

[BOOK III.]

N.B. June 3ᵈ, 1804. Mr. Vavasour gave Samuel Smithson permission to go over the Water thro' his Grounds after bringing the corpse of Elizabeth Pawson of Denton, in the Parish of Otley, to be inter'd in the Church yard of the Parish Church of Weston and the said Samˡ Smithson paid to Mr. Vavasour one Penny as an acknowledgement for taking his Hearse thro' the Water in Mr. Vavasour's Lands.

N.B. March 31, 1810. Mr. Vavasour gave Joseph Whitehead Permission to pas and repas through his ground from Otley to Weston Church Yard to set up a tomb stone and the said Joseph Whitehead paid to Mr. Vavasour one shilling as an acknowledgement for the said permission.

Witness, Edmund Greenwood, Parish Clerk.

[The above are on the flyleaf.]

BURYED	1739	
William Greenwood,	March yᵉ	29
Theodocia the Wife of Isaac Huddlestone,	April	2
Ann England,	May	6
Elin Wife of Edward Smith,	May	9
Mary Wife of Marmaduke Foster,	Sepᵇʳ	1
Mary Kendell,	Octoᵇʳ	25
Robert Walker,	November	11
Alce Brown,	March	2
Thoˢ Son of Joseph Farmer,	March	16

MARRIAGES.		
Stephen Buck & Catherine Flesher,	Sepᵇʳ	16
Thoˢ Mawson and Frances Harrison,	Sepᵇʳ	24
Thoˢ Mason and Margaret Greenwood,	Sepᵇʳ	27
Mark Nickleson and Susan England,	Noveᵇʳ	13
Jonathan Tod and Margaret King,	Feb:	10

BAPTIZ'D.		
Richard Son of Richard Kendel,	June	29
Ann Daughter of Thoˢ West,	Sepᵇʳ	9
Mary Daughter of Joseph Thackwray,	December	9
John Son of John Darby,	December	27
Joshua Son of John Overing,	December	27
James son of Charles Swire,	January	6
Richard Son of Mary Bowlin,	January	6
Sarah Daughter of Moses Pawson,	January	6
Thoˢ Son of John Newsam,	Feb.	24

BAPTIZ'D 1740.		
John son of William Muschamp,	April	29
John son of Stephen Buck,	May	11
Jonathan Son of William Bramley,	June	*[torn off]*
Ann Daughter of Robert Procter,	June	..
Margaret Daughter of George Rhodes,	July	
John Son of William Walker,	Sepᵇʳ	
William Son of John Bramley,	Octo:	
John Son of Wilᵐ Soweden,	Novᵇʳ	

Richard Son of Mark Nickleson,	January ..
Thos Son of George Whitaker,	January ..
Thos Stead ye son of Thos farmer,	Feb^y ..
Margaret ye Daughter of Thos Askwith,	March ..

MARRIAGES 1740.

Thos Dale and Sarah Hardcasel,	May	4
John Bramley and Alce Brown,	May	6
Isaac Pickard and Cecile Wray,	May	15
William Willee and Mary Brown,	Nov^{br}	25
William Benson and Mary Walker,	December	3

BURY'D.

Barbary Wife of John Maud,	May	11
William Maud,	June	9
Margaret Wife of John Newsam,	Nov^{br}	19
John Son of Stephen Buck,	December	3
Ann Dale,	Feb:	17

1741.

BURY'D. James Pickard,	April	4
Ann Mann,	June	3
Eliz: Pawson,	June	13
Rowland Jakes,	June	20
John Oldfield,	July	10
William Son of Richard Kendel,	Sep^{br}	18
William Mawson,	Sep^{br}	23
John Son of Willm Sowden,	January	4
Eliz: Wife of Thos Scerray,	January	22
Joseph Son of Thos England,	January	23
Chris: Son of Anthony Ward,	January	24
Henry Jackson,	Feb:	11
MARRIAGES. George Whitaker and Ann Kachen,	July	14
Robert Rowlinson, Mary Simson,	Aug^t	24
George Pickard and Cattren Stocks,	October	12
Nicholas Pawson and Ann Clark,	March	28
BAPTIZ'D. Alce Daughter of Thos Dale,	April	18
Roger Son of Andrew Moss,	May	10
William Son of Joshua Calvert,	May	16
John Son of Zackaray Hartley,	May	31
William Son of John Pawson,	July	19
Robert Son of Robert Hemsley,	Aug^t	9
Alce Daughter of James Pickard,	Sep^{br}	6
Willm Son of Richard Kendel,	Aug^t	29
Thos Son of Thos West,	October	11
Ann Daughter of Willm Catton,	Nov^{br}	22
Ann Daughter of John Watter,	Nov^{br}	29
Francis Son of Thos Robinson,	December	22
Chris: Son of Anthony Ward,	January	16

1742.

BAPTIZ'D. Thos Son of Thos Barber,	March	28
Mary Daughter of George Newsam,	June	6
Thos Son of Charels Swire,	July	18

John Son of Willm Sowden,	July	24
Hannah Daughter of Willm Holden,	Aug^t	7
Maudlen Daughter of George Whitaker, Junr,	Aug^t	22
John Son of Willm Crook,	Aug.	12
Ann Daughter of George Pickard,	Sep^br	12
Sarah Daughter of Stephen Watmuff,	Nov^br	11
Charles Son of Mr Weake,	December	19
William Son of Chris: Smith,	December	26
Mary Daughter of Willm Hudson,	Feb:	3
Janet Daughter of John Newsam,	December	26
Mary Daughter of William Hudson,	Feb^y	3^d [inserted]
Mary Daughter of William Hall,	Feb:	3^d
Sarah Daughter of Richard Kendell,	March	20
BURY'D. Frances Torner,	March	29
William Son of John Pawson,	March	29
George Mawson,	April	4
Jane Dixson,	April	4
Margaret Thackwray,	April	9
Ann Wife of Thos Teall,	April	17
John Newsam,	May	6
Francis Son of Thos Robinson,	May	11
William Hudson,	June	24
John Maud,	July	12
Eliz: Kendell,	July	15
Sarah Wife of Francis Kendell,	Aug^t	11
William Wharton,	Aug^t	23
Eliz: Daughter of Thos Kendell,	Aug^t	25
Jonathan Son of Robert Harrison,	October	15
John Askwith, Husbandman,	January	29
William Son of Marmaduke Foster,	Feb:	19
John Watter,	Feb:	27
MARRIAGES. William Hudson and Jane Kendel,	April	20
Chris: Smith and Catthren Whitaker,	April	20
William Thackwray and Eliz: Bailey,	July	2
George Hudson and Sarah Maud,	December	12

1743.

BAPTIZ'D. Eliz: Daughter of Michael Lamb,	April	10
Joseph Son of James Pickard,	April	17
Joseph Son of Joseph Farmer,	April	17
Thos Son of Thos Dale,	April	17
Sarah Daughter of Willm Thackwray,	May	12
Anthony Son of Anthony Pawson,	May	15
Robert Son of George Whitaker,	May	22
Mary Daughter of Mark Nickols,	June	19
Mary Daughter of Robert Proctor,	June	25
Eliz: Daughter of John Mawson,	July	26
Susan Daughter of John Pawson,	Aug^t	29
Thos Son of Thos Robinson,	Aug^t	29
Sarah Daughter of Thos Thackray,	Sep^br	25
William Son of Thos West,	December	13

William Son of Wm Cattan,	January	14
John Son of John Proctor,	March	4
MARRIAGES. Joseph Rhodes and Dority Furnis,	Nov^{br}	16
John Brown and Mary Bowling,	Nov^{br}	21
John Dixson and Mary Scurrah,	Feb.	3
BURY'D. Richard Vavasour,	Aprill	13
William Cryer,	July	20
Robert Son of George Whitaker,	July	21
Eliz: Daughter of John Mawson,	Aug^t	11
Sarah Daughter of Richard Kendel,	Sep^{br}	9
Thos Scurrah,	December	6
Elizabeth Thackray,	April	19th
Ellen the wife of Christopher Kendal,	July	16th

1744.

BAPTIZ'D. Joseph Son of William Sowden,	April	22
Henry Son of William Chaplin,	May	1
Cathren Daughter of George Pickard,	Aug^t	19
John Son of John Watter,	Sep^{br}	23
Major Son of John Simpson,	Sep^{br}	23
John Son of Wm Thackray,	October	28
Joseph Son of Joseph Rhodes,	Nov^{br}	4
Edward Son of John Dixson,	December	26
Mary Daughter of Richard Lofthouse,	January	27
Catthren Daughter of Chris: Smith,	Feb:	3
Eleniner Daughter of George Whitaker,	Feb:	3
George Son of Richard Kendel,	Feb:	17
John Son of William Hudson,	Feb:	17
Mary Daughter of James Pickard,	Feb.	24
John Son of George England,	March	24
BURY'D. Thomas Son of Thos Robinson,	Decem.	1
Eliz: Watter,	March	19

1745.

BAPTIZ'D. Martha Daughter of John Newsam,	April	14
John Son of Robert Proctor,	April	21
Samuel Son of Mark Nicholes,	April	21
Joseph Son of George Newsom,	May [page torn]	
Thos Son of George Whitaker,	May [3 or 5, top part torn off]	
Mary Daughter of Thos Askwith,	May	12
Eliz: Daughter of Andrew Moss,	May	26
Eliz: Daughter of Charles Swier,	Aug^t	4
Ann Daughter of Thos Thackray,	Aug^t	11
Eliz: Daughter of Thos Dale,	Aug^t	11
William Son of Joseph Farmer,	Aug^t	25
Edward Son of Wm Brogden,	Aug^t	25
Thomas Son of Wm Crooke,	December	6
Barbary Daughter of Wm Pickard,	December	15
Eliz: Daughter of Wm Sowden,	December	29
Thos Son of Samuel England,	January	21
Joseph Son of Wm Thackray,	Feb:	11
Thos Son of John Proctor,	Feb:	16

Tho⁸ Son of George Mawson,	Feb:	19
Margaret Daughter of Tho⁸ Robinson,	Feb:	19
Ann Daughter of Robert Robinson,	March	2
James Son of James Pickard,	March	16
John Son of Wᵐ Vavasour, Esqʳ,	March	22
Bury'd. Marmaduke Foster,	April	14
Elener Mawson of Askwith,	November	8
Marriage. Robert Robinson and Mary Pawson,	April	29

1746.

Bapt. John Son of Wᵐ Catton,	June	29
Hannah Daughter of Wᵐ Thompson,	June	29
Margaret Daughter of George Newsam,	July	4
Eliz: Daughter of Robert Kendel,	Sepᵇʳ	21
Tho⁸ Son of Richard Kendel,	January	18
James Son of Tho⁸ West,	March	1
George Son of John Dixson,	March	8
Bury'd. Eliz: Daughter of Charles Swire,	Oct.	1
Susan Daughter of George Newsam,	Oct.	7
William Son of George Newsam,	Oct.	11
Mary Daughter of Susan Becroft,	Oct.	23
Mary Daughter of Tho⁸ Asquith,	Novᵇʳ	8
Ann Daughter of Robert Robinson,	Novᵇᵉʳ	25
Hannah Daughter of Wᵐ Thompson,	January	15
Caleb Son of Caleb Pawson,	Feb:	8

1747.

Bapt. Anthony Son of George Pickard,	March	29
Francis Son of John Pawson,	April	26
Tho⁸ Son of Robert Hemsley,	April	26
Mary Daughter of Tho⁸ Dale,	May	17
Mary Daughter of Wᵐ Sowden,	Oct.	4
Ann Daughter of George Rhodes,	·Oct.	11
Abraham Son of James Pickard,	Oct.	18
Mary Daughter of Samuel England,	Novᵇʳ	18
George Son of George Mawson,	January	6
John Son of George Whitaker,	January	10
John Son of Robert Kendel,	January	16
William Son of Wᵐ Thackray,	January	17
Betty Daughter of Charles Swire,	January	31
Peter Son of Robert Proctor,	March	13
Bury'd. Jsabella Atkinson,	March	27
Margaret Daughter of Chris: Greenwood,	May	5
Frances Vavasour,	June	13
Francis Son of John Pawson,	June	28
Mary Walker,	July	21
Suson Daughter of John Genings,	Augᵗ	30
William Son of Wᵐ Walker,	Novᵇʳ	20
Anthony Ward,	Novᵇʳ	29
Margaret Mawson,	January	14
Eliz: Wife of John England,	Feb:	5
Joseph Son of Wᵐ Thackray,	Feb:	17

MARRIAGE. John Gill and Ann Pawson,   January 19

1748

BAPT. John Son of Joseph Farmer,   May 11
Sarah Daughter of Alce Polard,   June 5
George Son of Wm Crook,   June 28
Mary Daughter of John England,   Augt 21
Mary Daughter of Robert Robinson,   Oc^t 9
Margaret Daughter of John Pawson,   Oc^t 16
William Son of Wm Thompson,   January 27
Ann Daughter of John Newsam,   Feb: 12
Grace Daughter of John Dixon,   March 5
William Son of Wm Brogden,   March 5
Eliz: Daughter of Susan Becroft,   March 19
BURY'D. Ann Oldfield,   May 9
William Hudson,   May 16
Mary Wife of John Snowden,   July 13
Mary Daughter of Mark Nickoles,   Augt 4
Thomas Foster,   Oc^t 9
Eliz: Sowden,   Feb: 23
MARRIAGES. Thomas Kendel, Martha Maud,   June 1
John Ratliff and Sarah Kendel,   December 26

1749.

BAPT. Ann Daughter of Wm Sowden,   April 30
Eliz: Daughter of George Pickard,   May 7
Mary Daughter of Thos West,   May 7
Sarah Daughter of William Hudson,   May 21
Margaret Daughter of Thos Dale,   May 21
Sarah Daughter of John Watters,   June 11
Edward Son of David Rhodes,   June 11
Eliz: Daughter of Wm Thackray,   Augt 13
Alce Daughter of John Brown,   Augt 13
Eliz: & Ann Daughters of Richard Kendel,   Augt 20
Mary Daughter of John Ratliff,   October 22
Robert Son of Robert Kendel,   Decem: 3
Henry Son of Thos Thackray,   Decem: 24
Eliz: Daughter of Thos Robinson,   January 7
Mary Daughter of Paul Stubs,   Feb. 4
Isaac Son of Isaac Bowton,   March 6
Mark Son of Mark Nickoles,   March 24
MARRIAGES.—William Oldfield and Ann Ward,   [no date]
Isaac Bowton and Mary Ryecroft,   Oct. 12
John Moyses and Elin Dobson,   Oct. 22
BURY'D. Eliz: & Ann Daughters of Richard Kendel, Sep. 14 & 17
Richard Brown,   Oct. 1
Samuel England,   Feb: 12
John Pawson,   March 7
Edward Rhodes Son of David Rhodes,   March 22
Susan Wife of Mark Nickols,   March 24

1750

BAPT. John Son of Wm Oldfield,   April 28

Robert Son of George Whitaker,	May	27
John Son of Robert Hemsley,	June	29
Jutey the Doughter of Wm Catton,	July	16 [*an insertion*]
Jsaac Son of James Pickard,	Sep^{br}	29
Mary Daughter of George Hudson,	Nov^{br}	4
Major Son of Wm Vavasour,	Nov^{br}	12
Sarah Daughter of Joseph Farmer,	Decem.	26
Francis Son of Wm Thackray,	March	31
Bury'd. Thos Lister,	June	3
Thos Son of Wm Crook,	Aug^t	19
Major Son of Wm Vavasour,	March	18
Marriages. Francis Simpson and Mary Foster,	June	4
Thomas Holmes and Mary Mason,	Janu:	25

1751

Bapt. Sarah Daughter of John Ratliff,	April	14
Robert Son of Robert Kendel,	April	17
William Son of Thos Dale,	April	21
Mary Daughter of Francis' Simpson,	April	28
Walter Son of Wm Sowden,	Aug^t	4
Simon Son of John Brown,	Aug^t	17
William Son of George Newsam,	Aug^t	25
John Son of Zackra: Farrah,	Sep^{br}	1
Joseph Son of John England,	Sep^{br}	29
Sarah Daughter of Wm Oldfield,	December	27
Mary Daughter of Thos Brotherton,	January	10
Bury'd. Eliz: Daughter of Thos Dale,	May	15
Eliz: Daughter of Susan Becroft,	May	29
Eliz: Greenwood,	Sep^{ber}	28
Hannah Wife of John Proctor,	Nov^{br}	10
William Crook,	Nov^{br}	23
Mark Son of Mark Nickoles,	January	25
Marriages. Zackra: Farrow and Eliz: Kilner,	May	29
William Dawson and Mary Jackson,	Sep^{br}	16
Samuel Taylor and Rachel Askwith,	Decem.	2

1752

Martin the son of Thos West was bapt. Novem. 24

1753

Bapt. Ann Daughter of George Whitaker,	May	20
William son of Wm England,	June	24
Margaret Daughter of Thos Thackray,	July	8
Martha Daughter of George Pickard,	July	10
William Son of Wm Teall,	July	10
William Son of James Mitton,	July	22
Margaret Daughter of Joseph Farmer,	Sep^{br}	9
Frances Daughter of William Found,	Decem.	25
Eliz: Daughter of John Scerrow,	January	20
[Nancy the Doughter of Zacharay Farrow,	Do.	27 *inserted*]
Joseph Son of Richard Kendel,	Feb:	10
Henry Son of Isaac Boulton,	March	17
Bury'd. Henry Son of Thos. Thackray,	April	26

William England,	May	27
John Bean,	Aug^t	7
William Vavasour, Esq:	Nov^r	16
Chris: Kendel,	Decem.	15
William Son of Joseph Farmer,	Feb.	18
MARRIAGES. Thomas Pawson & Ann Crook,	April	22
Abraham Maud & Ann Rhodes,	April	23
Michael Donell, Mary Greenwood,	May	3
Dinis Longstrap & Sarah Newsam,	July	11
Thos Dale & Sarah England,	Aug^t	2
George Abbatt & Margaret Watmuff,	Feb:	13

1754

BURY'D. Richard Brown,	April	3
William Walker,	April	7
Thomas Kendel,	May	27
James Hoghson,	June	1
Major Son of Thos Thackray,	July	5
John Shiers,	July	25
Thomas son of Robert Kendel,	July	25
John son of Michael Lamb,	Aug^t	11
John son of Zackariah Farrow,	Oct^t	3
Sarah Daughter of Wm Thackray,	Oct^t	30
John Foster,	Nov^{br}	8
Edward Wharton,	Decem.	11
John son of Wm Thackray,	Decem.	16
Eliz: Bramley,	March	6
BAPT. Mary Daughter of John Moon,		
Tho: son of Wm Teal,	March	23
Geo: son of Geo. England,		
Martin son of John Brown,	March	31
Eliz: Daughter of James Pickard,	April	21
Eliz: Daughter of Joseph Bland,	April	21
John son of Robert Robinson,	April	28
Zachariah son of Robert Hay,	June	16
William son of Wm Hudson,	Sep^{ber}	29
Ann Daughter of Wm Oldfield,	Oct^t	26
John son of Richard Whiteley,	Decem.	1
Eliz: Daughter of John England,	Decem.	22
Francis son of James Standeven,	Janu:	12
Francis son of Robert Kendle,	Janu:	15
Thomas Son of Wm Thompson,	Feb:	16
Ann Daughter of Thos Pearsonson,	Feb:	23
MARRIAGES. John Proctor and Hannah Foster,	May	13
Henry Cauthera & Mary Brown,	Sep^{br}	26
William Parat & Mary Fairbank,	Nov^{br}	15
John Moon & Mary Shires,	Nov^{br}	20

1755

BAP^T. John son of Thos West,	March	30
Mary Daughter of John Proctor,	June	1
John Son of Wm Parat,	June	1

Francis Son of Francis Simpson,	July	20
Hannah Daughter of Thos Hudson,	July	27
James Son of Wm Cotton,	October	26
Ann Daughter of Joseph Farmer,	Nov^{br}	16
Elin Daughter of Wm Sowden,	January	11
Henry son of Thos Thackwray,	January	11
Margaret Daughter of Thos Thackwray,	January	11
John Son of Wm Thackwray,	January	16
John Son of John Skirow,	Feb:	19
John son of Thos Holmes,	Feb:	22
Grace Daughter of Joseph Mitton,	Feb:	22
Martin Son of Martin Bowling,	March	14
BURY'D. Sarah Wife of Dinnis Longstreph,	April	19
Elin Wife of Martin Bowling,	May	2
John Son of Mary Cotton,	May	6
Mary Foster,	May	29
Stephen Watmuff,	June	12
Mary Wife of Andrew Moss,	Octo:	16
Eliz: Wife of Thos Thackwray,	January	25
Margaret Daughter of Thos Thackwray,	Feb:	12
Thos Son of Mary England,	Feb:	26

1756

BAP^T. Samuel Son of Zacha: Farrow,	April	4
Jsaac Son of George Pickard,	April	25
Ann Daughter of John Brown,	May	4
Ann Daughter of John Ratliff,	May	4
Febe Daughter of Jsaac Bowton,	July	4
Hannah Daughter of Joseph Bland,	July	25
Thos Son of James Standeven,	Aug^t	15
Robert Son of John Harrison,	Sep^t	11
Sarah Daughter of Wm Found,	Nov^{br}	14
Mary Daughter of Robert Kendel,	January 1 [sic]	
Joseph Son of George Whitaker,	Nov^{br}	14
Thomas Son of Eliz: Barber,	March	6
BURY'D. John Son of Wm Parat,	April	22
Ann Merser,	April	24
Margret Wife of George Hardisty,	July	13
Susan Daughter of Charles Swier,	July	16
Ann Daughter of John Brown,	Sep^{br}	26
Mary Wife of Wm Pickard,	Octo:	12
Caleb Pawson,	Nov^{br}	10
Mary Vavasour, Widow,	January	11

1757. [No entries.]
1758

BAP^T. Charles Son of John Spence,	June	18
Wm Son of Thos Pawson,	Aug^t	27
Benjamin Son of Ann Cotton,	Sep^{br}	3
Wm Son of Wm Blahah,	Sep^{br}	3
Margaret Daughter of George England,	Sep^{br}	17
John Son of Richard Elis,	Nov^{br}	5

D

John Son of Zacha: Farrah,	Nov^{br}	12
Hannah Daughter of Wm Thackwray,	Nov^{br}	12
Eliz: Daughter of James Handeven [Standeven],	Nov^{br}	19
Thos Son of Francis Simpson,	Decem:	9
John Son of Francis Hainswith,	Decem:	17
Dinah Daughter of Wm Found,	January	14
Thos Son of Thos Rhodes,	January	28
John Son of Thos Preston,	Feb:	8
James Son of Wm Thompson,	Feb:	11
Richard Son of Richard Whitley,	March	4
BURY'D. Thos Scrow,	June	20
Mary Wife of Wm Kendel,	June	24
Edmund Smith,	July	12
Major Son of Thos West,	July	13
George Hardestey,	Aug^t	27
Mary Wife of John Brown,	Sep^{br}	12
Eliz: Wife of Chris: Greenwood,	Octo:	18
George son of George England,	Nov^{br}	13
Thos Grunell,	Decem.	2
George Terner,	Decem:	28
Robert England,	Feb:	18
James Pickard,	Feb:	25
Ann Daughter of Joseph Farmer,	March	13
MARRIAGES. Jonathan Fairbank & Mary Moon,	June	6
Thomas Preston & Sarah Ward,	June	19
William Callender & Mary Vavasour,	Dec:	11

1759

BAP^t. Ester Daughter of Robert Kendel,	May	13
Jarvis Son of Susannah Becroft,	May	27
John Son of Wm Teal,	July	10
Robert Son of Robert Robinson,	July	10
Wm Son of Maudlan Whitaker,	Decem:	30
Richard Son of George Hudson,	Feb:	10
George Son of Thos Hudson,	Feb:	17
John Son of John Lucas,	Feb:	24
Ann Daughter of Wm Harrison,	March	16
Ann Daughter of John England,	April	6
MARRIAGES. Wm Dibb & Mary Maud,	Aug^t	6
John Rhodes & Eliz: Newsam,	Decem:	1
Charles Swire & Ann Clark,	Decem:	11
BURY'D. Mary Stead,	May	13
Wm Son of John England,	May	18
George Whitaker,	May	30
Betty Daughter of Wm Standeven,	Aug^t	15
Isaac Son of George Pickard,	Octo:	10
Thos Hall,	Octo:	12
Isaac Huddlestone,	Octo:	17
Martin Bowling,	Nov^{br}	17
Martha Pickard,	Decem:	10

1760

BAP^T. Ann Daughter of John England,   April   17
John Son of Samuel Parrots,   May   11
Matthew Son of John Riley,   June   1
Wm Son of Jossias Whitehead,   June   1
John Son of Thos Riley,   June   15
James Son of James Standeaven,   July   10
Betty Daughter of Charles Swires,   Sep^{br} 14
Nansey Daughter of Wm Found,   Octo: 19
Jonas Son of John Spence,   Octo: 19
Wm Son of Robert Maud,   Decem: 21
Sarah Daughter of John Scirow,   December 21
Betty Daughter of Zacha: Farrow,   Decem: 24
Mary Daughter of Richard Ellis,   January 8, 1761
Mary Daughter of Thos West,   January 18
Joseph Son of Richard Whitelock,   January 25
Alce Daughter of Martin Bowling,   Feb: 15

MARRIAGES. Chris: Holmes and Mary Brogding, June   2 [1760]
Joseph Thackwray & Ann Sowding,   July   11
Joab Hobson & Alce Pickard,   Sep^{br} 7
John Fallis & Ann Hornbey,   Octo: 13
Richard Knapton & Ann Proctor,   January 21/1761

BURY'D. Jane Mawson,   May   1 [1760]
James Son of Wm Thompson,   May   12
Richard Son of George Hudson,   May   25
Michael Lamb,   July   12
John Atkinson,   Aug^t   8
Eliz: Huddlestone,   Aug^t   24
Robert Harrison,   January 27
Mary Pawson,   March 20
Eliz: Kilner,   March 21

1761

BAP^T. William Son of Francis Simpson,   May   17
Thos Son of Wm Thackwray,   May   24
Richard Son of Richard Whitelock   May   24
John Son of John Burnill,   July   6
John Son of John Harrison,   July   10
Joseph Son of Wm Teal,   Octo: 24
John Son of George Hudson, Husbandman,   Nov^{br} 8th
MARRIAGES. John Smith and Ann Leming,   May   28
Thos Cryer and Ann Taylor,   Aug^t   13
Wm Loftas and Mary Grunel,   Nov^{br} 17
John Harrison and Ann Bean,   January 6/1762

BURY'D. Ann Daughter of John England,   March 31 [1761]
Joseph Farmer,   April 3
Richard Son of Richard Whitelock,   May   24
Ann Daughter of Jonathan Summers,   June   3
Ann Wife of Wm Catton,   July   5

Isabella Thackwray,	Nov^{br}	24
Eliz: Daughter of Samuel Walker,	Nov^{br}	30
Christeanah Daughter of Wm Thackwray,	Decem:10	
John Swires,	March	21

1762

Bap^t. Sarah Daughter of John England,	March	7
Margaret Daughter of Wm Blacah,	March	6
Thos. John Moon,	May	2
Easter Daughter of Thos Hudson,	May	30
John Son of John Harrison,	May	30
John Son of John Riley,	July	10
Mary Daughter of John Smith,	July	10
Sarah Daughter of Robert Maud,	Aug^t	8
John Son of Wm Atkinson,	Octo:	24
Joseph Son of James Standeven,	Decem: 26	
Joseph Son of Jonathan Summers,	January	1
Ann Daughter of John Burnel,	January	1
Ann Daughter of Richard Whitelock,	Feb:	27
Chris: Son of Joseph Hardestey,	March	20

Ellen Daughter of Walter Vavasour Esqr, May 14th 1762 & Bap: at St.
Maries in York [an insertion].

MARRIAGES. Wm Atkinson and Susan Smithson,	May	14
Joseph Hardcastle and Sarah Sowden,	Aug^t	17
Wm Catton and Ann Smith,	Sep^{br}	20
Wilfred Scerrow and Lidia Holmes,	Nov^{br}	19
Thos Riley and Mary Barrit,	Feb.	15
Bury'd. Ann Thorn,	April	9
Wm Loftas,	May	14
Jane Wife of Thos Riley,	May	20
Francis Kendel,	May	22
Mary Wife of John Simpson,	May	24
Mary Cryer,	Sep^{br}	12
Wm Kendel,	January 10	
Wm Hardcastle,	January 13	
Jane England,	Feb:	21
Charles Vavasour,	Feb:	7
Betty Daughter of Zacha: Farrow,	March	5

1763

Bap^t. Joseph the Son of Jonathon Sumarsgil,	Jeⁿ	1
Ann the Daughter of John Burnil,	Jeⁿ	1
Ann the Daughter of Richard Whittah,	Feb.	27
Christopher the son of Joseph Hardcastle,	March	20
Ann the Daughter of John Harrison,	Ap^r	10
Mary the Daughter of John Bean,	April	24
John the Son of Marting Bowling,	May	8
Ann the Daughter of Zacriah Farrow,	Jun.	29
Edmund the Son of William Caton,	July	5
Thomas the Son of Charls Swiers,	July	10
William the Son of Robert Robison,	July	10
Thomas the son of John Scirrow,	Sep^t	4

Bettey the Daughter of Joseph Jackson,   O^c   30
Richard the Son of Richard Burton,   Jen^n   24
George the Son of John Smith,   Jnuary 1764, 24

MARRIAGES. John Suttil and Ann West,   April   5 [1763]
Joseph Jacson and Margarit Askwith,   April   18th
Andrew Procter and Francis [*sic*] Elinworth,   Ju   18th
William Moss and Sarah Thackwray,   Au^gst   26th
Jams Jacson and Jane Greenbank,   Jenuary 19, 1764

BURY'D. Samuel the son of Zacha: Farrow,   August   6 [1763]
John the Son of John Burnil,   August 12
Margarit Picard,   August 18
John Jennings,   Jenuary 18, 1764
                    1764
BAP^r. Isaac the Son of John Fallis,   Jenuary ye 21
Bety the Daughter of William Found,   March 25
Walter Asyscough [Fawkes *inserted*] the Son of Walter Vavasour Esqr,
    April the 4
Bettey the Daughter of Joseph Teal,   April ye 29
Mary the Daughter of John Burnil,   May ye 27
Liddey the Daughter of John Ward,   June   2
Ann the Daughter of William Atkinson,   June   9
Tibey the Daughter of Andrew Procter,   June   9
John the Son of William Moss,   July the 29
Thos. the Son of William Blacah,   August 12
Thomas the Son of Jams Jackson,   September 23
Ann the Daughter of Abraham Moon,   Sep^t ye 26
Sarah the Daughter of John Bean,   Novr ye 26
Ann the Daughter of Thomas Rilah,   March 17, 1765

MARRIAGES. Joseph Leming and Elisabeth Walter, August 13 [1764]
BURY'D. Sarah the Daughter of William Jewit [Jowett], August 18
John Dixon,   October the 7
                    1765
William Crook,   March the 15
Ann Wife of Wm Oldfield,   Nov^r   13
BAP^r. Ann Daughter of Thos Riloh,   March 15
William Son of John Rilah,   July   11
Mary the Daughter of John Harison,   July   11
John Son of John Ratlif,   July   21
Robert the Son of Andrew Procter,   Oct.   13
Mary Daughter of James Standeven,   the 13th
Ann Daughter of John Smith,   Oct^r   13
Richard Son of Mary Moss,   Dec^r   15
Betty Daughter of Joshua Myres bapti: Decr 28th 1765, Snowdon

    [*This leaf is torn and partly destroyed, but the entries are repeated in another
    form and by another hand, but they vary somewhat, see pp. 54 and 55.*]
                    1766
BURIALS. Ann Daughter of John Burnel bur'd Jany 6, of Weston
Mary Daughter of John Burnel bured Jany 21, of Weston

Mary Daughter of Ninus Leming bur. Jan. 21
Ann Teal Dau[r] of Manuel Teal of Askwith was bu[d] Feb[y] 3
John Son of W[m] Atkinson of Weston bur[d] Feb[y] 5th
Ann Dau: of W[m] Atkinson of Weston buried Feb[y] 12th
John England of Snowden buried   April
Mary the Daughter of John Bean of Askwith
Richard Son of Mary Moss of Snowdon,   Sep.
Henry Harper of Askwith,   Octobe
John Moon of Askwith,   Nov.
Mary the Wife of Thomas C . . . . Ask

176 . . .

MARRIAGES. Jonathan Bramley and Eliz: Gar . . . . Dec[r]
George Ingland and Eliz: Walker,   Jen. 5th 1767
John Walker & Suana Becroft,   July 19th in.
Joseph Cundlif and Grace Dixon,   Jen. 24th
William Sowdin and Ann Holms,   Jen. 26th
William Whitteker and Jane Newsam,   June 11th

[End of damaged leaf.]
From Lady Day, 1765, to Lady Day, 1766

BAPTISMS. William Son of John Rilah,   March 11th
Mary Daughter of John Harrison,   July   11th
John Son of John Ratcliff,   July   21st
Robert Son of Andrew Procter,   October 13th
Mary Daughter of James Standeven,   October 13th
Ann Daughter of John Smith,   October 13th
Richard Son of Mary Moss,   December 15th
Betty Daughter of Joshua Myers,   December 28th

1766

Mary Daughter of Ninus Leeming,   Jan[y] 5th
Elizabeth Daughter of William Moss of Snowden, Jan[y] 19th
Tho[s] Son of Tho[s] West of Weston,   March 9th
William Son of John Suttel of Weston,   March 9th
Benjamin Son of Zackariah Farrah,   March 9th
Joseph Son of Zackariah Farrah,   March 9th
Jane Daughter of John Burnel of Weston,   March 9th

1765

MARRIAGES. Andrew Shires and Ann Tenant,   Novem[br] 21st

1766

Joseph Hobson and Rachel Taylor,   Febru[y] 3[d]
Joseph Pickard and Ann Hunter,   Febru[y] 3[d]

1765

BURIALS. Ann Wife of William Oldfield,   Novem[br] 13th

1766

Ann Daughter of John Burnel,   . January 21st
Mary Daughter of John Burnel,   January 21st
Ann Daughter of Manuel Teal of Askwith,   February 3[d]
John Son of William Atkinson of Weston,   February 5th
Ann Daughter of William Atkinson of Weston, February 12th
BAPTISMS. April 6th John Son of Rachel Farmer of Weston, a Bastard
April 20th James Son of John Skirrow of Askwith

July   6. Martha Daughter of Joseph Teal of Askwith
Oct.   19th William Son of William Atkinson of Weston
                                    1767
Jany.   4th Edward Son of William Blakey of Askwith Scales
                                    1766
MARRIAGES. Septembr 1st John Walker and Susannah Beecroft
Decembr 8th Jonathan Bramley and Elizabeth Garth
                                    1767
Jany   5th George England and Elizabeth Walker
Jany   23d Joseph Cundliff and Grace Dixon
Jany   26th William Sowden and Ann Holmes
                                    1766
BURIALS. April 12th John England of Sowden [Snowden]
April   21st Mary Daughter of John Bean of Askwith
Septembr 23d Richard Son of Mary Moss of Snowden
October 28th Harper of Askwith (Henry)
Novembr 12th John Moon of Askwith
                                    1767
March   18th Mary wife of Thomas Robinson of Askwith
BAPTISMS. Mary Daughter of Andrew Procter of Snowden, April 5th
Joseph Son of John Riley, Askwith,   April   17th
Mary Daughter of John Fallis,   April   17th
Hannah Daughter of Joseph Myers of Dob Park, September 13th
[Rebeckah the Doughter of John Smith, Askwith, october 15th, *an insertion*]
Margaret Daughter of William Catton of Weston, Novbr 15th
                                    1768
John Son of John Burnel of Weston,   March 13th
                                    1767
MARRIAGES. William Whitaker and Jane Newsome, June   16th
Joseph Pickard and Mary England,   October 27th
Jonas Mann and Agnes Kidson,   Novembr 20th
                                    1768
William Gott and Ann Andrew,   Februy 23d
Joseph Holmes and Magdalen Greenwood,   March   1st
George Whitaker and Sarah Hobson,   March 15th
BURIAL. John Brogden,   March 20th
BAPTISMS. April 24th William Son of Joseph Hobson
June   26th Jane Daughter of William Oldfield
August   28th Sarah Daughter of Joseph Teal
Novembr 6th Jonas Son of Jonas Mann
Decembr 18th John Son of Abraham Moon
                                    1769
Januay   8th Thos Son of John Ratcliff
Jany   8th Czarina Daughter of Joseph Bland
Jany   29th John Son of William Atkinson
March   12th Mary Daughter of William Found
March   12th Anna Daughter of Jonathan Bramley
March   12th Hannah Daughter of Andrew Procter
                                    1768
BURIALS. April 5th Thos Foster

April   17th George Pawson
April   22^d   William Tidswell
April   27th Elizabeth Mawson
April   27   Frances Rhodes
                              1769
Janu^y 30th Thomas Riley
BAPTISMS. Sarah Daughter of Joshua Tezzeman, July   2^d
Mary Daughter of John Suttel,   Augst 25th
William Son of Walter Vavasour, Esqr,   Septem^{br} 12th
Francis Son of John Falliss,   October 17th
Joseph Son of John Hobson,   Novem^{br} 19th
John Son of Thomas West,   Decem^{br} 3^d
                              1770
Sally Daughter of Joshua Myers,   March 18th
                              1769
MARRIAGE.   Richard Smithson & Margaret Illingworth, Novem^{br} 20th
BURIALS. Ann Wharton,   May   14th
John Lamb,   ⎱   May   19th
William Lamb, ⎬Nunnery,   May   28th
Sarah Lamb,   ⎰   July   6th
Edward Son of Wm Blakey,   Novem^{br} 28th
Elizabeth Sheldon, Widow of Thos Sheldon,   Decem^{br} 28th
                              1770
Ann Wife of Thos Pawson, Askwith,   March 23^d
BAPTISMS. April 1st Mary Daughter of John Burnel, Weston
April   22^d   Joshua Son of Mary Newsome, a Bastard, Snowden
May   27th Sally Daughter of George Whitaker, Snowden
June   10th George Son of George England, Snowden
June   17th Thos Son of Mr Richard Burton, Askwith
July   10th John Son of William Dibb, Schoolmaster, Askwith
July   10th Sarah Daughter of John Harrison, Farmer, Askwith
July   10th Hannah Daughter of Joseph Jackson, Weaver, Scales
July   10th Betty Daughter of Zachariah Farrah, Woolcomber, Askwith
July   10th Ann Daughter of Joseph Teal, Labourer, Askwith
July   29th Thos Son of Andrew Procter, Innkeeper, Snowden
Sep^{br} 16th Betty Daughter of Martha Newsome, a Bastard, Snowden
                              1771
Jan^y   6th Ann Daughter of William Blacah, Scales
Feby 10th Andrew Son of William Moss, Snowden
Feby 10th Hannah Daughter of William Harrison, Askwith
March   24th Stephen Son of Thos Gill, Weston
                              1770
MARRIAGES.. June 24th Joseph Johnson and Ann Arbuthnot, Weston
August 12th Thos Pawson and Elizabeth Sowden
Novem^{br} 11th James Burnell and Mary Brown, Weston
Nov^{br} 19th William Teal and Isabella Thackray, Askwith
Nov^{br} 28.   James Bradley and Tabitha Leeming, Askwith
BURIALS. May 15th Thos Lockwood, Weston
Augst 31.   Abraham Bayley, Weston
Sep^{br}   9th Thos Booth of Otley. Paid an acknowledgem^t for coming
               through Mr Vavasour's Ground

Sep^{br} 11th Elizabeth Wife of Wm Teal, Askwith
Octob^r 13th Elizabeth Wife of Robert Procter, Snowden
Octob^r 19th Joseph Harrison, Askwith
Dec^{br} 15th Mary Lamb, Nunnery
Dec^{br} 21st Thos Askwith, Scales
Dec^{br} 31st Mary Harper, As:

1771

Mar^h 17th Fanny Flesher, As:
BAPTISMS. Sally Daughter of Edward Morrel, Snowden, May 5th
Hannah Daughter of Isabella Whitaker, Snowden, Bastard, May 5th
Mary Daughter of William Chowler, Scales, May 20th
Betty Daughter of Wm Atkinson, Weston, July 7th
Betty Daughter of Thos Pawson, Askwith, July 10th
Wm Son of James Standeven, Askwith, July 10th
Lucy Daughter of John Smith, Askwith, July 10th
Wm Son of William Whitaker, Snowden, Augst 11th
Jane Daughter of James Burnell, Weston, Augst 18th
Sarah Daughter of Andrew Procter, Snowden, Octob^r 1st
Betty Daughter of Joshua Tezzeman, Askwith, Octo^{br} 20th
James Son of Thos West, Weston, Nov^{br} 10th
Hannah Daughter of Joseph Hobson, Scales, Dec^{br} 8th
Betty Daughter of Joseph Robinson, Askwith, Dec^{br} 25th

1772

Ann Daughter of John Burnell, Weston, Feby 23^d
John Son of Wm Rowlinson, Snowden, Feby 23^d
Pally Daughter of Joshua Myers, March 15th
George Son of Joseph Teal, Askwith, May 10th

1771

MARRIAGES. Richard Barrit of Weston and Martha Newsome, Sno^{dn},
May 23^d. Certi: John Gill, W. & M^y Hardesty
George Hey of Denton & Ann Pickard of Weston Parish [*an insertion*]
BURIALS. Hannah Harrison, Carr-House, April 18th
Thomas Robinson, Askwith, July 28th
Ann Widow Lowcock, Askwith, Augst 4th
Sarah Daughter of Andrew Procter, Octo^{br} 18th
Rebecca Booth of Otley, Widow, Dec^{br} 1st

1772

Ann Pawson, Widow of William Pawson, Feby 8th
Mary Dunnell, March 3^d
Mary Hall, March 15th
Margaret Farmer June 6th
BAPTISMS. October 18. John Son of John Procter
Novem^{br} 15. Ann Dau. of John Faless
Decem^r 12. Hannah Dau. of George Whitaker

1773

Janu^y 21. Joseph Son of Andrew Procter
Febru^y 14. Benjamin Son of Anthony Ward
D^o 25. Stephen Son of William Moss
MARRIAGE. Feby 24. John Butterfield & Elizabeth Moss

1772

BURIALS.   June 6.   Margret Farmer
Novem^{br} 10.   Alice Wife of Joseph Harrison

1773

Janu^y   21.   Michael Son of John Todd
D^o   28.   Hannah Cooper
Febru^y 11.   Mary Smith
D^o   25.   James Standeven

1774

BAPTIZED.   May 29th Thos & Joseph Sons of Jonathan Bramley
June   1st Nancy Daughter of William Dibb
July   4.   William Son of John Gill
D^o   5.   Henry Son of William Atkinson
D^o   5.   Ann Dau. of Thomas West
Septem^{br} 5.   Hannah Dau. of John Smith
Feb^y   13.   Mary Dau. of Thos Kendall
D^o   19.   Margret Dau. of Edwd Greenwood

1773

MARRIAGES.   Novem^{br} 19.   Mark Lofthouse & Sarah Water

1774

Janu^y   5.   William England & Elizabeth England
Feb^y   12.   John Ward & Mary Thackeray
March   14.   James Shaw & Mary Farmer

1773

BURIALS.   April 25th Judith Wife of John Moon
May   28th Mary Robinson
June   14.   John Newsholm of Snowden
D^o   26.   Thos Son of Jonathan Bramley
July   10.   Richard Sowden
D^o   17.   Joseph Son of Jonathan Bramley
Augst   9.   William Son of Willm Whitaker
D^o   15.   Ann Wife of Luke Overend
D^o   16.   William Pickard
D^o   20.   John Simpson
Sep^r   2^d   Hannah Dau. of John Newsholm
Oct^r   1.   Christiana Wife of James West

October 1st 1773. N.B. That Two pence was paid for the use of Walter
Vavasour Esqr of Weston as acknowledgement for leave given by the
s^d Walter Vavasour to bring the deceased Body of Christiana the wife of
James West over the Ford & thro' his grounds leading from Burley
the nearest Road to be interr'd at Weston Church.   J. Bailey, Minister.

1774

Janu^y   2.   Elizabeth Dau. of Willm Atkinson
Do   3^d   Hanna Dau. of Willm Harrison
D^o   5.   Elisabeth Dau. of Willm Harrison
Do   7.   Alice Wife of Willm Thompson
Do   9.   Elisabeth wife of John Mawde
D^o   17.   Jane Dau. of John Smith
March   7.   Willm Sowden of Asquith
D^o   16.   John Newsholm of Snowden

1774

Bap^t. June 6.   James Son of James Shaw
July   12.   John Son of Mark Loftass
          12.   John Son of John Butterfield
          12.   Peggy Dau. of Joshuah Tassy
          12.   Nancy Dau. of Joseph Robinson
          12.   Joseph Son of Andrew Procter
          12.   Jane Dau. of Joseph Teal
Sep^r   18.   Hannah Dau. of William Harrison
          25.   William Son of John Burnell
          25.   William Son of Thos Gill

1775

Janu^y   1st   Mary Dau. of John Harper
March   1st   Thos Son of Isabel Thompson

1774

Burials. April 6th Susannah Jennings of Asquith
          11.   John Son of Abraham Moon   D^o
          25.   Margaret Dawson, Otley
Sep^r   22.   Hannah Dau. of William Harrison, Asquith
          23.   John Bean, Asquith

1775

Feb^y   14th   Andrew Proctor, Snowden
March   22.   Henry Small of Weston Hall
March   23.   George England, Snowden
April   22.   William Oldfield
May   3^d   Simon Smith
          7.   Mary Newsom
          28.   Thos the Son of Geo. England
Aug^t   10.   Elisabeth Walker
          16.   Mary Dau. of Thomas West
Sep^r   30.   William Candler Esqr
Oct^r   16.   Willm Son of Willm Whitaker
Nov^r   15.   Sarah Bean
          30.   Judy Wife of Ric^d Kendall

1776

Jan^y   4.   Ellen wife of Walter Vavasour of Weston, Esqr
Feb^y   8.   Sarah Wife of George Hudson

1775

Baptisms. April 30.   Hanah Dau^r of Jonathan Bramley
May   7.   Martha Dau. of Joshuah Myres
June   18.   Rachel Dau. of James Harrison
July   5.   Mary Dau. of Thos West
          9.   John son of John Smith
          9.   Benjamin son of Joseph Hobson
          30.   Mary Dau. of Willm Moss
Sep^r   24.   Christopher Son of Edward Greenwood
Dec^r   7.   James Son of John Land
          31.   James Son of Willm Atkinson
          31.   Saml Son of John Burnell

1776

Jan^y   21.   Jonathan Son of Thomas Kendall
BURIALS. William Howden, April 4th, of Snowden
April   8.   Walter Sowden, Asquith
  D^o   30.   Betty Dau. of Joseph Robinson, Asquith
May   16.   Ann Wife of John Fallis, Asquith
          26.   William son of Maudland Whittaker
July   27.   Elisabeth Dau. of William Thackeray, Weston
          30.   Richard Kendall of Weston
Nov^r   13.   Samuel Lamb of Horsforth
          17.   James son of Widow Standeven of Asquith

1777

John Ratcliff of Asquith, Janu^y 1st
Christopher Greenwood of Asquith

1776

BAPTISMS. May 26. Thomas Son of John Gill of Asquith
July   21.   William son of John Butterfield of Asquith
          21.   John son of John Ward of Snowden
Oct^r   27.   James son of Thomas Gill, Weston
Nov^r   17.   William son of Joseph Robinson of Asquith
Decem^r   22.   Martha Dau. of Jonathan Bramley, Weston
          22.   Lidia Dau. of Frances Fooler of Weston

1777

Jan^y   12.   Nancy Dau. of Robert Emsley of Asquith
Feb^y   25.   Lidia Dau. of Anthony Ward of Asquith
March   9.   Thomas Son of Thomas Robinson of Asquith
          16.   Ann Dau. of Joseph Robinson of Asquith
BURIALS. April 3^d Christopher Son of John Greenwood
May   4.   James Son of John Burnell
June   20.   Jane Lamb
July   8.   Jane Daughter of Charles Swires
July   24.   William Found
Nov.   9.   John Dixon
Nov.   19.   John Vavasour Esqr
Dec.   2.   Sarah Wife of John Land
Dec.   28.   Rachel Asquith, Widow

1778

March   4.   Sarah Gray, Widow
           6.   Jane Wife of William Hudson
          11.   John Kitchen

1777

BAPTISMS. April 6. Sarah Daughter of James Harrison
           6.   Sarah Daughter of William Moss
May   25.   John ye Son of John Greenwood
          25.   Mary Daughter of Joseph Pickard
July   5.   John Dawson Son of Edward Dixon
           6.   Grace Daughter of Joseph Teal
Au'st   13.   Mary Daughter of Thomas West
Dec.   25.   Sarah Daughter of Thomas Kendall
          25.   Richard Son of John Sowden

1778

Jan.	25.	Grace Daughter of Robert Emsley
March	1.	Christiana Daughter of Joseph Bentley
	15.	Susanna Daughter of William Atkinson
	22.	John Son of John Harper

BURIALS. 26 Mar: Eleanor Wife of Edward Dixon of Weston

Jun: [sic]17.		George Rhodes of Arthington
4 May.		George Son of John Burnell, Weston
14 Au'st.		Jane Tidswell of Asquith
8ber	1st	Sarah Dau. of Dinah Found, Weston
9ber	22.	Sarah Huddleston of Denton

1779

March   21.   George Mawson, Weston

1778

BAPTISMS. 24 May. Martha Dau. of Edward Greenwood, Asquith

21 June.		Eliz: Dau. of Henry Thackwray, Snowden.
July	5.	George Son of Thomas Mawson, Weston
	6.	George Son of John Burnell, Weston
	10.	Mary Dau. of Mark Loftus, Asquith
	10.	Jane Daughter of John Smith, Asquith
8ber	16.	Richard Son of Thos Kendall, Weston

1779

Jan.	3d	Elizabeth Dau. of William Dibb, Asquith
	24.	Katharine Dau. of John Barret, Scales
July	4.	Jane Dau. of Robert Emsley of Scales, Husbandman
Aug:	1st	Joseph Son of John Green of Snowden, Husbandman
	1st	Thomas Son of William Moss of Snowden, Farmer
	1st	James Son of Henry Thackwray of Snowden, Farmer
	1st	Timothy Son of Joshua Myers, Snowden
Sep.	12.	Jane Dau. of John Dibb of Snowden, Farmer
Octr	31.	Hannah Dau. of John Burnhill of Weston, Farmer

1780

Jany	9th	Thomas Son of Thomas Kendall of Asquith, Carpenter
Feby	24.	Sarah Dau. of Thomas Dale of Snowden, Farmer
	28.	Ann Dau. of Joseph Pickard of Snowden, Farmer
	28.	Saml Son of William Atkinson of Weston, Farmer
	27.	Joseph Son of James Harrison of Asquith, Wool-comber

1779

BURIALS. May 27th Hannah Dau. of Jonathan Bramley, Weston, Labourer

July	9th	Grace Cundliffe, Weston
Octr	14.	Hannah Daughter of John Burnhill, Weston
Nov.	27.	Robt Proctor of Otley, lately from Snowden

1780

Jany	27th	Mark Nichols of Weston, Husbandman
March	31.	John Mawson of Weston, Labourer
May	4.	Major Brown of Weston, Husbandman
	14.	Elizabeth Ashton, Housekeeper to W: Vavasour Esqr
July	8·	Ann Wife of George Teal, Farmer
	12.	Joseph Pickard of Snowden, Farmer
	14.	Jonas Son of Jonas Mann of Asquith, Farmer

August   5.   Elizabeth the Wife of Joseph Leeming, Cordwainer
Nov^r   17.   Walter Vavasour Esqr, Weston

1781

Jan: 17.   John Harrison of Carr-House, Farmer
Feb.   6.   John Dale, Born blind
March   15.   George Whitaker of Snowden, Farmer

1780

BAPTISMS.   April 2^d Joseph Son of Edward Greenwood of Asquith, Wool-
Comber [Born March 3rd *inserted*]
16th   Jane Dau. of William Thompson of Asquith, Taylor
16th   Martin Son of Thos West of Weston, Husbandman
May   7.   Mary Daughter of John Butterfield of Asquith, Wool-
Comber
July   16th   Hannah Dau. of Joseph Bentley of Asquith, Farmer
Sep^r   3^d   Thomas Son of Thos Mawson of Weston, Black-smith
10th   William ye Son of William Brogden of Asquith, Black-smith
Nov.   5th   William Son of John Harper of Asquith, Farmer
Dec^r   31.   Mary Dau. of Francis Simpson of Weston

1781

April   27th   Joseph Son of John Smith, Asquith
June   10th   Henry Son of William Moss, Snowden
July   5th   James Son of John Burnhill, Weston
29th   Mary Daughter of Thomas Dale, ⎫
29th   Ann Daughter of John Dibb,   ⎬Snowden
Aug: 6th   Hannah the Daughter of John Walter
Ann the doughter of Nathan torner, September the 18 [*an insertion*]
Nov.   4th   Judith Daughter of Joseph Teal
18th   Betty Daughter of William Blakey
Dec: 2^d   Thomas Son of Henry Thackwray
23^d   George Son of John Butterfield
23^d   Elisabeth Daughter of William Metcalfe
26th   John Son of John Crooke, Asquith

1782

Feb: 3^d   Betty Daughter of John Barrett
3^d   Robert Exley Mawson Son of Thos Mawson

1781

BURIED.   April 13th Charles Son of John Swires of Asquith
May   20th   John Procter of Asquith, Farmer
June   21st   Ellen Wife of William Kitchen
23^d   Betty Daughter of William Kitchen
July   9th   George Smith
Aug: 6th   Sarah the Wife of John Walter
Sep: 2^d   Martin Bowling of Asquith
29th   Thomas Thackwray of Snowden
30th   Sabina Bland Dau. of Joseph Bland of Weston
Oct^r   12th   William Thackwray, Parish Clerk of Weston 40 yrs.

1782

BAPTIZED.   April 1st Samuel son of Jonathan Bramley of Weston
28.   Margaret the Daughter of Thomas Kendall, Askwith
28.   Sarah Daughter of William Harper, Askwith

May   5.   Joseph Son of Ann Harrison, Askwith
July   10.   Edmund son of Edmund Greenwood, Askwith
         10.   John son of John Ashley, Askwith
Aust   25.   Mary Daughter of William Atkinson, Weston
Sep\u02b3   29.   Betty Daughter of Thomas Dale, Snowden
                        1783
Feb\u02b8   8\u1d57\u02b0   Enon Son of William Dibb of Asquith
Feb.   23\u1d48   Joseph Son of William Thompson, Askwith
March   14\u1d57\u02b0   Edmund the son of John Greenwood, Newall
                        1782
BURIED.   May 1\u02e2\u1d57 Mary Smith
May   23\u1d48   Edward Dixon of Burley, Gentleman
August   13\u1d57\u02b0   George Dixon of Burley, Yeoman
         15\u1d57\u02b0   Elizabeth Burton
October 14\u1d57\u02b0   Betty Dale
November 24\u1d57\u02b0 Susanna Burnhill
                        1783
February 1\u02e2\u1d57   Thomas Tackwray
         19\u1d57\u02b0   Susanna Jeffrey
March   14\u1d57\u02b0   Jarvis Greenwood
         23.   Elizabeth Swire
BAPTISED.   March 30\u1d57\u02b0 William the Son of John Forrest, Askwith
         30\u1d57\u02b0   William the Son of William Barrett, Snowden
May   11.   Easter the Doughter of John Dibb, Snowden
D\u1d52   11.   George the Son of John Linfot, Weston
July   11.   James the son of Fransis Standevin, Askwith
D\u1d52   11.   Nancy the Doughter of William Blakah, Askwith
October 12.   William the Son of Thomas West, Weston, firs [sic] after the
              new act
         19.   Marey the Doughter of William harper, Askwith
         19.   Ann the Doughter of John harpr, Askwith
Novm.   15.   Ann the Doughter of Thomas Dale, Snowden
D\u1d52   30.   Thomas the Son of Thomas Robinson, Weston
                        1784
Feb.   8.   Marthay the Doughter of John Eshlay, Askwith
D\u1d52   22.   Fransis the Son of Fransis Simpson, Weston
                        1783
BURIED.   Sarah Newsom, 30\u1d57\u02b0 March
April   1\u02e2\u1d57   Ann Newsom Daughter of the above
June   25.   Sarah Dibb, Snowden
July   7.   Easter Dibb, Snowden
September 10. Marey Dixon, Weston
Octobr   19.   hanah West, Burley
D\u1d52   25.   James Skirrow, poor, Askwith
Novm.   15.   Charls Swiers, Askwith
Decm.   17.   Rachil harrison, Askwith
D\u1d52   20.   James harrison, Askwith
                        1784
Jan\u02b8   13.   Jane Smith, Askwith
D\u1d52   21.   Marey Lofthous, Askwith

D^o   30.   Joseph thompson, Askwith
March   23.   Joseph greenwood, Askwith
Anthony Pawson of Bland hill, April y^e 5
Elener Shires of Snowden, April y^e 17th
James Pickerd of Snowden, April y^e 30th
Elener Whitacar of snowden, may y^e 27
Sarah sowden of Askwith, August 22nd
BAPTIZED. May ye 9.   Elizabeth the Daughter of John Butterfield
         Askwith

D^o   27.   James the son of w^m moss, snowden
August   8.   W^m the son of John Bawdon, Weston
D^o   22.   Ann the Daughter of Wm Medcaf, Askwith
Sep^{tm}   5.   John the son of Wm Barrett, snowden
D^o ye 19.   samuel the son of stephen moss, snowden
D^o   27.   Catron the Daughter of John Crook, Askwith
October ye 3.   Ann the Daughter of Wm Adkinson, weston
D^o   10.   John the son of John Dibb, snowdon
D^o   18.   John the son of Thomas mawson, weston
December 12. George the son of John Barrit, Scales
                    1785
January   9. Elizabeth the Doughter of Edward grenwood, Askwith,
             Born October the 30 in 1784
March   6.   Elin the Doughter of Wm Whitaker, Snowden
D^o   John the son of Joseph Ingland, Snowden
BURIED. August. Elizabeth Moss Daughter of William Moss of Snowden, 7th
September. Elizabeth Daughter of Mary Hudson of Asquith, 16th P.
Novem^r. Robert Robinson of Asquith, Labourer,   28th
                    1786
March.   Ellen Daughter of William Whitaker of Snowden, 5th
                    1785
BAPTIZED. July. Mark the son of Mary England of Snowden, 3^d
July.   Natty Son of William Blakey of Asquith,   10th
Au'st.   Hannah Daughter of Thomas Dale of Snowden, 1st
          William Son of Thomas Kendall of Asquith,   1st
          Hannah Daughter of James Harrison, Asquith, 14th
          Henry son of Henry Thackwray of Snowden,   14th
Sept^r   William Son of Francis Standeven, Asquith,   11th
          James Son of John Gill of Asquith,   25th P.
October. John Son of Eli Burton of Asquith,   9th
          Nathanael Son of John Ashley of Asquith,   18th
                    1786
Jany.   Tryhana Daughter of John Crook, Asquith,   22^d
March.   Thomas Son of William Barret, Snowden,   5th
BURIED.   May. John Walter of Asquith, Labourer,   6th
May.   Hannah Daughter of James Harrison,   7th
May.   Thomas Barrett Son of William Barrett of Snowdon, 29th
June.   Mary Brogden of Denton, Widow,   7th
June.   Jane Wife of Robt Helmsley of Asquith,   11th
June.   John Son of Joseph England of Snowden,   19th
July.   Joseph son of William Harper of Asquith,   17th

Novem^r Sarah Wife of William Moss of Snowden,   18th
BAPTIZED.   June.   Ellen Daughter of John Dibb of Snowden, 18th
July.   Joseph Son of William Harper of Asquith,   10th
Au'st.   William Son of William Bowling, Weston,   13th
Au'st.   Joseph Son of John Harper of Asquith,   13th
Septr Mary Daughter of Sarah Todd of Dobb Park,   24th
Decemb^r Miles Son of Edwd Greenwood, Asquith,   30th

1787
March.   Jonathan Son of John Barrett of Scales,   11th
BURIED.   April.   Walter Ayscough Fawkes Vavasour Esqr, aged 22, 1st
June.   Ellen Moorhouse of Weston, Widow,   7th
October. Major Son of Thomas West of Weston, ⎱ Twins 3^d P.
         Matthew Son of Thomas West of Weston, ⎰   15th P.

1788
January. Thomas Pawson of Barrowby Psh. of Kirkby Over^w,   24th
February. Elizabeth Daughter of Charles Swire of Asquith,   25th
March.   John Son of John Crook of Asquith,   9th

1787
BAPTIZED. April.   John son of William Metcalf of Asquith,   22^d
July.   Matthew and Major sons of Thomas West,   5th P.
         Anne Daughter of William Harper of Asquith,   10th
         Betty Daughter of Mark Lofthouse of Asquith,   10th
         Elizabeth Daughter of John Waite of Weston,   15th
         Betty Daughter of William Barret of Snowden,   29th
August.   Sally Daughter of Joseph England of Snowden,   20th
Septem^r John Son of James Harrison of Asquith,   23rd
Novem^r Mary Daughter of John Mountain of Asquith,   18th

1788
Februa^{ry} John son of William Bowling of Weston,   4th
March.   Thomas Son of Francis Standeven, Asquith,   23^d
         William Son of Thomas Mawson of Weston,   24th
BURIED. March. Margaret Daughter of Joshua Tazzy of Asquith, 27th
May.   Thomas Son of William Moss of Snowden,   2^d
June.   Anne Wife of John Pulleyne of Stank, Psh. of Harewood, 7th
August.   Andrew Son of William Moss of Snowden,   23^d
Septem^r Sally Daughter of John Forrest of Asquith,   10th
Novemb^r Martin Son of Martin Bowling of Newhall, Psh. of Otley, 25th
         Thomas Standeven of Asquith, Mason,   29th
Decem^r George England of Snowden,   2^d P.

1789
January. Anne Daughter of John Crook of Asquith,   11th
Febr^y Anne Daughter of Joseph Hobson of Scales,   3^d

1788
BAPTIZED.   April.   Hannah Daughter of William Blakey of Asquith, 6th
         William Son of John Dibb of Snowden,   6th
July.   Thomas Son of Francis Simpson of Weston,   5th
Septr Thomas Son of William Illingworth, Dobb Park,   21st
         Edmund Son of Ursula Fieldhouse of Asquith,   25th
Octr Anne Daughter of Thomas Tewksbury, Asquith,   5th
Novr Anne Daughter of John Crook of Asquith,   30th

E

1789

Janu^y	Mary Daughter of Henry Thackwray of Snowden,	25th ·
Feb^y	John Son of Thomas Dale of Snowden,	22d
March.	Sarah Daughter of Joseph Land of Asquith,	8th
	Hannah Daughter of Anne Harrison of Asquith,	8th
	Abraham Son of Abraham Holmes, Asquith,	8th
BURIED.	March. James Son of William Atkinson, Weston,	28th
May.	Elizabeth Ingland of Snowden, Widow,	13th
August.	John Atkinson Son of John Atkinson of Weston,	30th
Sep^tr	Elizabeth Wife of Edward Morril of Weston,	13th

1783

Decem^br Annah Daughter of Jonathan Bramley, Weston, Poor, [3^d *date struck out*]

1790

Feb^ry	Thomas Robinson of Weston,	8th

1789

BAPTIZED.	April. Robert Son of Thomas Robinson, Askwith,	5th
April.	Joseph Son of William Todd, Dog-Park,	20th
April.	Wilfred Son of Thomas Skirrow, Askwith,	26th
May.	William Son of Edward Greenwood, Askwith,	3d
June.	Ellin Daughter of James Lun, Snowden,	14th
July.	Mary Daughter of John Forrest, Askwith,	10th
August.	Elizabeth Daughter of John Harper, Askwith,	2d
Sep^tr	Mary Daughter of Thomas Simpson, Scales,	20th
Nov^r	Hannah Daughter of John Gill, Askwith,	19th P.

1790

Jan^y	Martha Daughter of John Barrit, Scales,	24th
Ditto	Lidia Daughter of John Mountain, Grass-garss,	24th
March.	William Son of Benjamin Waugh, Snowden,	7th
BURIED.	May. Richard Kendell, Asquith,	31st
July.	Nathan Turner, Asquith,	11th
Sep^tr	Ann West, Newall,	9th
Sep^t	Elizabeth Pawson, Denton,	15th
Octo^br	Robert Robinson, Aquith,	8th

1791

Feb^ry	Peter Dale of Snowden,	24th
March.	Martha Bramley of Weston,	10th P.

1790

BAPTIZED.	July. Richard Son of Wm Bowling, Weston,	5th
July.	W^m s. of Thomas Duxberry, Weston,	5th
July.	Ann D. of Wm Skirrow, Weston,	5th
August.	Ann D. of Thomas Howden, Asquith,	1st

1791

Jan^ry	Thomas S. of Abraham Holmes, Asquith,	2d
	John S. of Thomas Kendall, Asquith,	Ditto
Feb^ry	Thomas S. of Thomas Robinson, Asquith,	20
	Elizabeth D. of James Harrison, Asquith,	Ditto
\ March.	Eli son of Eli Burton, Asquith,	13th
	Jane D. of John Gill, Asquith,	13th

BURIED. April. Mary Robinson of Askwith,   22^d
May.   Elizabeth Farrow of Askwith,   2^d
May.   Ann Simpson of Askwith,   17th
July.   Joseph Bland of Weston,   13th P.
Augst Joseph West of Weston,   9th P.
Augst Mary Land of Askwith,   29th
Septr Elizabeth Swire of Askwith,   19th
Novr George Teal of Timley [Timble or Timblings] in the
            Parish of Fewston,   25th

1792

Feb^{ry} Ann West of Otley,   21st Poor
Feb^{ry} Hannah Hobson of Asquith,   26th

1791

BAPTIZED. April. Mary D. of William Atkinson of Dob park, 24th
May.   John son of George Hudson of Askwith,   8th
May.   Francis s. of Francis Standeven, Askqwith,   15th
July.   James Burnell Atkinson s. of William Atkinson of Weston, 4th
July.   William s. of Wm Skirrow, Weston,   4th
July.   Joseph s. of Ann West, Weston,   4th Poor
July.   Sarah D. of Thos Skirrow, Asquith,   10th
July.   Nancy D. of John Richardson, Grass garrs,   31th
Augst Sarah D. of Joseph Verity, Weston,   7th
October. Mary Clarkson D. of Thos Wilkinson, Weston,   2^d
Novr Francis Son of Wm Simpson, Scales,   20th
Decr Margaret D. of John Crook, Askwith,   18th

1792

January. Mary Daughter of Wm Moss, Snowden,   1st
February. Hannah Daughter of John Todd junior, Dogpark,   19th
March.   Martin Dibb Burnel Son of John Burnell of Weston,   18th
April.   Ann Daughter of John Mounton, Grass-gars,   22^d
April.   John Son of Thomas Howden of Askwith,   29th
May.   Sarah Daughter of Thomas Simpson, Askwith,   6th
May.   Ann Daughter of Francis Simpson, Weston,   20th Poor
July.   Sarah Daughter of Thomas Duxberry, Weston,   5th
July.   John son of Henry Thackray, Snowden,   15th
September. Mary Daughter of Wm Atkinson, Weston,   2^d
October. John Son of Joseph Land, Askwith,   14th
October. Hannah Daughter of Edmund Greenwod of Askwith,   21st
October. Mary Daughter of Rebecca Smith, Askwith,   21st
October. Joseph Son of Thomas Todd, Dogpark,   28th
Novr William Son of George Hudson, Scales,   25th
Novr Abraham Son of John Barret, Scales,   25th

1793

Jan^{ry} Jonas Son of Christopher Mann, Askwith,   6th
Jan^{ry} Sarah Daughter of Abraham Holmes, Askwith,   27th
Feb^{ry} Thos Son of Thos Skirrow of Askwith,   24th
April.   Rosemary Daug^r of John Todd of Dogpark,   7th
April.   Willm Son of Joseph Verity of Weston,   28th
May.   Markale [Michael] Son of James Clay, Askwith,   12th
May.   Willm Son of John Jennings, Kirskhill,   22

1792

BURIED. Augst Joseph Hobson of Askwith,   5th
Septem^r Thomas swire of Askwith,   2^d
Octo^{ber} Thomas Standeven of Askwith,   9th
Dec^r   Henry Tachraw [Thackray] of Snowden,   13th
Dec^r   Joseph Forrest of Askwith,   29th

1793

Jan^{ry} Elizabeth Lamb of [Arthington] Nunnery in the Parish of Haddle, 7th
Jan^{ry} William Lamb of Nunnery in the Parish of Haddle,   26th
Feb^{ry} Jane Harrison of Askwith, ·   1st Poor
Feb^{ry} Agnes Mann of Askwith,   12th
April.   Francis Standeven of Asquith,   8th April
May.   Ann Catton of Weston,   4th P.
May.   Ann Robinson, Askwith,   9
May.   Sarah Standhaven, Askwith,   22
June.   Joseph Robinson, Askwith,   21
         John Skirrow, Weston,   26
Sept.   Joseph Standhaven, Askwith,   8
D^o   Sarah Lofthouse, Askwith,   20
Oct^r   6th John Mawson Son of Thos Mawson, Weston,   18 [*sic*]
Novr 14. Sarah Pawson, Widow of Anthony Pawson of Norwood, P.
Decr 23^d Susanna West, Wife of   ^s West, Weston,   P.

1793ho

Jan.   18. John Houldin, Askwith [son of Thos Howden]
Feb.   28. Mary Bland, Askwith
April   28. Mary D. of Benj: Warf [Waugh], Otley
May   15. Zachariah Farrow, Askwith,   P.
June   30. Mary wife of ɪ. Skirrow, Weston
August 9th Thomas Gill of Weston,   P.

1793

BAPTISED. June. Jane Daught^r of Lucy Smith (Illegit.), Askwith, 21
July.   John Son of Will. Skirrow, Weston,   5
   D^o   Benjamin Son of Ann West, Weston,   D^o Born Jan. 2^d
Aug.   18. William Son of William Atkinson, Weston,   18
             John Son of Hannah Smith (Illegit.), Askwith,   18 Poor
Sept.   Hannah Daughter of John Harper, Askwith,   8
Oct.   13th Mary D. of Jos^h Ward, Weston
Oct.   20. Joseph S. of Will. Atkinson, Dobb Park
Nov.   10. John S. of John Moss, Snowden
Nov.   24. Ann D. of John Ratcliff, Askwith
No.   24. Ann D. of Thos Simpson, Askwith
Dec. · 25. Hannah D. of Will. Illingworth, Dobb Park

1794

Apr.   20. Elizabeth D. of T. Houldin [Howden], Askwith
July   10th William Son of John Crook of Asquith
August 3.   Rachael Skirrow of Asquith, an adult Person
        24. Ann D. of Abr^m Holmes, Askwith
Sept.   7.   John S. of Thos Deuxbery, Weston
        14. Wilfred S. of Willm Moss, Snowden
        28. Mary D. of Thos Robinson, Askwith

Oct.   26. Martha D. of Ann Todd, Dobb Park
Nov.   2. Thos S. of Joseph Land, Askwith

1795

Jan.   25. Richard S. of Richd Mann, Askwith
March 1. Rachael D. of Henry Thackwray, Snowden
Mar.   15. Joseph S. of Joseph Verity, Weston
Mar.   22. Christopher S. of Christ^r Mann, Askwith
Mar.   29. Nelly D. of John Mountain, Grass-Garths
Apr.   5. Ruth D. of Edward Greenwood, Askwith
Apr.   19. John S. of Joshua Robertshire, Northouram
     Matthew S. of John Todd, Dobb-Park
May   10th Betty D. of John Forest, Askwith
    17th Hannah D. of George Hudson, Scales, near Askwith
July   5. John S. of Francis Simpson, Weston
July   5. John S. of William Atkinson, Jun., Weston

1794

BURIED. Augt 27. Elizabeth D. of Thos Newsome, Snowden
Sept.   7. James S. of Thos Newsome, Snowden
Oct.   23. Ellen Wid: of Will: Water, Askwith
Nov.   5. John S. of Ann West, Weston
Nov.   6. Eliz. Thackwray, Newhall
Dec.   2. James S. of Will. Catton, Weston

1795

Jan.   1. Ann D. of Saml Smithson, Burley
    3. Sarah W. of Jno. England, Snowden
    26. William Catton, Otley
April   14. Elizabeth W. of John Proctor, Askwith
May   9. Lucy W. of Willm Thompson, Askwith
May   21. Stephen Moss, Snowden
June   18. John Dibb, Snowden
July   28. Elizabeth Howden, Askwith
Augst 11. George S. of Thos Newsome, Snowden
Octr 28. Margret W. of John Crook, Askwith
Nov.   5. Francis Simpson, Scales

1796

Jan.   9. Jane D. of John Dibb, Snowden
Feb.   8. Sarah D. of Thos Simpson, Scales
    24. Hannah D. of Benjn Waugh, Otley
June   2. Wm Son of Thos Newsom, Snowden
July   4th Mary Ingland, Leathley
    4th Mark Lofthouse, Asquith
Augst 7th Mary Howden, Snowden
Oc^r 14th Sarah Widow of Richard Kendall, Asquith

1797

Jany 10th Joseph Hobson of Asquith
April 28th Martha Greenwood, Asquith
May   14th Thos Ratcliffe, Asquith
June 11th Ann England, Leathley
July   3^d Sarah Ratcliffe, Asquith
July   17th Hannah Proctor, Asquith

1795

BAPTISED.   Aug. 9th John S. of Thos Simpson, Askwith
Septr   6th Betty D. of James Clay, Askwith
                John S. of Ann Moon, Askwith, Illegit:
Octr   4th Mary D. of Jno. Ratcliffe, Askwith
          25th James Son of Joseph Pickard, Snowden

1796

Jan.   17th Elizabeth D. of Thos Skirrow, Askwith
March 27th Thomas S. of Thos Young, Askwith
April   17th William Son of Wm Simpson, Scales
May   1st Thomas Hudson Son of Mary Ingland, Scales (Illegit.)
           8th Rachael Daughter of Thos Todd, Dob-park
          29th Joseph S. of Tho. Holden [Howden], Asquith
Do   John S. of Susanna Tempest, Weston, Illegit.
June   19th Henry S. of John Moss, Snowden
July   10th George S. of Abraham Holme, Asquith
          10th Mary D. of Ralph Holden, Snowden
Novr   6th Thomas S. of Wm Pawson, Asquith
      ·\13th Richard S. of Eli Burton, Asquith
Decr   4th Sarah D. of Joseph Farmer, Asquith
          18. Hannah D. Henry Thackray, Snowden

1797

Feby   26th Ann Dr of Mary Harrison, Weston, Illegit:
March   5th Thomas S. of Thomas Simpson, Askwith, Born Jany 15th
April   30th Thomas S. of Thos Duxbury, Weston, Born March 1st
May   21st Robert Son of Thos Newsom, Snowden, Born April 10th
June   4th Mary Dr of John Todd, Dog Park, Born May 5th
          18th George S. of Joseph Pickard, Snowden, Born May 14th
July   9th Ann D. of Richard Mann, Askwith, Born March 27
          23. Henry Son of John Harper of Askwith, Born June 26th
Ocr   8. Ann D. of Joseph Proctor, Dob-park, born Sepr 2
          29. Philemon Son of Joseph Land, Asquith, born Sepr 24

BURIED.   Aug: 15. Elizabeth Mawson, Bradford
Sep.   27th Elizabeth Bramley, Weston
Decr   11th John Tackwaray [Thackwray], Newhall

1798

Jany   9th Luke Overend, Weston
          16. Mary West, Weston
May   18. Thos West, Weston
June   12th Edward Elmsall Vavasour of Weston Hall, Esqr
Sepr   9th Robert Elmsley, Asquith
Ocr   7th Susan Newsome, Snowden
          15th Hannah Smith, Asquith
Novr   10th Ann Moyses, Leathley

1799

Jany   7th Ann Swyeres, Asquith
May   13th Thomas Thompson, Grass Garths
Sepr   1st Ann Smith, Asquith
Decr   17th William Waufe [Waugh], Otley
          22d John England, Snowden

1800

April   3^d Andrew Moss, Snowden

        22^d James Gill, Asquith

May   11th Joseph Standaven, Asquith

        12th Elizabeth West, Staningley

1801

March 12th Ann West, Weston

April   3^d Joseph Leeming, Asquith

May   9^d Jane Rodes, Ardington

May   30th Sarah Moon, Askwith

June   26th Charles Son of Robert Wardle, Weston

July   2^d Rachael Daughter of Wm Daniel, York

October 11th John Smith (Clark of this Parish), Asquith

1802

March 7th Sarah Booth, Bradford

April 25th Thomas Ratcliffe, Asquith

May   18th Margaret Whitehead, Windhill

June   27th Ann Simpson, Weston

1803

March 27th James Burnell, Weston

June   12th Sarah Whitaker, Snowden

December 9th Sarah Dixon, Burley

1804

Jan^y   18th Mary Bowling, Weston

April   8th Sarah Standaven, Asquith

June   3^d Elizabeth Pawson, Denton

August 1st Jonas Mann, Asquith

        23. Charles Swire, Asquith

Nov^r   10th Catharine Todd, Dob-park

        18th Elizabeth Todd, Dob-park

1805

April 26th Ann Moon, Asquith

July   19th Mary Burnell, Weston

July   24th Sarah Land, Asquith

Oct^r   10th Andrew Shires, Leeds [late of Snowden]

        30th Ann Dale, Snowden

Dec^r   29th Sarah Ratcliffe, Asquith

1806

Jan^y   26th Ellen Bolland, Dob Park

May   17th David Smith, Asquith

June   18th Elisabeth Harrison, Asquith

July   27th James Land, Asquith

July   27th John Johnson, an Infant, Weston

Septr 28th Mary Robinson, Idle

Oct^r   12th Samuel Simpson, Asquith

        19th Sarah Ratcliffe, Asquith

        31st Elizabeth Walker, Weston

Nov^r   7th Thomas Skirrow, Asquith

1807

March 11. Margaret Newsome, Snowden

1797

BAPTISED.   Novr 19th Mary D^r of Jas. Clay of Asquith, born Octr 3^d

Decr 24th James Son of George Hudson, Scales, born Novr 20th

1798

Jany 28th John Son of William Illingworth, Dob park, born Decr 20th
               1798 [sic]

Feby 18th James Son of Francis Simpson, Weston, born Jany 12th

March 11th Walter Son of Thos Dale, Snowden, born Feby 10th

April   1st James Son of John Moss, Snowden, born Feby 28th

       29th Ann D^r of Lucy Smith, Asquith, illegit: born April 4th

Sep^r   9th Ruth D^r of Thos Todd, Dob-park, born Aug^st 3^d

       30th Thomas Son of Thomas Howden, Asquith, born Sepr 5th

Octr 28.   John Son of John Ratcliffe, Asquith, born Octr 8th

Novr 11th James Son of Abraham Holmes, Asquith, born Octr 23^d

1799

March   3^d Elizabeth D^r of Joseph Pickard, Snowden, born Jany 19th

       24.   William Son of Thomas Simpson, Scales, born Jany 12th

June   2^d Joseph Son of Henry Thackwaray, Snowden, born March 26th

Sep^r   1st Hannah D^r of John Moss, Snowden, born July 21st

Sep^r   1st Hannah Daughter of John Smith, Asquith, born July 23^d

        8th John Son of Benjamin Hobson, Asquith, born Aug^st 15th

       15.   John Son of Grace Teale, illegit., Asquith, born June 30th

Octr 20th Mary Daughter of Jonas Fox, Weston, born Sepr 20th

Nov^r   3^d Elizabeth D^r of Joseph Todd, Dob-park, born 25th Sep^r

1800

Jany 19th Elizabeth Daughter of Thos Dawson, Asquith, born 8th Dec^r
               1799

       26th Elizabeth D. of Elizabeth Moss, Snowden, born Novr 25th,
               Illegit.

March 23^d Samuel Son of James Clay, Asquith, born Feby 18th

April 27th Rachael Daughter of William Daniel, York, born March 21st

June   8th John Son of Robert Procter of Snowden, born May 3^d

July   13th John Son of Thomas Skirrow, Asquith, born June 11th

       27th Sarah Daughter of John Forrest, Asquith, born July 4th

       27th Mary Daughter of Joseph Pickard, Snowden, born July 6th

August 31st John Son of John Todd, Dob-park, born July 24th

Octr 12th William Son of Thomas Young, Asquith, born Septr 18th

Octr 26th Elizabeth Daughter of John Smith, Asquith, born Sepr 28th

1807

BURIED.   April 3^d Sarah Todd, Dob-Park

       21st Ann Simpson, Scales

May   28th Ann Hemsley, Asquith

June   4th William Moss, Snowden, an infant

September 4th John Dawson Dixon, Burley

Novr 24th John Skirrow, Weston

Decr 24th Mary Simpson, Asquith

1808

Jany 26th John Ward, Weston

March   4th Mary Smithson, Burley

June   12th Joseph Procter, Dobpark

Oct^r   29th John Holmes, Asquith

1809

February 28th Sarah Dixon, Burley
April   12.   John Booth, Drighlington, late of Bradford
June   4.   John Son of Thomas Mawson, Yunger, Weston
June   26th Joseph Hardesty, Asquith
July   2^d Christopher Kendall, Asquith
        3^d Joseph Farmer, Otley
       18th John Burnell, Weston
September 17. Sarah Todd, Dobpark
        21. William Atkinson Pape, Weston
Dec^r   3^d William Standaven, Asquith
       20th Thomas Young, Asquith

1810

Jan^y   7th Esther Atkinson, Weston
March 25th Abraham Pickard, Snowden, an Infant
April   1st Isaac Pickard, Snowden, an Infant
May   6th William Todd, Askwith
May   7th Edward Dixon, Burley

1800

BAPTIZED.   Nov. 2^d James Son of Joseph Land, Asquith, born Sepr 28th
Dec^r   7th John Son of John Mountain, born Nov. 1st

1801

Jany 25.   Sarah D^r of Thos Simpson, Asquith, born Decr 25th 1800
Feb^y   8th Elizabeth Daughter of Joseph Proctor, Dob park, born
             Decr 27th 1800
       15th Charles Son of Robert Wardle, Weston, born Jany 6th 1801
March   8th William Son of Eli Burton, Asquith, born Feby 10th
May   24.   James Son of Thomas Howden, Asquith, born 1st Inst
       31st Nancy Daughter of William Swaine, Asquith, born 1st Inst
June   14.   Thomas Son of John Ratcliffe of Asquith, born 15th of May
       21st John Son of Thomas England, Addingham, born May 25th
August 23^d Elizabeth D. of John Bolton, Asquith, born July 18th
Sep^r   6th James Son of Christopher Hardesty, Asquith, born May 31st
       20th Lucy Daughter of Wm Thompson, Asquith, born Augst 23^d
       25.   Elizabeth Daughter of Benjⁿ Hobson, Asquith, born Octo^r
             [sic] 4th

1802

Jan^y   3^d Mary Daughter of Robt Proctor, Snowden, born Octo^r 5
       31st Wilfred Skirrow Son of Thomas Dawson, born Decr 1st 1801
Feb^y   7th George Son of William Todd, Asquith, Jany 5th 1802
March   7th John Son of Joseph Todd, Dob-park, born Feby 6th
April 18th Hannah Daughter of John Mountain, Grass Garth, born
             26 Mar.
       25th Ann Daughter of James Clay, Otley, born March 28th
May   2^d Ann Daughter of Joseph Ward, Weston, born April 7th
July   6.   Mary Ann [Daughter of Robert] Wardle, Weston, born
             June 17th
July   6th Samuel [Son of John] Burnell, Clifton, born June 8th
       18th Agnes Daughter of Christ^r Mann, Asquith, born June 9th

[BAPTIZED.]   [July] 25. John Son of Thomas Lambert, Asquith, born
June 30th

August 29th John Son of James Land, Asquith, born Aug[st] 5th

Sept[r] 19th Elizabeth Daughter of Jonas Fox, Weston, born Aug[st] 29th
  26. John Son of Joseph Pickard, Snowden, born Aug[st] 20th

Oct[r] 17th Hannah Daughter of William Illingworth, Dob-park, born
28th Aug[st]

Nov[r] 7th Sally Daughter of Joseph Proctor, Dob-Park, born Oct[r] 12th
  14. Joseph Son of Thomas Simpson, Asquith, born Oct[r] 16th

1803

March 6th Rebekah Daughter of John Smith, Asquith, born Feb[y] 9th

April 10th Joseph Son of Christopher Hardesty, Asquith, born Feb[y] 8th

July 10th John Son of George Petty, Asquith, born June 1st
  10th Hannah Daughter of Abraham Holmes, Asquith, born April 13th
  31st Thomas Proctor Son of Elizabeth Johnson, Weston, Illegit.,
born July 17th

August 14th William Son of John Mountain, Grass Garths, born July 15th

September 18th Rachael Daughter of W[m] Hudson, Asquith, born Aug[st] 19th

Oct[r] 16th Joseph Son of Susanna Newsom, Snowden, Illegit., born Sep[r] 1st

Nov[r] 8th James Son of Sarah Newsom, Snowden, Illegit., Oct[r] 1st
  6th Robert Son of Christ[r] Paley, Snowden, born Nov. 12th 1802

Dec[r] 25th Robert Son of Robert Proctor, Snowden, born Nov[r] 22[d]

1804

January 1st Ann Daughter of John Todd, Dob-park, born Nov. 28th 1803
  8th William Son of Thomas Howden, Asquith, born Dec[r] 8, 1803
  15. Lydia Daughter of Thomas Dawson, Asquith, born Nov. 25th
1803

Feb[y] 19th Jonas Son of Christ[r] Mann, Asquith, born Jan[y] 10th

March 4. James Son of James Clay, Otley, born Jan[y] 31st

April 1st Joseph Son of Joseph Pickard, Snowden, born Feb[y] 28th
  8th Hannah Daughter of Benjamin Hobson, Asquith, born March 7th
  22[d] Catherine daughter of Joseph Todd, Dob-park, born March 18th

July 8th Joseph Son of Joseph Proctor, Dob-park, born April 13th

August 5th James Son of James Land, Asquith, born July 10th

Oct[r] 7th Enos Son of Martha Farrer, illegit[e], Asquith, born Sep[t] 1st

Oct[r] 21st Joseph Son of Francis Simpson, Weston, born Sep[t] 26th

Nov[r] 25th Francis Son of Thomas Simpson, Asquith, born Oct[r] 20

Dec[r] 9th John Son of John Smith, Asquith, born Nov[r] 8th
  23rd Joseph Son of John Mountain, Grass Garths, born Nov[r] 20th
  23rd William Son of William Thompson, Asquith, born Nov. 12th

1805

May 26. Samuel Son of John Moss, Dobb park, born April 11

June 30th Sarah D[r] of John Ratcliffe, Asquith, born June 1st

July 7th William Son of Robert Wardle, Weston, born May 2[d]
  7th Mary Daughter of John Burnell, Clifton, born June 8th
  14. Hellin Daughter of George & Mary Petty, Seacroft, b. June 1.

Oct[r] 27th John Son of Christopher Mann, Asquith, born Sep[r] 26th

Nov[r] 3[d] Thomas Son of Thomas Lambert, Asquith, born Oct[r] 8th
  3. Sally Daughter of John Todd, Dob park, born Oct[r] 3[d]
  10. Joseph Son of Joseph Todd, Dob park, born Oct[r] 9th

1806

[BAPTIZED.] Jany 26th Thomas Son of William Fieldhouse, Asquith, born Decr 5th 1805

Feb^y   2^d Robert Son of Thomas Dawson, Asquith, born Decr 24th 1805
            2^d William Son of Samuel Moss, Snowden, born Decr 31st 1805
            2^d Ann Daughter of Robert Procter, Snowden, born Decr 23^d 1805

March   2^d John Son of James Clay, Otley, born Feby. 1st 1806
            9th Robert Son of William Parker, Asquith, born Feby 3^d 1806
            16th Eliza Daughter of John Skirrow, Weston, born Feby 2^d
            16th Ann Daughter of James England, Esholt, born Jany 31st
May   4th Robert Son of Jonas Fox, Weston, born April 4th
June   15th John Son of John Dibb, Snowden, born May 25th
            15th Joshua Son of Christopher Hardesty, Asquith, born April 2^d
            15th Sarah Daughter of James Land, Asquith, born May 10th
July   6th James Son of Joseph Procter, Dob Park, born May 1st
July   20th John Son of Joseph Ward, Weston, born June 16th
Oct^r   19th Sarah Daughter of John Ratcliffe, Asquith, born Octr 5th

1807

Jan^y   7th Hannah Daughter of Joseph Pickard, Snowden, born Nov. 22
January 25. Sarah Daughter of Thomas & Esther Kendall, Askwith, Born January 3rd
July   12th Joshua Son of Thomas Holden, Asquith, born June 18th
Sep^r   6th David Son of John & Sarah Todd, Dobpark, Born August 15th
Nov^r   8.   William Atkinson Son of Joseph Pape, Weston, Born August 18
Nov^r   8.   Elizabeth Daughter of Christopher Mann, Askwith, Born Septr 27

1808

Jany 24. Andrew Son of Robert Proctor, Snowdon, born Novr 29th 1808 [sic]
Feb^y   7th Mary Daughter of Susannah Newsome, Scales, illegit^e, born Jany 7th
May   8th Amos Son of William Smith, Asquith, born Jany 23^d
May   8th Joseph Son of William Parker, Asquith, born April 5th
June   12. Joseph Son of James and Elizabeth Land, Askwith, Born May 4th
July   10th Rachael D^r of Thos Dawson, Asquith, born April 14th
            31st Joseph Son of Joseph Ward, Weston, born July 5th
            31st Sarah Daughter of John Moss, Dob-Park, born June 9th
August 21. Mary Daughter of Elizabeth Gill, Weston, Born August 2
Sep^r   11th James Son of John Dibb, Asquith, born Aug. 17th
Oct^r   2^d Hannah Daughter of Joseph Proctor, Dob-park, born Sepr 2^d
            16th Sarah Daughter of Thomas Acomb, Asquith, born Sepr 14th
            23^d Ann Daughter of John Mountain, Grass Garths, born Sepr 26th
Nov^r   6th Sarah Daughter of Christopher Hardesty, Asquith, born Octr 21st
            27th Ann Daughter of Joseph Pickard, Snowden, born Octr 19th

1809

Jan^y   15th Thomas Son of John Ratcliffe, Asquith, born Decr 16th 1808
Feb^y   12th Daniel Son of Joseph Todd, Dob-park, born Jany 18th
February 26. John Son of James Moss, Snowden, born Jany 24

[BAPTIZED.] March 19th John Son of Thomas Smith, Asquith, born Feb. 14th

          19th William Son of Stephen Hudson, Weston, born Feby 23^d

July   23^d John Son of Samuel Moss, Snowden, born June 18th

          30th Joseph Son of Robert Proctor, Snowden, born May 17th

Sep^t   10th Susanna Daughter of Joseph Pape, Weston, born June 29th

          10th William Son of Thomas Kendall, Snowden, born Augst 9th

Oct^r   22^d Mary Daughter of Thos Hudson, Asquith, born Sep. 27th

October 29. Sarah Daughter of Christopher Mann, Asquith, born Sep^t 19

Nov^r   28th Thomas Holmes, Adult

Dec^r   24th William Son of Thomas Lambert, Asquith, born Novr 27th

1810

May   27th John Son of Francis Simpson, Junr, Weston, born May 4th

July   22^d Mary Ann Daughter of Joseph Procter, Dob-park, born June 30th

September 16. Mary Daughter of William Smith, Askwith, Born August 15

Oct^r   7th Hannah Daughter of Joseph Ward, Weston, Born Augst 29th

          28th Nancy Daughter of John Dibb, Asquith, born Octr 10

1811

March 17th Betty Daughter of Robert Proctor, Snowden, born Feby 21st

April   28th Maria Daughter of Jane Dibb, Asquith, Illeg., born April 7th

July   7th Rebekah Daughter of Thomas Acomb, Asquith, born May 20th

          14. Mary Daughter of Thomas Dawson of Asquith, born June 3^d

1810

BURIED. July 29. James Pawson, Denton

Nov^r   3^d George Kendall, Asquith

         3^d William Moss, Snowden

Dec^r   1st Thomas Dawson, Asquith

1811

Feb^y   3^d James Harrison, Asquith

April   15th Ann England, Snowden, an Infant

         19th John Newsome Luty, Snowden

         28th Hannah England, Snowden

May   12th Alice Blakey, Asquith

July   30th Mary Moss, Snowden

Oct^r   31. Susan Greenwood, Otley

1812

Jan^y   15th Nancy Dibb, Asquith

April   14th Joseph [son of Joseph] Ward, Weston

May   5th John [son of Christopher] Mann, Asquith

June   18th Elizabeth Robinson, Asquith

August 2. Joseph Kendell, Asquith

September 12. John Swire, Askwith

October 3^d James [son of John] Atkinson, Newall, aged 22 years

Novemb. 23. Mary Cockshott, Snowden, aged 80 years

Decemb^r 22. Mary Gill, Askwith, aged 66 years

1811

BAPTISMS. Augst 4th Grace Daughter of John Ratcliffe, Asquith, born July 14th

          11th Mary Daughter of James Moss, Snowden, born July 20th

Oct^r   27th James Son of James Land, Asquith, born Sep^t 26th

Novr 24th James Son of Joseph Todd, Dob-park, born Octr 5th
Decr 21st Elizabeth Daughter of Joseph Pape, Weston, Augst 31st
     21st Ann Daughter of Francis Simpson, Asquith, born Sept. 24th
     29.   Harriot Daughter of John Kirkby, Weston, Born January 14th

1812

Jany 12th Martha Daughter of Christ^r Hardesty, Asquith, born Decr 12th
Feby 2^d Maria Daughter of Christopher Mann, Asquith, born Augst 31st
1811
Feby 16th James Son of William Dibb, Snowden, Dee^r 22^d 1811
     23^d William Son of Joseph Pickard, Snowden, born Jany 10th
April   12th Mary Daughter of Betty Forrest, Asquith, illegit., born Feby 25th
May   3^d Rachel Daughter of Saml Moss, Snowden, born April 3^d
July   12th Mary Daughter of Thomas Kendall, Snowden, born June 22^d
     12th Sarah Daughter of Michael Wilson, Asquith, born June 19th
August 23rd Joseph Son of Joseph Proctor of Dob or Dog Park, born July 25
     30th James Son of John Harrison of Askwith, born July 28th
September 20th Ann Daughter of Mary Simpson of Weston, illegitimate, born 22nd August
October 18th Sarah Daughter of William Parker of Weston, born 29th August
December 6th Hannah Daughter of Thomas Lambert of Weston, born 6th Nov^r
     27.   William Son of John Bowling of Askwith, born October 17th

Memorandum.—I hereby certify that I did induct the Reverend William Carter into the real actual and corporal possession of the Vicarage of Weston on Saturday, the third day of October 1829.—John Horsfall. Witnesses, Wm Horsfall, Thos Lancaster.

[BOOK IV.]

Banns of Marriage between Thos Grunwell, Husbandman, & Mary Cryer, Spinster, both of this parish, were publish'd the 5, 12 & 19 of September by me R^d Haighton.

> Thos Grunwell, Husbandman, and Mary Cryer, both of this Parish, were Married in this Church by virtue of Banns this twentieth Day of September in the Year One Thousand Seven Hundred and fifty six by me R^d Haighton.
>
> This Marriage was solemnized between Us { Thomas Grunnill [sic]. / Mary Cryer.
>
> In the presence of Robt Kendall,
>   Richard Sowden.

[The subsequent entries are given in an abbreviated form. Unless otherwise stated, the parties are "both of this Parish" and the marriage is "by Banns."
From here to the 13th August, 1764, the officiating minister is the Rev. Richard Haighton, the Vicar.]

1756. Novr 29th. John Hartley, Milner, of the Parish of Leathley and Mary Atkinson of this Parish, Spinster. Witnesses, Wm Atkinson, Willm Thackwray.

1757. Jany 17th. Samuel Parrot, Husbandman, & Sarah Fairbank, Spinster. [No witnesses.]

June 6th. Robert Holliday of Baildon in the parish of Otley, Labourer, and Anne Watmoth of this Parish, Widdow. Wits., George Mawson, Thomas Langran.

Septr 4th. William Blacow, Husbandman, & Allice Askwith, Spinster. Wits., Joseph Holdsworth, William Thackwray.

Novr 21st. William Harrison, Husbandman, & Jane Reynard, Spinster. Wits., John Simpson, William Thackwray.

1758. 6 June. Jonathan Fairbank of Burley in the Par. of Otley, Worset Weaver, and Mary Moon of this Par., Spinster. Wits., Samuel Parrat, Abraham Moon.

29 July. Thomas Preston of the Par. of Gargrave, Batchelor, and Sarah Ward, Spinster, of this Par. Lycence. Wits., Willm Wetherill, William Oldfield.

1760. [sic] 7th Sept. Joab Hobson of the Par. of Fewstone, Carpenter, and Alice Pickard of this Par., Spinster. Wits., Wm Heclas, Joshua Hobson.

1758. 11th Dec. Wm Candler Esq. & Batchelor and Mary Vavasour, Spinster. Licence. Wits., Walter Vavasour, John Ward, Sarah Clough.

1759. 6th August. William Dibb, Schoolmaster & Batchelor, and Mary Mawd, Spinster. Wits., Geo. Mawson, Wm Thackwray.

24th Nov. John Rhodes of the Par. of Fewston, Husbandman, and Elizabeth Newsom of this Par., Spinster. Wits., Henry Robinson, William Thackwray.

17th Dec. Charles Swire, Husbandman, & Anne Clark, Spinster. Wits., George Mawson, William Thackwray, Wilfrid Skirrow.

1760. 2nd June. Christopher Holmes of Denton in the Par. of Otley, Husbandman, and Mary Brogden of this Par., Spinster. Wits., Christ^r Marshall, William Wetherill.

11th July. Joseph Thackwray of Otley Par., Blacksmith, and Anne Sowden of this Par., Spinster. Wits., Richard Sowden, William Sowden.

13th Oct. John Fallis, Husbandman, and Anne Hornby, Widow. Licence. Wits., Geo. Mawson, Wm Thackwray.

1761. 21st Jan. Richd Knapton of the Par. of Harwood, Husbandman, & Anne Proctor of this Par., Spinster. Wits., George Mawson, Andrew Prockter.

28th May. John Smith and Anne Leeming, by Lycence. Wits., Chris. Kendall, William Thackwra.

31st August. Thos Cryer, Milner, of this Par., and Elizabeth Taylor, Spinster, of Denton in the Par. of Otley. Wits., Wm Lofthouse, William Thackwray.

17th Nov. William Lofthouse and Mary Grunnel, Widdow. Wits., William Thackwray, George Cryer.

1762. 13th Jan. John Harrison of Askwith, Labourer, of this Par., and Anne Bean, Denter [sic], of the Par. of Otley. Licence. Wits., Sam. Bingley, Wm Oldfield.

14th June. Willm Atkinson, Husbandman, and Susanna Smithson, Spinster. Wits., Henry Robinson, John Burnell.

23rd August. Joseph Hardcastle of the Par. of Guiseley, Worset Weaver, and Sarah Sowden of this Par. Wits., Christopher Hardcastle, William Hardcastle.

20th Sept. William Catton of this Par., Labourer, and Anne Smith of the Par. of Guiseley. Wits., Edward Raimes, Thomas Dixon.

19th Nov. Wilfrid Skirrow, Farmer, and Lydia Holmes, Spinsr. Lycence. Wits., Mary Dixon, Richard Sowden.

1763. 15th Feb. Thomas Rilay, Linen Weavr, and Mary Barret. Wits., William Thackwray, John Procter.

5th April. John Suttell of the Par. of Addle, Malster, and Anne West of this Par. Wits., Tho: Gill, Thomas West.

18th April. Joseph Jackson of the Par. of Fewston, Worset Weaver, and Margret Askwith of this Par. Wits., John Jackson, John Wade.

18th July. Andrew Proctor and Frances Illingworth. Wits., Thomas Thackra, William Thackwray.

26th August. William Moss of Snowden, Husbandman, and Sarah Thackwray. [No witnesses, but in the following entry the names of Stephen Moss & Thomas Thackray appear, but are crossed out.]

1764. 19th January. James Jackson and Jane Greenbank, by Lycence. Witness, Edward Raimes.

13th August. Joseph Leeming, Shoemaker, and Elizabeth Walter. Wits., John Smith, William Thackwray.

1765. 21st Nov. Andrew Shires of the Par. of Weston and Ann Tenant of the Par. of Ripon (Licence), by Wm. Fryer, Curate of Leathley. Wits., Robert Bridbery, John Burnell.

1766. 3rd Feb. Joseph Hobson, Husbandman, and Rachel Taylor, by Geo. Benson, Curate of Ilkley. Wits., John Ryley, William Thackwray.

3rd Feb. Joseph Pickard, Husbandman, and Ann Hunter, Spinster, by G: Benson, Curate of Ilkley, Wits,, Thomas Dale, Joseph Farmer.

1st Sept. John Walker of the Par. of Otley, Batchelor, and Susannah
Beecroft of this Par., Spinster (Licence), by John Whinnerah, Vic^r of
Fewston. Wits., William Sowden, John Skirrow.

8th Dec. Jonathan Bramley & Elizabeth Garth, by Wm. Fryer, Curate of
Leathley. Wits., Thomas Steel, Willm Garth.

1767. 5th Jan. George England, Widower, and Elizabeth Walker, Spinster, by Wm. Fryer, Assistant Curate. Wits., Joshua Hardisty, William
Thackwray.

23 Jan. Joseph Cunliffe of the Par. of Ilkley, Shopkeeper, and Grace
Dixon of Weston, Spinster (Licence), by G. Benson, Curate of Denton.
Wits., Willm Robinson, William Thackwray.

26th Jan. William Sowden of Askwith in the Par. of Weston, Woolcomber,
and Ann Holmes of the same par. & Town (Licence), by G. Benson, Curate of Denton. Wits., Richard Sowden, Henry Bolton.

16th June. William Whittaker, Farmer, and Jane Newsan, by Licence
w^h consent of Parents, by Wm. Fryer, Curate of Leathley. Wits., W^m
Walker, Edward Raimes.

27th October. Joseph Pickard, Carpenter, and Mary England (w^h consent
of Parents), by Wm. Fryer, Curate of Leathley. Wits., Wm Walker,
Edward Raimes.

20th Nov. Jonas Mann and Agnes Kidson, by Wm. Fryer, Curate of Leathley. Wits., John Burnell, George Mawson.

1768. 23^d Feb. William Gott, Wool Comber, and Anne Andrew, Spinster
(Licence), by Ed. Beeston, Vie^r of Ilkley. Wits., Edmund Greenwood,
Richd Kendall.

1st March. Joseph Holmes, Wool Comber, and Magdalen Greenwood,
Spinster (Licence), by J. Ellinthorp, Curate of Otley. Wits., Edmund
Greenwood, William Gott.

15th March. George Whittaker, Husbandman, and Sarah Hobson, Spinster, by Wm. Fryer, Curate of Leathley. Wits., Thomas Whittacker,
George Dixon.

1769. 30th November. Richard Smithson of the Par. of Addle and
Margaret Illingworth of this Par., Spinster, by J. Ellinthorp, Vicar.
Wits., Joseph Johnson, John Atkinson.

1770. 18th June. Joseph Johnson & Ann Arbuthnot, Spinster, by J.
Ellinthorp, Vicar. Wits., John Aked, Edward Raimes.

12th August. Thomas Pawson and Elizabeth Sowden, Spinster (Licence),
by J. Ellinthorp, Vicar. Wits., John Burnell, Chris: Kendall.

11th Nov. James Burnell & Mary Brown, Spinster, by J. Ellinthorp, Vicar.
Wits., Edwd Dixon, Thos Mawson.

19th Nov. William Teal & Isabella Thackray, Spinster, by J. Ellinthorp,
Vicar. Wits., William Thompson, Abraham Moon.

28th Nov. James Bradley & Tabatha Leeming, Spinster, by J. Ellinthorp,
Vicar. Wits., Chris: Kendall, John Smith.

1771. 23rd May. Richard Barrit and Martha Newsome, Spinster, by J.
Ellinthorp, Vicar. Wits., Richard Kendall, Isaac Bolton.

1st September. George Hey of the Par. of Otley & Ann Pickard of this
Par., Spinster, by J. Ellinthorp, Vicar. Wits., William Thackwray,
Michael Wilson.

1773. 24th Feb. John Butterfield & Elisabeth Moss (Licence), by Jas. Bailey, Minister. Wits., William Tidswell, William Thackwray.

19 Nov. Mark Lofthouse and Sarah Water (Licence), by Ja^s Bailey, Minister. Wits., Joseph Leemin, John Watter.

1774. 5th Jan. William England & Elisabeth England, by Ja^s Bailey, Minister. Wits., George Dixon, Thomas Mawson.

21st Feb. John Ward of ye Par. of Fewston and Ann Thackeray of ye Par. of Weston, by Ja^s Bailey, Min^r. Wits., William Dibb, Ja^s Bailey.

28th March. James Shaw of Denton in ye Par. of Otley and Sarah Farmer of Asquith of the Par. of Weston (Licence), by James Bailey, Minister. Wits., George Dixon, Thomas Mawson.

3rd May. William Dale & Hannah Hudson, by Ja^s Bailey, Minister. Wits., Edward Dixon, Thomas Mawson.

27th May. William Thompson of the Par. of Asquith in the Par. of Weston and Lucy Leeman of the Par. of Weston afores^d (Licence), by Ja^s Bailey, Minister. Wits., John Smith, Joseph Leemin.

31st Oct. Thomas Todd & Mary Jennings, Spinster, by Ja^s Hartley, Curate of Otley. Wits., Henry Small, William Thackwray.

12th Dec. Michael Wilson of the Par. of Otley and Mary Simpson of the Par. of Weston, by Ja^s Bailey, Minister. Wits., John Dixon, Richard Taylor.

1775. 3rd Jan. John Sowden & Hannah Thompson, by Ja^s Bailey, Min^r. Wits., Walter Sowden, Thomas Thompson.

1st August. Thomas Hudson & Isabella Whitaker, by James Bailey, Minister. Wits., George Dixon, Thomas Mawson.

1776. 20 Feb. James Pullen of the Par. of Otley and Alice Brown of Par. of Weston, by James Bailey, Minister. Wits., John Skirrow, William Taylor.

1st Sept. Thomas Robinson and Ann Bland, by James Bailey. Wits., Edmund Greenwood, George Dixon.

1777. 31st March. George Hudson & Sarah Moon, by James Bailey, Junr. Wits., Thomas Kendall, Abraham Moon.

19th May. John Verity of ye Par. of Hampsthwaite and Mary Moon of ye Par. of Weston, by Ja^s Bailey, Junr. Wits., Willm Taylor, George Maltas.

23rd June. Samuel Smithson of ye Par. of Weston, yeoman, and Mary Oldfield of the Par. of Otley, Spinster (Licence), by James Bailey, Junr. Wits., Thomas Mawson, Nathl Aked.

8th Oct. John Smith, Husbandman, and Hannah Riley, Spinster, by J. Bailey, Curate of Otley. Wits., Richard Smith, Abraham Watter, James Smith.

1778. 20th Jan. Thos Kendall, Cordwainer, and Mary Leah, Spinster (Licence), by J. Bailey, Curate of Otley. Wits., Thos Whitley, Thomas Kendall.

2nd Feb. Henry Thackray and Hannah Todd, Spinster, by J. Bailey, Curate. Wits., William Moss, Stephen Moss.

10th March. George Dixon of the Par. of Weston and Sarah Oldfield of the Par. of Otley (Licence), by Ja^s Bailey, Minister. Wits., Wilfred Skirrow, William Taylor.

30th July. William Taylor & Susannah Chapman, by James Bailey, Mm^r. Wits., William Atkinson, Wm Craven.

26th Oct. Samuel Howgate of ye Par. of Calverley & Mary Sowden of this Par., Spinster, by J. Bailey, Curate of Otley. Wits., John Sowden, Jons Kendall.

19th Nov. William Buckden, Blacksmith, & Elisabeth Bean, Spinster, by J. Bailey, Curate of Otley. Wits., Edm Greenwood, Thos Kendall.

1779. 2nd Feb. John Green of Haverah Park, an extra parochial Place, and Hannah Rowlinson of the Par. of Weston, Spinster, by J. Bailey, Junr. Wits., John Taylor, Willm Thackwray.

30th March. Thos Gill, Miller, & Mary Clayton, Spinster, by J. Bailey, Junr. Wits., Willm Taylor, Chris: Kendall.

20th May. Thomas Dale, Farmer, and Ann Hobson, Spinster, by James Bailey, Junr. Wits., William Hobson, William Thackwray.

3rd August. William Hodgson of the Par. of Otley, Tallow-Chandler, and Jane Dibb of the Par. of Weston, Spinster, by James Bailey, Junr. Wits., William Dibb, John Crooke.

1780. 4th May. Francis Standeven, Mason, and Sarah Jennings, Spinster, by J. Bailey, Junr. Wits., William Taylor, Jos Kendall.

14th May. John Crooke, Cordwainer, & Margaret Farmer, Spinster, by J. Bailey, Junr. Wits., Wm Hodgson, John Farmer.

15th May. Francis Simpson, Labourer, & Mary West, Spinster, by J. Bailey, Junr. Wits., Willm Taylor, Wm Craven.

7th August. Edward Morrel of the Par. of Otley, Husbandman, and Elizabeth Nichols of the Par. of Weston, Widow, by J. Bailey, Junr. Wits., Richard Walker, William Thackwray.

2nd Oct. William Kitchin of the Par. of Calverley and Ellin Sowdin of the Par. of Weston, Spinster, by Jas Bailey, Senr, Minister. Wits., John Sowden, Richard Windsor.

1781. 9th Jany. George Teal, Husbandman, and Hannah Bland, Spinster, by J. Bailey, Junr. Wits., William Taylor, James Holmes.

16th April. William Medcalfe of the Par. of Otley and Mary Ratcliffe of this Par., by J. Bailey, Junr. Wits., James Young, Thomas Ratcliff.

4th June. John Walker of the Par. of Bradford and Rachael Oldfield of this Par., by Jas Bailey, officiating Minister. Wits., Alexr Glendinning, William Thackwray.

12th June. Stephen Moss & Sarah Thrush, Spinster (Licence), by J. Bailey, Curate. Wits., John Dobson, Wm Thackwray.

13th August. Joseph England, Carpenter, & Mary Teale, Spinster (Licence), by J. Bailey, Junr. Wits., Bryan Moorhouse, Thos Kendall.

1782. 23rd Nov. John Baldwin of the Par. of Fewston, Husbandman, and Barbara Pickard of this Par., Spinster (Licence), by Jas Bailey, Junr. Wits., George Teal, John Smith.

17th Dec. William Barrett, Mason, & Mary Stele, Spinster, by J. Bailey, Junr. Wits., John Skirrow, John Smith.

1784. 2nd August. Eli Burton, Farmer, & Hannah Holmes, Spinster, by J. Bailey, Junr. Wits., Richard Holmes, Ann Morley.

5th August. Thomas Mawson of the Par. of Hampsthwaite and Ann Harrison of this Par., Widow, by J. Bailey, Junr. Wits., Chrisr Kendall, John Smith.

Feby 18th 1785. Recd the Duty thus far. Wm Maude, Junr Deputy Collector.

1785. 21st Nov. Thomas Todd & Sarah Teal, Spinster, by James Bailey, Minr. Wits., John Grunwell, William Henson.

1786. 28th Feb. William Bowling, Husbandman, & Mary Barret, Spinster, by Jas Bailey, Minister. Wits., Thos Kendall, Ann Langwith.

4th Sept. John Mountain & Mary Holmes, by Jas Bailey, Minister. Wits., Joseph Mountain, Mary Mountain.

14th Nov. William Illingworth, Farmer, & Sarah Todd, Spinster, by Jas Bailey, Ministr. Wits., Sarah Armitage, John Smith.

1787. 1st Feb. Thomas Young of this Par., Farmer, and Anne Moss of the Par. of Otley, Spinster, by Jas Bailey, Ministr. Wits., James Young, Mary Young.

13th Feb. William Henson, Taylor, & Anne Petty, Spinster, by Jas Bailey, Ministr. Wits., Thomas Todd, Sarah Todd.

20th August. John Holding of the Par. of Fewston, Husbandman, and Hannah England of this Par., Spinster, by W. Bawdwen, Curate. Wits., Francis Standeaven, S . . . . England.

24th Sept. William Mawson of the Par. of Otley, Blacksmith, and Elizabeth Mawson of this Par., Spinster, by Jas Bailey, Minr. Wits., Thos Mawson, Thomas Dunburn [?].

26th Dec. Thomas Tewksberry [*signed* Duxberry] and Mary Harrison, Spinster, by Jas Bailey, Ministr. Wits., John Skirrow, William Curtiss.

1788. 18th Jan. Thomas Newsome, Yeoman, & Mary Leuty, Spinster, by Jas. Bailey, Ministr. Wits., John Atkinson, William Harrison.

14th April. Joseph Land, Farmer, & Mary Young, Spinster, by Jas Bailey, Ministr. Wits., Philemon Land, Wm Chadwick.

19th May. Thomas Skirrow, Farmer, & Ruth Land, Spinster, by Jas Bailey, Ministr. Wits., Lydia Skirrow, Philemon Land.

5th Nov. Thomas Simpson of this Par. & Elizabeth Suttill of the Par. of Addle, by Jas Bailey, Minr. Wits., William Wyatt, John Stead.

1789. 12 Jan. Thomas Robinson, Husbandman, & Esther Horsman, Spinster, by Jas Bailey, Minister. Wits., John Walter, Joseph Leeming.

20th April. William Todd, Husbandman, & Hannah Teal, Spinster, by Jas Bailey, Ministr. Wits., John Grunwell, John Smith.

18th June. John Gill, Husbandman, & Anne Holmes, Single-woman. Wits., Marey Mountain, John Mountain.

23rd August. Thomas Howden, Linen Weaver, & Mary Robinson, Spinster, by Jas Bailey, Ministr. Wits., Sarah Robinson, John Swire.

30th Nov. Benjamin Waugh of the Par. of Otley, Ostler, and Mary Procter of this Par., Spinster, by Wm Anderton, Curate. Wits., Robert Procter, John Smith.

1790. 28th June. William Skirrow, Grazier, and Mary Burnhill, Spinster, by Jas Bailey, offg Minr. Wits., Sam: Smithson, Wilham Atkinson.

5th Oct. Thomas Wilkinson of the Par. of Otley, Farmer, and Ann Robinson of this Par., Spinster, by Wm Anderton, Curate. Wits., Edmund Greenwood, Joseph Stubbs.

13th Dec. William Simpson of this Par. & Anne Heathfield of the Par. of Otley, by Jas Bailey, officiatg Minr. Wits., Robt Taylor, John Smith.

29th Dec. Christopher Mann, Bachelor, & Ledia Skirrow, Spinster, by W. Webstr[?], ofst Minr. Wits., John D. Cunliffe, Wm Pawson, Joseph Holmes.

1791. 1st Jan. William Daniel of Par. St. Michael's, Spurriergate, York, and Jane Burnell of this Par., Spinster, by Jas Bailey, officiatg Minister. Wits., Wm Skirrow, Robert Wardle.

7th April. John Burnell, Farmer, & Sarah Dibb, Spinster (Licence), by Wm Anderton, Curate. Wits., Willm Atkinson, Willm Dibb, Junr.

23rd May. William Atkinson, Tradesman, & Jane Burnell, Spinster, by Wm Anderton, Curate. Wits., John Burnell, Henry Atkinson.

25th Dec. Joseph Ward, Husbandman, and Hannah Thompson, Spinster, by Wm Anderton, Curate. Wits., John Ratcliffe, Richard Kendall.

1792. 20th Nov. John Swiers, Husbandman, & Sarah Robinson, Spinster, by William Anderton. Wits., Eli Burton, William Standeaven.

31st Dec. John Ratcliffe, Husbandman, & Sarah England, Spinster, by Wm Anderton, Curate. Wits., John Dibb, John Smith.

1794. 24th Feb. William Pawson of the Par. of Otley, and Anne Robinson of this Par., by Thos Rye, Cur. Wits., John Crooke, Rachel Skirrow.

2nd June. David Smith of the Par. of Otley and Hannah Teale of this Par., by T. Rye, Cur. Wits., John Mountain, Christr Mann, Lydia Mann, Rachel Holmes.

9th June. Joseph Farmer of the par. of Otley & Mercy Land of this par., by Chris: Atkinson, officg Minr. Wits., Rachel Skirrow, Edward Smith.

5th August. Thomas Dawson of the Par. of Ilkley and Rachel Skirrow of this par. (Licence), by Jas Bailey, officg Min. Wits., Elizth Skirrow, John Tiplady.

25th August. Hugh Gardome of the Par. of Otley and Nancy Dibb of this Par., by Thos Rye, Cur. Wits., James Kendall, Geo. Blackburn.

1795. 23rd Feb. John Skirrow & Susanna Atkinson (Licence), by Thos Rye, Cur. Wits., John Atkinson, Samuel Atkinson.

3rd August. Joseph Procter & Hannah Whitaker, by Thos Rye, Cur. Wits., Robt Proctor, Mary England.

23rd Dec. Joseph Thornton of the Par. of Otley and Mary Gill of this Par., by Thos Rye, Cur. Wits., William Catton, Thos Wilkinson.

1796. 5th Jany. Jonathan Wilson of the Par. of Hampsthwaite and Margaret Blakey of this Par., by Thos Rye, Cur. Wits., Wm Randerson, William Thompson.

11th Dec. James Whitwham of the par. of Fewston and Ann Dibb of this par. (Licence), by Thos F. Wilson, A.B., Curate. Wits., Stephen Moss, John Smith.

[From here to May, 1812, the marriages are by Thos. F. Wilson, unless otherwise stated.]

1797. 22nd Feb. Samuel Oxley of the par. of Leeds and Ann Andcliffe of this Par. (Licence). Wits., John Shaw, Marmade Forster, Junr, Jno Dawson.

30th Oct. Thos Harper of the Par. of Otley and Mary Hardesty of this Par. Wits., Marmaduke Broadwith, John Smith.

1798. 20th Feb. John Smith and Sarah Ingland. Wits., Joseph Kendall, William Ingland.

10th Oct. John Holmes of the Par. of Guiseley and Mary Proctor of this Par. Wits., John Smith, Jane Thompson.

25th Dec. Benjamin Hobson and Elizabeth Todd. Wits., John Forrest, Joseph Land.

1799. 16th June. Robert Proctor and Ann Rowlinson (Licence). Wits., Wm Burnitt, John Smith.

30th Sept. George Stead of the Par. of Otley and Grace Overin. Wits., James Stead, Ann Stead.

1800. 10th April. John Forrest and Sarah Land (Licence). Wits., Joseph Land, John Smith.

28th Nov. William Thompson & Sarah Kendall. Wits., Wm Kendall, Thomas Kendall.

1801. 30th March. Christopher Hardesty & Grace Teale. Wits., Thos Skirrow, James Robinson.

6th April. Thomas England of the Par. of Addingham and Elizabeth Thackwray of this Par. Wits., Nathaniel Winn, John Smith.

4th August. Thomas Lambert & Lucy Smith, by Thos Hamilton, Curate of Guiseley. Wits., Jonas Fox, John Smith.

20th Nov. John Bowers & Elizabeth Standhaven. Wits., Thos Kendall, William Swain, Parish Clerk.

1802. 2nd March. William Standeaven and Ann Moon (Licence). Wits., William Swain, Parish Clerk, Joseph Thornton.

13th September. George Petty & Mary Hudson. Wits., Thos Freeman, Edmund Greenwood, Parish Clerk.

5th Oct. James Darnbrough and Mary Standhaven. Wits., Sarah Swires, Edmund Greenwood, Parish Clerk.

1803. 28th Feb. William Hudson & Mary Thompson. Wits., James Robinson, Thomas Hudson, Edmund Greenwood, Parish Clerk.

28th March. William Hutchinson of the Par. of Fewston and Sarah Rhodes of this Par. Wits., Joseph Ingland, Edmund Greenwood, Parish Clerk.

1804. 2nd April. Joseph Freeman of the Par. of Otley and Ellen Dibb of this Par. Wits., James Whitwham, James Freeman, Edward Flesher, Edmund Greenwood, Parish Clerk.

7th May. Thomas Robinson of the Par. of Ilkley and Margaret Kendall of this Par. Wits., Wm Netherwood, John Harper, Edmund Greenwood, Parish Clerk.

5th Nov. Samuel Moss & Mary Todd. Wits., John Ward, John Dickinson, Samuel Moss, Edmund Greenwood, Parish Clerk.

26th Nov. William Fieldhouse & Ann Ellis. Wits., Edmund Fieldhouse, Richard Ellis, Edmund Greenwood, Parish Clerk.

11th July, 1804 [sic]. William Parker & Alice Thompson. Wits., Richard Sowden, George Stead, officiatg Parish Clerk, William Standeaven.

1805. 7th Dec. George Whittacker & Ruth Watson. Wits., Wm Burnell, Thos Skirrow, Joseph Pape, Edmund Greenwood, Parish Clerk.

[Edmund Greenwood, Parish Clerk, *is a witness to all subsequent marriages in this book.*]

1806. 28th Jan. William Bradley of the Par. of Otley and Sarah Moss of this Par. Wits., William Moss.

3rd March. John Pawson of the Parish of Otley & Anne Atkinson of this Parish, by W. Smith, Cure of Pool. Wits., Wm Pawson, M. Smithson, Joseph Pawson.

21st April. Thomas Robinson & Martha Bramley. Wits., Thos Fieldhouse, Mary Newton, Thomas Mawson.

5th May. Samuel Burnell & Ellen Pawson. Wits., Wm Pawson, Mary Wardle, James Land, Elizabeth Smithson.

26th May. John Ratcliffe & Elizabeth Barrett. Wits., Robert Dibb, Thos Fieldhouse, Sarah England, Aanny Barrett.

1807. 17th Feb. Abraham Reynard of the Par. of Otley and Margaret Wilson of this Par. (Licence), by Robt Dyneley, officiat. Min. Wits., Wm Randerson.

13th April. Joseph Pape & Mary Atkinson. Wits., Samuel Atkinson, Wm Burnell, [. . . . . .].

27th April. William Wheelhouse of the Par. of Fewston and Sarah England of this Par. Wits., John Robinson, George Stirk.

9th June. George Hole of the Par. of Otley and Ann Bolton of this Par. (Licence). Wits., William Crament, Samuel Jennings.

27th July. Thomas Hudson & Elizabeth Mawson (Licence), by W. Smith, Cure of Pool. Wits., William Darnbrough, William Hudson.

9th August. Robert Dibb of this Par. and Ann Renton of the Par. of Otley (Licence). Wits., John Matson, George Renton, William Hodgson, Mary Dibb.

17th August. William Simpson & Charlotte Todd by Robt Dyneley, officiatg Minister. Wits., Thos Fieldhouse, James Robinson.

30th Nov. James Moss & Martha Butterfield. Wits., Wm Butterfield, John Moss.

1808. 18th April. Joseph Stubbs of the Par. of Otley & Mary Leuty, by W. Smith, cure of Pool. Wits., Mary Stbbs [sic], Ralf Robinson, John Leuty.

6th June. Joseph Smith of the Par. of Fewston, Bachelor, and Martha Thackwray of this Par., Spinster, by T. Rye, Curate of Leathley. Wits., Thomas Myers, John Ratcliffe, Jane Dibb.

12 June. John Greenwood of the Par. of Bradford, Cordwainer and a Bachelor [Widower *in banns*], and Ann Blakey of this Par., Spinster, by G. Benson, Minister of Denton. Wits., James Land, Abraham Rynard [sic], Margaret Reynard.

31st August. Samuel Swires, Bachelor, and Sarah McBane, Spinster, by W. Smith, Cure of Pool. Wits., William Swiers, Walter Todd.

10th Oct. Thomas Smith of the Par. of Kirkby-overblow and Mary Forrest of this Par. Wits., Ann Smith, Wilfred Skirrow.

1809. 23rd Jan. John Procter & Ann Todd. Wits., Wm Burnell, Joseph Pape.

21st May. William Thompson, Taylor and a Widower, and Elizabeth Dibb, Widow (Licence), by G. Benson, Vicar of Ilkley. Wits., Ann Dibb.

17th July. James Whittaker & Ruth Wigglesworth. Wits., Henry Thackwray.

28th Nov. Thomas Holmes of the Par. of Leeds and Tryphenia Crooke of this Par. (Licence). Wits., Wilfred Skirrow, Rachel Overend, Sarah Skirrow.

27th Dec. William Kendall & Ann Thackray. Wits., Mary Smith, Joseph Pape.

1811. 19th Feb. Benjamin England and Hannah Mawson. Wits., John Luty, John Ratcliff.

25 Feb. Simon Hartley of the Par. of Guiseley and Betty Moss of this Par., by W. Smith, Cur^e of Pool. Wits., William Dibb.

3rd Sept. John Harper & Mary Whittaker. Wits., Joseph Land, James Robinson.

1812. 17th March. Robert Exley of the Par. of Otley and Jane Gill of this Par. (Licence). Wits., Wm Mawson, Sarah Skirrow, Wm Westwood, Jane Westwood.

6th April. Richard Bowling & Betty Forrest. Wits., Ann Fox, John Bowling, Benjamin Holmes.

4th May. John Gill & Mary Kendall. Wits., Thomas Kendall, Edmund Greenwood, Parish Clerk.

INDEX OF PERSONS.

INDEX OF PLACES.

The asterisk (*) near the number of the page indicates that the name is repeated in the same page.

GENERAL INDEX.

J. Whitehead & Son, Printers, Leeds and London

Yorkshire Parish Register Society.

1917.

Subscription : **One Guinea per annum, due 1st January.**

Patrons.

REGISTERS PRINTED OR IN THE PRESS.

YORKSHIRE PARISH REGISTER SOCIETY.

Treasurer's Statement, *December 31st, 1914.*

RECEIVED.

	£ s. d.	£ s. d.
Balance in Bank, *Dec. 31st, 1913*... ...		185 17 1
Subscriptions 1911 to 1913	12 12 0	
Do. 1914	169 1 0	
Do. 1915	1 1 0	
		182 14 0
Donations—		
Per T. W. Skevington, Darrington Register	0 10 6	
Per W. A. Briggs, for Kildwick Register	15 6 2	
Per Rev. Canon H. S. Atkinson, for Darrington Register	8 8 0	
		24 4 8
Sales of extra copies to Members ...		14 3 0
Bank Interest—*June*, 1914	1 18 9	
Do. *Dec.*, 1914	1 7 4	
		3 6 1
		£410 4 10

PAID.

	£	£ s. d.
G. D. Lumb Postages and Payments in 1913		0 19 5
J. A. Hirst—ditto		0 10 9
W. H. Milnes, Ltd.—		
On account of Halifax Register ...	30 0 0	
Balance ditto ...	51 10 0	
John Whitehead & Son—		
Printing Kildwick Register ...	62 8 7	
Knight & Forster, Limited—		
Printing Darrington Register ...	50 11 2	
Yorkshire Printing Company, Limited—		
Printing Howden Register, Part IV ...	52 2 8	
		246 12 5
Balance in Bank		162 2 3
		£410 4 10

Audited and found correct.—S. DENISON, *Hon. Auditor,*
Jan. 25th, 1915

J. A. HIRST,
Hon. Treasurer.

REPORT for 1914.

THE Council of the Yorkshire Parish Register Society have the pleasure to present their Sixteenth Annual Report. The number of members on the roll is 183, a decrease of 7 compared with 1913.

During the year the second part of Halifax Register was issued to the members for 1912. The Registers of Garforth, Kildwick (Part I), Howden (Part IV), and Darrington have been issued to the members for 1913. Of the latter, Garforth has been presented, £15 6s. 2d. has been given towards Kildwick, and £8 18s. 6d. towards Darrington. For 1914, Harewood Register (Part I), which is being presented by Mr. William Brigg, is nearly ready, and will be the Fiftieth Volume issued by the Society. Rothwell Register is waiting for the Index, and Skipwith is ready for the printer. For 1915 St. Mary's, Bishophill Junior, is in the printer's hands, and it is hoped that Thornhill (Part III) and Thornton Watlass will be so shortly.

It is intended that the publications for 1916 shall be Easingwold, Rounton, and Kildwick.

The Registers of Aberford, Bilton near York, Brompton, Church Fenton, Crofton, Emley, Featherstone, Halsham, Hook, Hornby, Ilkley, Keighley, Kirby Ravensworth, Knaresborough, Saxton, Sowerby, near Thirsk, Wakefield, etc., either have been or are being copied. Donations have been promised towards the printing of Aberford, Batley, Crayke, Dewsbury, Easingwold, Husthwaite, Ilkley, Keighley, Kildwick, Rounton, Scarborough, Silkstone, and Snaith.

YORKSHIRE PARISH REGISTER SOCIETY.

Treasurer's Statement, *December 31st, 1915.*

RECEIVED.

	£ s. d.	£ s. d.
Balance in Bank, *Dec. 31st, 1914*... ...		162 2 3
Subscriptions 1913 and 1914 ...	12 12 0	
Do. 1915	166 19 0	
Do. 1916	3 3 0	
		182 14 0
Donation—		
J. B. Williams, towards printing		
Easingwold Register, 1916 ...		20 0 0
Sales of extra copies to Members ...		1 19 3
Bank Interest—*June* half-year	1 18 0	
Do. *Dec.,* ditto	3 5 2	3 2
		£371 18 8

PAID.

	£	£ s. d.
G. D. Lumb—Postages and Payments in 1914		1 17 2
J. A. Hirst— ditto		0 8 10
John Whitehead & Son—		
Post-cards and Postages	0 16 0	
Knight & Forster, Limited—		
Wrappers and Postages	3 13 8	
E. J. Arnold & Son—		
Cash Book	0 12 6	
		5 2 2
Balance in Bank		364 10 6
		£371 18 8

Audited and found correct.—S. DENISON, *Hon. Auditor.*
Jan. 24*th*, 1916.

J. A. HIRST,
Hon. Treasurer.

REPORT for 1915.

THE Council of the Yorkshire Parish Register Society have the pleasure to present their Seventeenth Annual Report. The number of members on the roll is 175, a decrease of 7 compared with 1914.

During the year the Register of Harewood (Part I) and Rothwell (Part III) have been issued to the members for 1914. The former Register was kindly presented by Mr. William Brigg, of London, a member of the Council. For 1915 the Register of St. Mary's, Bishophill Junior, and Thornhill (Part III) have been printed off as far as the index. Skipwith and Thornton Watlass are postponed. For 1916 Easingwold and Kildwick (Part II) are both in the hands of the printer, and Rounton will be so shortly. Twenty pounds has been given by Mr. J. B. Willans towards the cost of Easingwold ; £10 has been promised by Sir Hugh Bell, Bart., towards the cost of Rounton ; one quarter of the cost of Kildwick will be raised by Mr. W. A. Brigg.

It is intended that the publications for 1917 shall be Snaith, towards the cost of which 25 per cent. has been promised, and Sheffield, towards which it is believed that substantial assistance will be forthcoming locally.

The Registers of Aberford, Bilton, near York, Church Fenton, Crofton, Emley, Featherstone, Halsham, Hook, Hornby, Keighley, Kirby Ravensworth, Knaresborough, Saxton, Sowerby, near Thirsk, Wakefield, etc., either have been or are being copied.

A donation has been given towards the cost of printing Aberford, and promised towards Batley, Crayke, Dewsbury, Husthwaite, Keighley, Scarborough, and Silkstone.

The Council regret that the Society has lost two members by death during the year, namely, Mr. G. E. Weddell, an active member of the Council, who transcribed Howden and other Registers, and Mr. Lothrop Withington, who was drowned in the *Lusitania* disaster.

In this time of stress the Council appeals for members from descendants of Yorkshire families now in the British dominions beyond the seas, and in the American States, feeling that the publication of Registers materially assists in preserving their ancestral connexion with the Homeland, and kindly memories for the county where their forefathers lived and died.

YORKSHIRE PARISH REGISTER SOCIETY.

Treasurer's Statement, *December 30th, 1916.*

RECEIVED.

	£ s. d.	£ s. d.
Balance in Bank, *Dec. 31st, 1915* ...		364 10 6
Subscriptions 1913 ...	1 1 0	
Do. 1914 ...	1 1 0	
Do. 1915 ...	7 7 0	
Do. 1916 ...	160 13 0	
Do. 1917 ...	6 6 0	
Do. 1918 ...	1 1 0	
		177 9 0
Donation—		
Legh Tolson—Weston Transcripts ...	5 0 0	
Sales of extra copies to Members ...	7 0 0	
		12 0 0
Bank Interest—*June* half-year ...	2 18 6	
Do. *Dec.* ditto ...	2 17 8	
		5 16 2
		£559 15 8

PAID.

	£ s. d.	£ s. d.
John Whitehead & Son—		
Printing Rothwell Register and Postages	120 4 7	
Miss S. E. Bailey—		
Indexing ditto ...	20 10 0	
Knight & Forster, Limited—		
Printing St. Mary, Bishophill Junior Register and Postages ...	68 18 3	
Sanderson & Clayton—		
Printing Thornhill Register III ...	48 16 4	
		258 9 2
G. D. Lumb - Postages and Payments, 1915 ...		1 6 9
J. A. Hirst—Postages, 1915 ...		0 7 10
John Whitehead & Son—		
Post-cards and Postages ...		0 16 2
Robert B. Cook—		
Transcripts of Weston (Otley) Register ...		10 0 0
Balance in Bank ...		288 15 9
		£559 15 8

Audited and found correct—S. DENISON, *Hon. Auditor.*
Jan. 23rd 1917.

J. A. HIRST,
Hon. Treasurer.

REPORT for 1916.

THE Council of the Society have the pleasure to present their Eighteenth Annual Report. The number of members on the roll is 166, a decrease of 11 compared with 1915.

During the year the Register of St. Mary, Bishophill Junior, and Thornhill (Part III) have been issued to the members for 1915. For 1916 Easingwold, Kildwick (Part II), Weston, near Otley, and Rounton are in an advanced state of printing. Mr. Legh Tolson has promised £15 towards the cost of printing Weston, and has given £5 towards the cost of copying the Weston transcripts at York. The publications for 1917 are a volume of Sheffield Registers, which will be issued at the joint expense of this Society and the Hunter Archæological Society, and a volume of Snaith Registers, towards the cost of which 25 per cent. is given locally ; also the Register of Kilburn, towards the cost of which Mr. W. T. Lancaster has promised £10. It is intended that the publications for 1918 shall be a second volume of Sheffield Registers, to be issued jointly with the Hunter Society, and the Register of Richmond or Crofton.

The Registers of Aberford, Bilton, near York, Church Fenton, Crofton, Emley, Featherstone, Keighley, Knaresborough, Kirby Ravensworth, Saxton, Sowerby, near Thirsk, Wakefield, etc., either have been or are being copied.

The Council regret that the Society has lost four members by death during the year, namely, Mr. J. B. Kay, the Rev. John Newman, Mr. J. G. Ronksley, and the Rev. Canon W. R. Wilson.

If it were not for the donations which have been so kindly promised, the issue of Registers could not be maintained to the extent it has been, and the Council hope that further offers of donations may be forthcoming.

RULES.

1 That the name of the Society shall be "THE YORKSHIRE PARISH REGISTER SOCIETY," and the Society shall have for its objects the transcribing and printing of the Parish Registers in the County of York, and such Bishops' Transcripts as may be accessible.

2 That the affairs of the Society shall be governed by a Council, consisting of a President, two Secretaries, and a Treasurer, with not exceeding twelve other members.

3 That the officers and one-third of the members of the Council shall retire annually, but shall be eligible for re-election.

4 That three members of the Council shall form a quorum.

5 That the subscription of members of the Society shall be One Guinea per annum, which shall entitle them to the publications for the year; but the name of any member whose subscription shall be two years in arrear shall thereupon be removed from the Society, and shall not be re-admitted until all arrears have been paid. New members may be elected by either the Council or the Society.

6 That the subscription shall be due on the First of January in each year, and that no work shall be issued to any member whose subscription is in arrear.

7 That an Annual Meeting of the Society shall be held in the month of February in each year, of which at least seven days' notice shall be sent to all the members. At this meeting a report of the work of the Society, with a statement of the income and expenditure, shall be presented. These shall be annually published, together with a List of Members and the Rules of the Society.

8   That so long as the funds of the Society permit, three volumes at least shall be issued to the members in each year.

9   That copies of the publications of the Society shall be supplied to members only.

10   That no payment shall be made to any person for editing any work for the Society, but that the Editor of each volume shall be entitled to ten copies of the work so edited by him, and the Incumbent to two copies for the use of the parish.

11   That the Council may require any Transcript to be examined by them before publication.

12   That each volume of Registers published shall have a full index of both Christian and Surnames and of Places.

13   That the Treasurer's accounts shall be audited by a member of the Society, who shall be elected at a meeting of the members.

14   That no alteration shall be made in any of the above rules except at the Annual Meeting. Notice of any proposed alteration must be sent to the Hon. Secretaries a month before such Annual Meeting, and by them communicated to the members.

LIST OF SUBSCRIBERS for the year 1916.

Acum, W. H. ... . 107, Queen Victoria Street, London, E.C.
Aldenham, The Right Hon. Lord... Aldenham House, Elstree, Herts.
Anderton, H. F. ... ... S. Anderton & Sons, Limited, Bradford
Armytage, Sir G. J., Bart., F.S.A. . Kirklees Park, Brighouse
Ayrton, Wm. .. .. 10, Dale Street, Liverpool

Bateson, J. Edwin ... ... Brooke Lodge, North Stoke, Wallingford
Bedford, James Edward, F.G.S. ... Arncliffe, Shireoak Road, Headingley, Leeds
Bell, Sir High, Bart. ... ... Rounton Grange, Northallerton
Bolton, The Rt. Hon. Lord, F.S.A. Bolton Hall, Leyburn
Brierley, Henry ... . 26, Swinley Road, Wigan
Brigg, William, B.A. ... ... 1, James Avenue, Cricklewood, London, N.W.
Brigg, Wm. Anderton, M.A. ... Kildwick Hall, Keighley
Brogden, J. Henry ... ... 200, Leeds Road, Bradford ·
Brooke, J. A. ... .: Fenay Hall, Huddersfield
Brooksbank, Ed. ... ... Healaugh Manor, Tadcaster
Brown, Wm., B.A., F.S.A. ... The Old House, Sowerby, near Thirsk
Brumfitt, George ... .. 2, Pembroke Avenue, Hove
Burton, C. M. ... ... 27, Brainard Street, Detroit, Mich., U.S.A.

Cecil, Lady William (Baroness
  Amherst of Hackney) ... Stowlandtoft Hall, Bury St. Edmunds
Chadwick, S. J., F.S.A. ... ... Lyndhurst, Dewsbury
Charlesworth, John ... .. The Crofts, Horbury, near Wakefield
Cheesman, W. N. ... ... The Crescent, Selby
Cholmley, Alfred S. ... ... Place Newton, Rillington, York
Clark E. T., F.S.A. .. ... The Goddards, Snaith
Clay, A. T. ... . Rastrick, near Brighouse
Clay, J. W., F.S.A. ... ... Rastrick House, Brighouse
Clough, E. M. O. ... ... The Senate, Houses of Parliament, Cape Town,
                              Union of South Africa
Coates, Sir E. F., Bart , M.P. ... 99, Gresham Street, Bank, London, E.C.
Collins, Francis, M.D. ... .. St. Andrew's, Lyme Regis, Dorset (*Hon. Sec.*)
Comber, John ... ... Ashenhurst, Albury Road, Guildford
Cookson. Capt. Bryan ... ... Maxey House, Blenheim Avenue,
                              Southampton
Cresswell, Lionel ... ... The Hall, Burley-in-Wharfedale
Crisp, F. A., F.S.A. ... ... Grove Park Press, 270, Walworth Road,
                              London, S.E.

Crossley, E. W. ... ... Broad Carr, Holywell Green, near Halifax
Cuthbert, Major-General Gerald,
   C.B., C.M.G. ... ... Bingfield, Corbridge-on-Tyne

Denison, Samuel, F.S.A. ... Spenthorn, West Park, Leeds
Dent, H. H. C. ... ... Chapel Ash, Wolverhampton
Dixe, Rev. R. E. H. ... ... Maltby Rectory, Alford, Lincolnshire

Eckersley, J. C., M.A. ... ... Carlton Manor, Yeadon, Leeds
Ecroyd, T. B. ... ... Lomeshaye, Nelson, Lancashire
Eddison, J. E., M.D. ... .. The Lodge, Adel
Edmondson, Prof. T. W. ... University Heights, New York City, U.S.A.,
   c/o Alfred Hafner, 2, Star Yard, London, W.C.
Elvidge, J. T. ... ... 5, St. Albyns, Hove, Sussex

Ferrand, W. ... ... St. Ives, Bingley

Garforth, Sir W. E. ... .. Snydale Hall, near Pontefract
Gill, C. C. ... ... Westcroft, Cleveland Walk, Bath
Gill, Francis V. ... .. 139, Sunbridge Road, Bradford
Gleadow, F. ... . 38, Ladbroke Grove, London, W.
Gorton, Mrs. ... ... Walesby Vicarage, Ollerton, Newark
Grant, Rev. A. T. ... . The Red House, Wemyss Castle, Fife
Greenwood, J. A. ... ... Funtington House, near Chichester

Hall, T. Walter ... ... 6, Gladstone Road, Sheffield
Hansom, Joseph S. ... ... 110, Palace Gardens Terrace, Kensington, W.
Harding, W. A. ... ... Histon Manor, Cambridgeshire
Harland, John Crowe ... ...· Southfield Boulevard, Eltingville, Staten
   Island, New York, U.S.A
Hawkyard, Arthur, M.D. ... Rowland Road, Dewsbury Road, Leeds
Hepper, Major H. A. L. ... .. Mount Pleasant Road, Malabar Hill, Bombay
Hirst, John Andis ... ... 4, South Parade, Leeds (*Hon. Treasurer*)
Hirst, Thos. Julius .. ... Meltham Hall, near Huddersfield
Hirst & Capes ... ... Albert Chambers, Harrogate
Hull, The Right Rev. the Lord Bis-
   hop of (Francis Girdon) ... Hessle, Hull
Huntriss, E. ... ... West Field, Halifax

Ingham, E. T. .. .. Blake Hall, Mirfield
Ingle, W. L. ... ... Morley Grange, Churwell, Leeds

Jackson, Edward Walker ... Highcliffe, Thorne Road, Doncaster

Knight, A. L. .. .. Curer Hall, Langbar, Ilkley

Lancaster, W. T., F.S.A. ... 7, Clarendon Place, Leeds
Lathrop, Kirke , ... 44, Bramham Gardens, South Kensington,
   London, S.W.

Littledale, W. A., F.S.A. ...	21, The Boltons, London, S.W.
Longstaff, G. B., M.D., F.S.A. ...	Highlands, Putney Heath, London, S.W.
Limb, G. D., F S.A.	31, Lyddon Terrace, Leeds (*Hon. Sec.*)
Midgley, Rev. J., M.A.	Wood Cottage, Todmorden
Miles, James	34, Upperhead Row, Leeds
Miller, Rev. Canon N. J., M.A. ...	Winestead Rectory, Hull
Mills, J. Willis	Westwood, Beverley
Morkill, J. W., M.A. ...	Newfield Hall, Bell Bisk, *via* Leeds
Morrison, Walter	Malham Tarn, Settle
Musgrave, Percy	Brookland, Bolton, Lancashire
Oates, Mrs. C. A.	Gestingthorpe Hall, Castle Hedingham, Essex
Ormerod, Hanson, M.A. ...	Greenroyd, Rastrick, Brighouse
Parker, Col. John W. R., C.B., F.S.A.	Browsholme Hall, Clitheroe *(President)*
Peel, W. S.	Melling, near Carnforth
Pullein, Miss Catherine	The Manor House, Rotherfield, Sussex
Richardson, W. R., M.A. ...	" Lascelles," Kingswood Road, Shortlands, Kent
Saltmarshe, Col. P.	Saltmarshe, Howden
Sandwith, Major L.	Alvaston, Derby
Scattergood, B. P., M.A.... ...	Moorside, Far Headingley, Leeds
Scott-Gatty, Sir A. S., F.S.A. ..	Garter King of Arms, College of Arms, London, E.C.
Scott, John	7, West View, Ilkley
Scott, R. F., M.A.	The Masters' Lodge, St. John's College, Cambridge
Slingsby, F. W.	Thorp Underwood Hall, York
Smithson, G. R.	Thorniehurst, Wolverhampton
Stavert, Rev. W. J., M.A., F.S.A.	Burnsall Rectory, Skipton
Stocks, The Ven. Archdeacon J. E., D.D.	Foston Rectory, Leicestershire
Sigden, Thos. B.	Registrar, Deeds Registry, Wakefield
Tempest, Mrs.	Broughton Hall, Skipton
Tolson, Legh	Ravensknowle, Dalton, Huddersfield
Townend, William	St. John's, Wakefield
Ullathorne, William G.	9, Lansdowne Road, Tunbridge Wells
Waddington, John	131, Marine Parade, Kemp Town, Brighton
Wakefield, The Rt. Rev. the Lord Bishop of (G. R. Eden, D.D.)	Bishopgarth, Wakefield
Walker, Norman D.	Currergate, Steeton, Keighley
Warde-Aldam, W. W.	Frickley Hall, Doncaster
Watson, T. E.	St. Mary's Lodge, Newport, Mon.
Wheler, Capt. G. B. Hastings ...	Ledstone Hall, Castleford

Whitehead & Son, John ... ... Alfred Street, Boar Lane, Leeds
Willans, J. Bancroft ... ... Dolforgan, Kerry, Newtown, Mont.
Wilson, C. H. ... ... 5, Park Row, Leeds
Wilson, H. S. L. ... ... Crofton Hall, Wakefield
Wilson, Rev. Canon J. A., M.A. ... Taitlands, Stainforth, Settle
Winn, A. T., M.A. ... ... The Uplands, Aldeburgh, Suffolk
Worsley, Sir Wm., Bart. ... ... Hovingham Hall, York
Wood, Walter, A. ... ... Racine, Wisconsin, U.S.A.

York, The Most Rev. the Lord Arch-
  bishop of (Cosmo G. Lang, D.D.) Bishopthorpe, York

LIBRARIES.

Bingley Public Library, Bingley
Boston Public Library, Mass., U.S.A. (B. Quaritch, 11, Grafton Street, London,
  W., Agent)
Bradford Free Library, Darley Street, Bradford
British Museum, c/o Dulau & Co., 37, Soho Square, London, W.
College of Arms, Queen Victoria Street, London, E.C. (G. Woods Wollaston,
  Bluemantle, Librarian)
Dewsbury Public Free Library, Dewsbury
Edinburgh Public Library, Edinburgh
Edinburgh, The Signet Library
Guildhall Library, London, E.C.
Halifax, The Public Library
Harrogate Public Library, Raglan Street, Harrogate
Huddersfield Public Library, Huddersfield
Hull Public Library, Hull
Keighley, The Carnegie Public Library
Leeds Church Institute, Albion Place, Leeds
Leeds Institute of Science, Art, and Literature, Cookridge Street, Leeds
Leeds Library, Commercial Street, Leeds
Leeds Public Library, Municipal Buildings, Leeds
Leeds University, College Road, Leeds
Lincoln's Inn, The Library of the Hon. Society of, London, W.C.
Liverpool Free Public Library, Liverpool
Manchester, Chetham's Library, Hunt's Bank
Manchester Free Public Libraries, King Street, Manchester
Manchester, John Rylands Library, Deansgate
Middlesbrough Free Library, Middlesbrough
New England Historic Genealogical Society, 18, Somerset Street, Boston, Mass.,
  U.S.A (B. F. Stevens & Brown, 4, Trafalgar Square, London, W.C., Agents)
New York Genealogical and Biographical Society, 226, West 58th Street, New
  York, U.S.A.

New York Historical Society, 170, Central Park West, New York, U.S.A.

New York Public Library, Astor Library Building, New York City, U.S.A. (B. F. Stevens & Brown, 4, Trafalgar Square, London, W.C., Agents)

New York State Library, Albany, New York, U.S.A. (Alfred Hafner, 2, Star Yard, London, W.C., Agent)

Newberry Library, Chicago, Ill., U.S.A. (B. F. Stevens & Brown, Agents)

Oxford, Bodleian Library

Pennsylvania, Historical Society of, 1300, Locust Street, Philadelphia, Pa., U.S.A. (B. F. Stevens & Brown, Agents)

Pennsylvania State Library, Harrisburg, U.S.A.

Ripon Cathedral, Dean and Chapter of

Rochdale Free Public Library, Rochdale

Rotherham Free Library, Rotherham

Sheffield Public Library, Surrey Street, Sheffield

Sheffield University Library, Sheffield

Todmorden, The Free Library

Utah, Genealogical Society of, 60, East South Temple Street, Salt Lake City, Utah, U.S.A.

Victoria, The Public Library of, Melbourne (c/o Agent-General of Victoria, Melbourne Place, Strand, London, W.C.)

Wakefield Institute of Literature and Science, Wakefield

Washington, D.C., U.S.A., Library of Congress (E. G. Allen & Son, Ltd., King Edward Mansions, 14, Grape Street, Shaftesbury Avenue, London, W.C., Agents)

West Riding County Council, County Hall, Solicitor's Department, Wakefield

York Architectural Society, 33, Bootham, York

York Minster Library, c/o Chapter Clerk's Office, St. William's College, York

York Public Library, York

York Subscription Library, York

Yorkshire Philosophical Society, Museum, York

CPSIA information can be obtained
at www.ICGtesting.com
Printed in the USA
BVHW081302231118
533754BV00028B/2540/P